THE HERB GARDEN COOKBOOK

A basket brimming with a variety of summer's basils.

THE HERB GARDEN COOKBOOK

▶LUCINDA HUTSON◀

Photography by
COOKE PHOTOGRAPHICS

★
TexasMonthlyPress

Texas Monthly Press, Inc.
P.O. Box 1569
Austin, Texas 78767

B C D E F G H

Library of Congress Cataloging-in-Publication Data

Hutson, Lucinda, 1950–
    The herb garden cookbook / by Lucinda Hutson.
        p.   cm.
    Bibliography: p.
    Includes index.
    ISBN 0-87719-080-1 : $19.95
    1. Cookery (Herbs) 2. Herb gardening–Southwest, New. I. Title.
TX819.H4H88 1987
641.6'57–dc19 87-21490
CIP
Book design by Julienne McNeer

For my mother, who instilled in me an appreciation of good food; and my father, whose love of Mexico and the sea inspired my own travels. And to my grandmother, whose spirit is always with me.

▼▼▼▼▼▼▼▼▼▼▼▼▼▼▼▼▼▼▼▼▼▼▼▼▼

CONTENTS

▼▼▼▼▼▼▼▼▼▼▼▼▼▼▼▼▼▼▼▼▼▼▼

▼▼▼▼▼▼▼▼▼▼▼▼▼▼▼▼▼▼▼▼▼▼▼▼▼▼

ACKNOWLEDGMENTS

My warmest thanks to all of my friends and colleagues who helped make this book possible. John Dromgoole taught me organic gardening techniques, continually shared his expertise, and designed an enchanting garden for me which daily offers a new gift and brings me great pleasure.

Anne Norman, my editor, dedicated endless hours to this project, as did my copy editor, Marsia Hart Reese, whose constant enthusiasm helped me keep the faith when I grew weary. Sara Lord's creative ideas and inspiration, Lucia Gilbert's encouragement, and Melissa Airoldi's help with the source list, bibliography, and recipe development were of great value. Thanks to Ray Bard for advice and encouragement.

The color and clarity captured in the photographs taken by Richard and Mary Cooke, as well as their patience and many hours spent in the hot Texas sun are certainly appreciated. Special thanks also to my multi-talented friend, Jan Heaton, for her artistic contributions, to Trisha Shirey and Susie Smith for their photographs, and to Jim Schermele for his design of the basket filled with basils.

I am especially grateful to the many botanists, herbalists, and gardeners who so generously supplied information, notably: Dr. Robert Bye, Dr. Edelmira Linares, Dr. Gary Nabhan, Dr. Billie Turner, Dr. Guy Nesom, Gilbert Voss, Jim Bauml, Kevin Dahl, Tricia Shire, Sol Meltzer, Scooter Cheatham, Lynn Marshall, Catine Perkins, JoAn Martinez, Jean Andrews, Kim Kuebel, Diane Barnes, Chris Winslow, Renee Shepherd, Marilyn Hampstead, Fairman and Kate Jayne, Manuel Flores, Malcolm and Delphine Beck, J. L. Hudson, Holly Shimizu, Don Pylant, Carole Saville, Lorine Gibson, and Craig and Sue Dremann.

I also want to thank Richard and Barbara Cilley, Sara Aleshire, Marilou Morales, Mark Yznaga, Maurice Allen, David Lord, Judy Glenn, Genoveba Rios, and Christopher Peabody for advice in recipe development as well as the many friends who tested recipes. My gratitude to Robert Del Grande, Stephan Pyles, Paula Lambert, Amy Ferguson, Carla Wood, Dean Fearing, Mark Miller, Ann Clark, Minh Lien, Foo Swasdee, Mick Vann, Chris Shirley, Danny Paquette, and Ron Estill, and to all of the wonderful cooks I have had the fortune to meet upon my travels for graciously sharing their recipes.

I certainly appreciate the herbs given to me by Sol Meltzer, It's About Thyme, Taylor's Gardens, Gardenville, Sandy Mush Nursery, and other friends. Special thanks to Javier Aviles for the care he has given my garden.

And finally, my gratitude to my family for support and care: my sister, Christopher Peabody, a talented caterer and my mentor, who flew in from California to help with the recipes; my sister, Cynthia Forney, who offered optimism and cheer; my brother, Stuart Hutson, for his wonderful sense of humor; my *tia*, Hermila Contreras, who taught me how to cook; my parents, Patricia McAlmon and Stuart Hutson, for giving me so much opportunity and encouraging me to travel; and to my grandmother for leaving me with fond memories. *Muchísimas gracias*

Herbs also grow well in pots.

HERBAL INTRIGUE

What got you interested in herbs?" people often ask me. I attribute it to my travels in Mexico, where I often found myself in kitchens, talking and eating with friendly folks who readily shared what little they had. I quickly discovered the importance of herbs in peasant cuisines— how they enlivened otherwise mundane fare. A generous pinch of oregano in a pot of frijoles, several sprigs of yerba buena (mint) in chicken soup, and generous doses of chopped cilantro in the salsa picante added flavor to simple ingredients. Almost every home had a small herb garden, or at least some favorite herbs growing in rusted tin cans or weathered clay pots. Vendors in the colorful Mexican markets sold fresh herbs tied up in small bundles and dried herbs, just enough for a few meals, wrapped up in little paper cones.

For an anthropology class my senior year in college, I wrote a term paper on the medicinal herbs used by Mexican women. During my research, I again seemed to end up in the kitchen, chatting with the women who also shared their recipes. After all, many of the medicinal herbs have important culinary virtue as well. And so began my adventure of cooking with herbs.

THE LEGACY

Apparently, herbs intrigued an earlier member of my family as well. Just before completing this book, I found some old family papers handwritten by my grandmother. She wrote the following about Lucinda Duncan, her great grandmother after whom I was named, who crossed the plains to California in 1852. According to family records, her family was one of twelve in an ox train and were the first white settlers in Los Angeles County. Here is what my grandmother wrote:

She had auburn hair—wavey—parted in middle and wore black lace cap— buried in a white one—and nainsook— fine cotton—shroud. . . . Brought all her own herbs and had herb garden for medicine. . . . She had a stroke while milking—as her husband couldn't milk —and fell off the stool and died in five days. They were very devoted. . . . He married again—old widow Westfall who married him for his money and gave him ground glass which didn't kill him—so he divorced her giving her $50.00—he died of old age more or less—at 85.

And so the legacy continues. (Fortunately, I don't know how to milk a cow, so there is no danger of my falling off a milking stool, and none of my recipes includes ground glass!) The seed was planted over a century ago; I propagate the tradition. Today I spend much of my time gardening and cooking, while often thinking about that ox-pulled wagon bouncing across the country from Missouri with its precious cargo: herb seeds, perhaps even a plant or two, bound for their new home in the California sunshine.

▼▼▼▼▼▼▼▼▼▼▼▼▼▼▼▼▼▼▼▼▼▼▼▼▼▼▼▼▼▼

HERB GROWING IN THE SOUTHWEST

▼▼▼▼▼▼▼▼▼▼

With the renewed interest in herbs today, many books about these delightfully aromatic plants are available. Unfortunately, however, most of them are geared toward gardening in England or New England, and their information seldom applies to gardening situations we face in the South and Southwest. Herbs that flourish in a Cape Cod garden sometimes cannot abide the summer's heat in the Southern and Western states; cultivation practices differ as well. For instance, many current herb books say to plant cilantro in the spring; to do so in our area causes the plant to bolt prematurely, whereas planting seeds in the fall assures us of healthy plants.

And so I decided to write about growing herbs in the Southwestern states. But what exactly is the Southwest? I don't want to conjure up images of cacti and desert mesas, and I certainly do mean to include the sunny state of California. New Mexico and Colorado are surely the Southwest, although their more severe winters and shorter growing seasons pose different gardening problems from those of their Texas neighbors. And to cause more confusion, the state of Texas alone has five gardening zones, with winter temperature extremes ranging from -5 to 30 degrees.

Herbs that grow in the Southwest also grow in the Southeastern and South Central states of the Sunbelt–areas with plenty of sunshine and relatively mild winters. So don't let the word *Southwest* limit you. Many of the herbs in this book will grow in Northern states as well, providing they are given winter protection. Most of the herbs I have chosen, however, grow especially well in the Southwest; for instance, several sun-loving Mexican and Oriental herbs are quite at home here. Still, we are talking about a large area with many gardening zones and various types of soils, so it is best to consult your local agricultural extension agency, an almanac, or local nurseries to find out the first and last freezing dates for planting, harvesting, and planning the herb garden.

WHY FRESH HERBS?

▼▼▼▼▼▼▼▼▼▼

Once you have walked into the garden and brushed against a fresh, pine-scented rosemary plant, gently rubbed the leaves of lemon thyme, releasing its citrus perfume, or picked a bouquet of spicy, clove-scented basil, you will understand why fresh herbs offer such delight. Not only do they have an inviting aroma, but they look beautiful growing, providing color, texture, and fragrance to the garden. And the gourmet and novice chef alike will marvel at how quickly and deliciously herbs enhance even the simplest meals, pleasing the eye as well as the palate.

With today's emphasis on health and sensible eating, fresh herbs provide culinary options. Freshly chopped herbs may be substituted for rich sauces and salt. Using fresh herb sprigs as flavoring and garnishes certainly makes diet fare more appealing, and they taste good as well. Combining mineral water and fruit juice in an iced glass and garnishing it with a fresh sprig of mint can replace a cocktail. And a big salad of various greens and sprigs of fresh herbs is fun to eat but not fattening! The added benefit is that many herbs contain vitamins and minerals. But mostly, it's simply amazing what a burst of flavor and freshness these aromatic plants give to food.

Although dried herbs serve their purpose (I prefer to use oregano and thyme in their dried form when a recipe needs a more intense flavor), the flavor of fresh herbs in incomparable. Unfortunately, many people do not store dried herbs properly. I cringe when I enter kitchens where jars of dried herbs and spices are stored next to a hot stove or exposed to direct sunlight, thinking of the worn-out flavor they will impart to food. I despair to think how long people have kept them on their shelves, how long they sat on grocery shelves before purchase, and how long in warehouses before that. And few people seem to realize that many commercially grown herbs are heavily fertilized with chemicals, which increase the yield but decrease the flavor, or that many herbs come from countries indiscriminately using dangerous insecticides.

My advice? Discard those jars of herbs that have sat on the shelf for months or years, and replace them with fresh ones from a reliable source. Better yet, plant an herb garden. In the sunny Southwest, you can have herbs almost year round!

WHERE TO GROW HERBS

For optimum growth, herbs require six hours of sunshine daily. Gentle morning sun is ideal, to dry the morning dew from the leaves and to prevent the possibility of leaf disease. The afternoon summer sun in the Southwest is quite harsh, although adequate mulching can help maintain the moisture level. Certain herbs tolerate more shade than others. Specific growing information is given on each herb in the following chapters.

Before choosing space for an herb garden, make sure that trees or buildings will not block sunshine. Because I have a shady back yard, I used all available space in the front by making 2-foot beds along all borders and the path to the front door. This arm's-length-size bed enables me to reach the front and the back with ease. Larger, curved beds line the front sidewalk, and a low limestone wall contains shade-growing herbs beneath the front windows of the house. A 5-foot dry-stack limestone wall, hollow in the center, makes a well-draining planter for herbs and flowers. One side of the wall has creeping thymes, rosemaries, and other herbs growing between the irregularly shaped honeycomb rocks.

Upon visiting my garden, Dolores Latorre, author of *Cooking and Curing with Mexican Herbs* (Encino Press), appreciated the way I grow herbs intensively in a small space. "After all," she commented, "herbs are gregarious. They love to be around each other and people as well." She's right. Herbs have brought much personal joy to me as well as to visitors and passersby.

Space-saving devices include cedar or redwood trellised window boxes, half barrels, and other clay or wooden containers. Apartment or condominium dwellers may plant herbs on patios or decks, providing they have enough sunshine; in fact, containers often allow the good drainage necessary for the healthy growth of herbs.

When planting herbs, keep in mind their ultimate size and needs so that plants requiring similar conditions are grown together. Taller herbs should be grown in the background to prevent their shading lower-growing plants. Remember that perennial herbs continue to grow year after year and need a permanent location. Because many herbs are companion plants to vegetables— that is, they mutually benefit one another— they should be planted in close proximity. For more information, consult the individual herb chapters.

The versatility of herbs, their variety of fragrance, color, and shape, make them valuable as ornamental plants. Interspersing them among bright flowers and vegetables gives a lovely cottage garden effect, brimming with color and texture. Many herbs not only tolerate our mild winters, but also are the first plants to pop their heads up in early spring, so herbs supply year-round beauty and fascination to the garden.

SOIL AND RAISED-BED GARDENING

As there are already many books devoted to the subject, I do not intend to discuss formal herb garden design; instead, I wish to concentrate on several basic ways to prepare an herb garden. For those choosing to till a garden space, it should be done

▼▼▼▼▼▼▼▼▼▼▼▼▼▼▼▼▼▼▼▼▼▼▼▼▼▼▼▼▼

twice if possible. Till in compost, organic fertilizer, and other nutrients (bone meal, rock phosphate, seaweed meal, etc.) and allow the garden to sit a few weeks. Till again to a depth of 12 inches, taking caution to remove any roots of insidious weeds. This method works especially well when herbs and vegetables are grown together.

John Dromgoole, frequent contributor to *Organic Gardening* magazine, and manager of Gardenville of Austin (a vanguard nursery specializing in soils, compost, and natural pesticides as well as plants and seeds), taught me the importance of healthy soil years ago. "The soil," he says, "is the stomach of the plant. You feed it, it feeds you." Healthy soil promotes healthy plants and discourages insects and disease. But most important, using organic matter and natural insect control (if necessary) produces herbs that are safe to eat!

Dromgoole also taught me the importance of raised-bed gardening, which promotes good drainage and enables you to build the soil. This is especially beneficial in parts of the country where black gumbo and caliche soils become soggy and unworkable when wet, but compacted and cracked when dry. Raising the beds allows you to fill them with a good mixture of approximately 50 percent sandy loam, 25 percent aged compost, and 25 percent sand. In more arid regions, raised beds tend to dry out frequently, so gardeners there may choose to recess their beds to catch any available water. Still, a good soil mixture is important; a neutral to slightly alkaline soil is preferable for most herbs.

Look for reputable local sources for soil and compost, or make your own. Don't be persuaded to buy cheap soil (it's often full of weeds and lacks nutrients); the initial expense for superior products will be well worth it. The main thing to remember is that herbs require a loose and well-draining soil. Working plenty of organic matter into the beds is the best way to improve soil. Find the best available organic material in your area: aged compost, composted rice hulls, wood shavings, stable beddings, and so forth. I also mix in some rock phosphate or bone meal, which promote strong root growth and supply valuable phosphorous to the plants.

Many herb books say that herbs like poor soil, but that statement is misleading. The "poor" soil of the Mediterranean, where many herbs thrive, is sandy and well-draining, not heavy and compacted like other "poor" soils. True, herbs don't require an overly rich soil, simply one that is loose and porous, and they do tolerate arid, rocky, sandy, and limestone terrain better than most plants. Still, the healthier the soil, the healthier the herbs. Once the beds are planted, however, your work is not done. Occasionally turning the soil gently and working in compost and other nutrients keeps it in good shape.

My garden, designed by John Dromgoole, has raised beds made of dry-stack white limestone in a style common to walls in the Hill Country of Central Texas; however, there are several easier and more economical methods for building raised beds. Three cedar or redwood boards (each 2 inches by 10 inches by 8 feet) may be made into a rectangular bed; cut one board in two to form the ends. Many nurseries now sell cedar landscape timber edging with flexible galvanized tin backings that can be molded into desired shapes with little effort. Railroad ties also may be used, but make sure that they are not treated with creosote, which is toxic in the food chain, and smells terrible when warmed by the sunshine. For more elaborate ideas for herb garden design, consult specialty books now available.

SEEDS VERSUS PLANTS

▼▼▼▼▼▼▼▼▼▼

Occasionally, problems occur in direct sowing of seeds in our part of the country. An unexpected 90-degree day in April will fry tender seedlings, if hungry worms have not already done their damage. Keeping seedlings evenly moist is imperative. Renee Shepherd, owner of Shepherd's Garden Seeds in California, recommends planting herb seeds indoors in flats in sterilized potting soil, then transplanting them in the garden once established. She also recommends planting seeds in a small "seed bed" area, tending them carefully, then transplanting them into the larger garden. Remember that the vulnerable young plants must be "hardened off" (gradually exposing them to increased amount of direct sunlight) before transplanting. This holds true for nursery transplants as well. Overzealous gardeners too often buy young plants from nurseries where they have been kept in semishade, then rush home and plant them in full sun, only to see the plant go into shock or even perish. Instead, expose tender plants gradually to sunshine.

Certain herbs grow especially well from seeds. Herbs in the Apiaceae (Umbelliferae) family including coriander, dill, fennel, and parsley generally do best when planted in the fall. Because they develop a taproot, I plant them directly in their permanent location, making successive plantings throughout the season. The umbrella-shaped flowers in this family look attractive ornamentally, producing seeds with culinary use.

Arugula and sorrel also grow well from seeds planted in the fall. Basil, on the other hand, should not be planted until the soil and air are sufficiently warm. Cool weather stunts their growth, and they are quite susceptible to frost. But basil flourishes in warm weather, and successive sowings may be made throughout the spring and summer. I love to plant a variety of basils ranging in color from deep purple to pale green and in spicy, citrus, and floral fragrances.

With the renewed interest in herbs, local herb growers as well as mail-order catalogs offer a wide selection of herb transplants. Do encourage these sources to grow their herbs organically; after all, you eat what you plant. Unfortunately, many herb nurseries tend to use chemical fertilizers and pesticides (one of the reasons to grow your own!). Look for reliable sources in your area, as it is always good to find plants already adapted to their environment. Although herb transplants may seem rather expensive, remember that many herbs are perennials, and often only one or two of each plant is needed per garden. One package of seeds may go a long way, but how many gardens need a whole row of oregano? Even if you are able to find the necessary herbs in your area, do send off for the catalogs listed at the back of this book. They offer gardening tips, wonderful advice, recipes, and other valuable herbal information as well as seeds and live plants.

Diane Barnes of Its About Thyme herb nursery in Austin, Texas recommends planting seeds in a sterilized soil mixture in flats or pots. Her greenhouse situation is ideal for propagating seeds: a misting device keeps the seedlings moist but never soggy. The home gardener may improvise a greenhouse by covering the flat or pot with plastic. Avoid direct sunlight and make sure that the seedlings don't dry out. Gently spraying with a diluted seaweed spray (a natural nutrient now available at nurseries) is quite beneficial. Using an English-style watering can with an upturned "rose," or spout, provides a gentle spray without damaging the delicate seedlings. Within a week to 10 days, most seeds germinate; remove the plastic and give them diffused sunlight to help them grow. Remember that these seedlings dry out quite easily and must sometimes be gently watered twice a day, but that overwatering causes damping off or fungal disease. Once the first true sets of leaves appear, the herb seedlings may be transplanted into small pots with well-draining soil, kept well watered, and given indirect sunlight. When they are strong enough to be transplanted to the garden, remember to harden them off.

For those gardeners too busy to propagate herbs from seeds, herb transplants offer an easy solution. Because these plants are well established, they are more

▼▼▼▼▼▼▼▼▼▼▼▼▼▼▼▼   ▼▼▼▼▼▼▼▼▼▼▼▼▼▼▼▼

drought tolerant and more resistant to disease and insects if grown under proper conditions. And they give you more choice. For instance, there's no telling which oregano you will get if you plant from seed, but you may order a particular variety from a catalog or choose one at a nursery.

PROPAGATION OF HERBS
▼▼▼▼▼▼▼

Some of the propagation techniques frequently referred to in the following chapters include: cuttings, layering, and root division.

CUTTINGS Making cuttings is the easiest way to share herbs with friends. Certain herbs root readily in a small jar of water; mints, pineapple sage, basil, epazote, and Mexican marigold mint fare especially well. Remove the bottom leaves from a 4–5-inch cutting and place in water, refilling the jar as the water evaporates. Place on a window sill with gentle morning light until it has developed a hardy root system, then transplant into pots or the garden.

Semisoft tip cuttings, about 3–4 inches long and cut just below a leaf node, may be used for propagation. Remove the leaves from the bottom few inches of the stem, leaving a few healthy ones at the top, and root them (rooting powder may be used) in a good rooting medium. (Sol Meltzer, author of *Herb Gardening in Texas*, recommends a mixture of one-half sharp sand, perlite, or vermiculite and one-half peat moss.) Make sure to keep the cuttings moist, but remember that overwatering may cause root rot; give them adequate light (a greenhouse is ideal). Diane Barnes says that these cuttings or "slips" generally root in about a month, and she recommends rooting them in the fall or very early spring. Oreganos (including the Mexican oreganos), marjoram, rosemary, sage, winter savory, thyme, lemon verbena, tarragon, and Mexican marigold mint grow especially well by this means of propagation.

LAYERING Another method of propagation employed in the herb garden is layering. (Actually, in many cases, nature does this on its own.) Well-established herbs such as rosemary, sage, tarragon, and thyme especially lend themselves to this technique, which involves bending a low-growing branch to the ground, securing it with a piece of bent wire (even an old-fashioned hairpin will do), and covering it lightly with soil. I usually secure the branch with a few rocks to hold it down. Within about 6 weeks, roots should have formed, and you may cut the "new plant" from its mother plant and transfer it to another place in the garden.

ROOT DIVISION Root division is also an effective means of propagation. In the fall or very early spring (late February), clumps of perennial herbs may be dug up and easily divided. Or simply cut away a portion of the mother plant's root-system with a sharp knife, and transplant immediately. Mints, oreganos, marjoram, thymes, winter savory, Mexican marigold mint, and lemon balm are easy to divide in this manner.

When making these divisions, cut away dead or woody branches and roots, and transplant the new plants into pots or to other places in the garden. Trim the top of the plant by one-third to make up for the root loss, and water well. Clumps of alliums and lemon grass may also be carefully lifted, making sure not to damage the bulbs. Separate the bulbs and transplant. I like to plant alliums in clumps or as an ornamental border around the vegetable garden. Because they have lovely flowers ranging in shades from bright pinks to white, they also provide excellent contrast in the herb garden.

WATERING/MULCHING
▼▼▼▼▼▼▼▼▼▼▼▼▼

One of the main problems associated with growing herbs comes from overcare: overwatering, overfertilization, and overly rich soil. Generally, herbs require less water than other plants; in fact, some of the most flavorful herbs grow on Mediterranean and Mexican hillsides with only moderate natural rainfall. Remember, though, that summers are not as intensely hot there as they are in the Southwest, where herbs require especially consistent watering; mulching helps maintain moisture. In my garden, I have installed a drip-irrigation system, which provides deep soaking as opposed to frequent shallow waterings. Because it waters the roots, there is not as much loss of water to evaporation. With the increased incidence of water rationing during the summers in many Southwestern cities, drip irrigation is most beneficial, as it is usually exempt from watering restrictions, and it certainly cuts down on the time spent with a hand-held hose! It also diminishes the incidence of leaf disease, as the leaves are not apt to remain wet (basil and lemon balm are especially susceptible to leaf spots). Even if you don't have a drip system, a deep soaking is better than frequent light spraying with the hose. Look for soaker hoses, which are commonly available.

Root disease and fungal disease are common among herbs such as sage, rosemary, thyme, and lavender when they are overwatered or not planted in a well-draining soil. I usually plant these herbs in beds that don't require as much water as other herbs and place limestone rocks at the base of the plants to keep water off the roots. Some of my hardiest rosemarys grow in rather neglected areas. Remember to water herbs on a wet-to-dry cycle so they don't get "wet feet." Sticking your finger into the soil near the plant is the best way to gauge its need for water.

Remember that container-grown herbs (including hanging baskets) are apt to dry out and must be checked daily, but do not overwater them! Top dressing the containers with compost helps them retain moisture.

Mulching or top-dressing the soil with organic material such as aged compost, leaves (run over them with a lawn mower to break them down), wood shavings, or fine pine bark not only adds nutrients to the soil but helps moderate the soil temperature, keeping it cooler in the summer and warmer in the winter. During summer droughts, mulching is crucial in retaining precious water, just as in the winter it helps protect roots from freezing. Although I keep a compost bin outside where kitchen scraps, grass clippings, and leaves decompose, I also purchase aged compost. Look for sources in your area that sell ready-made compost, or collect materials such as stable beddings, cottonseed meal, rice hulls, grass clippings, and leaves. The finer the mulch, the better to discourage insects and to give a tidy appearance to the garden. Continually mulching the soil adds nutrients, helps prevent weeds, and conserves precious water.

FERTILIZER

Remember that fertilizing herbs often causes lush growth at the expense of flavor; however, mixing small amounts of fish emulsion and liquid seaweed (about 1 tablespoon of each) to a gallon of water and feeding about twice a month gives young herb plants a good start. Fish emulsion is a good source of nitrogen, and seaweed supplies important trace minerals as well as makes the plants more resistant to disease and insects. Once the plant is well established, there is really no need to feed it unless it shows signs of weakness and except after a heavy harvest.

After a mild winter, many perennial clumps of herbs still have much green growth. I usually cut the plants back, removing woody branches, and feed it with the same fish emulsion/seaweed combination. After heavy harvesting of an herb, I feed it in order to give it a boost. Herbs such as fennel, dill, sorrel, chives (and other alliums), and parsley can stand a richer soil and more frequent feedings than other herbs (mix some composted manure into the soil around them). Manure tea also makes a good organic fertilizer. Using a small hand shovel, place about two scoops of composted manure in a gallon container, fill the container with water, and let set for a few days before using as a liquid fertilizer.

INSECTS AND DISEASE

Part of the joy in growing herbs is their low maintenance. Providing they are grown under proper conditions, they are generally not prone to serious damage by insects or disease, although herbs that are grown in a poorly draining soil or over-watered are susceptible to root rot and fungal disease. Too much shade also may cause leaf and root diseases. As insects often attack weaker plants, check the plant's environment if you detect pests. Is there enough sunshine? Is the soil too dense? Has the plant been underwatered or overwatered?

In the early springtime (especially after a mild winter), hungry worms and caterpillars do some serious munching on leafy herbs, especially sorrel. I go foraging at night with a flashlight, picking them off and discarding them in a merciless manner. Another method is to spray or dust the plant with bacillus thuringiensis (sold under many trade names and commonly referred to as BT), a natural bacteria, that destroys the digestive system of worms without harming people or beneficial insects. The caterpillar of the swallowtail butterfly can ravage dill, fennel, and parsley overnight if not controlled (see chapter on dill).

Aphids occasionally cause problems, especially for herbs in a greenhouse environment, although they are seldom a serious threat outdoors. Look for these tiny (usually green, white, or black) creatures clustered together sapping the life out of tender new growth or on the underside of broad-leafed herbs such as sorrel. If you see leaves curled up, unwind them and you will see lots of aphids, or perhaps a worm. Where there are ants, expect to find aphids, because ants feed on a sugary secretion called honeydew that aphids produce. Usually a blast of hose water dislodges the aphids (if our helpful ladybug friends have not eaten them for supper), but serious infestation may have to be eradicated with a spraying of insecticidal soap, a product that is available at nurseries and is not hazardous to people or wildlife.

During hot and humid months, spider mites are a nuisance, especially if the herbs are not kept properly watered. These pests (in the spider family) are very tiny but may be detected by the damage they do to foliage. If you notice an herb that looks rather "burned," with mottled and pale discoloration and a general weak appearance (new growth often looks crinkled and deformed), spider mites are probably the cause. Hold a piece of white paper under the damaged leaves and tap the plant; the tiny (usually red) mites then become apparent. Sometimes close observation of the plant shows their small webs as well. If a plant shows extreme damage, I cut it back, then spray it with a light application of insecticidal soap once every 3 days over a nine-day period to break the egg cycle. Look for spider mite damage on lemon verbena, rosemary, lemon balm, Mexican marigold mint, mint, oregano, marjoram, and thyme. Top-dressing these herbs in the summertime with compost helps them retain moisture, which in turn might discourage spider mites.

Have you ever seen a slug siesta? In mid morning, lift up the leaves of sorrel and other leafy herbs that may be touching the ground and you are bound to find these chubby creatures napping (along with pill bugs and snails). Some people walk around with a can of kerosene and plop the poor creatures in it—instant death. I prefer to set traps, although I have been known to round them up and relocate them to a dark corner of the yard. Place overturned grapefruit, cantelope, or orange halves randomly in the garden: slugs, snails, and pill bugs will rest there during the day, when they may be captured and discarded. Or sink in the garden lids of jars filled with beer, which drowns these creatures in a state of inebriated bliss.

Because slugs and snails crawl around on their bellies, sand or diatomaceous earth, which contains an abrasive silica, scratches their undersides, causing them to desiccate. If you go to the garden at night with a flashlight, you can really see slugs, snails, and pill bugs feasting. Slugs adore chives, onions, and shallots, slithering down their hollow tops. The best way to discourage them is to keep the garden clean, as they hide in debris. Remove yellowed and decaying leaves and anything else that provides a hiding place. This also helps prevent disease.

One of the pleasures of an organic garden—that is, one free of chemicals—is that it encourages beneficial insects, which prey upon pests. Butterflies, bees, and other insects are crucial in pollinating the garden. I love to watch the formidable-looking praying mantis stalk his prey, the chameleons changing colors, and lady bugs and bees flitting from flower to flower. Although insecticidal soap is a natural product, it is harmful to beneficial insects as well as to detrimental ones. Unless an infestation is serious, don't spray; instead, let the beneficial bugs feast.

COMPANION PLANTS

Planting herbs among flowers, vegetables, and ornamental plants just seems to make them grow better. Many herbs actually add trace minerals to the soil, and some herbs improve the growth and flavor of certain vegetables. The pungent and pervasive aroma of many herbs seems to repel insects from the garden, so interspersing herbs among plants more susceptible to insect attack is quite beneficial. I always plant garlic and chives around my roses to repel aphids, for example, and I border vegetable beds with the strong-scented alliums. I seldom have significant insect damage in my garden.

Many vegetables are commonly associated with specific herbs. These partners require the same growing conditions and usually complement one another in the kitchen as well. For instance, basil and tomatoes bask in the sun together, and in cooking, basil is the tomato herb *par excellence*. Savory is reputed to improve the flavor of beans as they grow, and it certainly perks up their flavor in the bean pot.

Tomato lovers may prefer that the tomato horn worm munch on dill or parsley instead of precious tomatoes; that's a tough decision for me! But what I especially enjoy about growing herbs, flowers, and vegetables together is that it breaks the monotony of traditional rows, giving color, texture, and fragrance to the garden. And it makes harvesting more pleasurable: pop a cherry tomato in your mouth and a complementary basil leaf is within hand's reach!

HARVESTING, STORING, AND USING HERBS

Herbs are best gathered at mid morning, when the dew has dried off the leaves but before the sun has sapped their volatile oils. The flavor of most herbs is at its peak right before flowering; however, once the herb has flowered, it generally tastes bitter and too strong. Although frequent pruning is advisable (in fact, "topping" the emerging tender growth promotes new growth), never cut the plant more than halfway, in order to allow for a second growth. In the kitchen, rinse lightly, discarding any yellowed or damaged leaves.

Herbs such as mint, basil, parsley, cilantro, epazote, pineapple sage, and Mexican marigold mint may be stored several days in a jar of water, making attractive bouquets. Pinch off the bottom leaves to prevent their touching the water, and change

▼▼▼▼▼▼▼▼▼▼▼▼▼▼▼▼▼▼▼▼▼▼▼▼▼▼

the water daily. Store in a cool place away from direct sunlight. Cilantro and parsley store well for over a week in a jar of water in the refrigerator, covered loosely with a plastic bag. Just remember to change the water every few days.

If you must store herbs, I suggest placing them is a single layer in a tightly sealed plastic container. Dill, fennel, mints, marjoram, oregano, parsley, thyme, rosemary, sage, and tarragon keep well this way. Or place some sprigs in a tightly sealed plastic bag (squeeze out excess air) and store in the refrigerator standing up instead of lying flat. Make sure that there is no moisture on the leaves or they will mold or rot. And don't accidentally store other refrigerated goods on top of the bag, or you will bruise the leaves. This holds true for the fresh herbs packaged in sealed plastic bags now available at many supermarkets across the United States.

The best way to use herbs, of course, is fresh from the garden. Often, a walk through the garden inspires a meal, and it's fun to collect a fragrant bouquet and use as needed. Herbs with woodier stems, such as rosemary, winter savory, sage, lemon verbena and Mexican oreganos, are easily removed from their stems by stripping off the leaves in a downward motion from the top, then discarding the stem. The tender green stems of fennel, dill, coriander, salad burnet, summer savory, parsley, and basil may be chopped with the herb; in fact, they are quite flavorful and contain minerals and vitamins.

Many herb books recommend using fresh herbs judiciously. On the contrary, it is my opinion that you rarely can use too much of a fresh herb, perhaps with the exceptions of the pungent oreganos, rosemary, epazote, mouth-puckering sorrel, or strongly anise-flavored Mexican marigold mint. A myth seems to surround sage — that it tastes strong and medicinal, perhaps true for dried sage. But fresh sage offers a clean, refreshing, and uplifting flavor. Granted, it is best to use fresh herbs cautiously at first; you can always add

more if desired. But once you succumb to their seduction, it's farewell to bland meals and to the lifeless, ancient jars and tins of dried herbs on the shelf.

There is no real rule in using fresh herbs — just what tastes good! To me, that means at least three times as much of a fresh herb as dried, although others may be contented with less. Don't be alarmed if my recipes call for three tablespoons of a fresh herb; be pleasantly surprised. When doubling or tripling a recipe, however, don't necessarily double or triple the herbs and spices, or their flavors may be overpowering.

Add fresh herbs to soups, stews, and other long-simmering dishes the last 10–15 minutes of cooking to retain their flavor and prevent bitterness. Winter savory, rosemary, and thyme, are the exceptions; they can withstand longer cooking. The full flavor of herbs in cold foods is enhanced when they are added several hours or days before serving (cheese spreads, herbal butters, pasta and rice salads, taboulleh, marinated salads, cold drinks, and such). Citrus juice, wine, and vinegar used in salad dressings often cause herbs to darken or to fade, so it is best to add fresh herbs just before serving.

Always use a sharp knife and work quickly when chopping herbs, as they darken and bruise easily. Sharp kitchen scissors are especially useful for snipping chives, parsley, basil, fennel, and dill. And I like to use the gentle rocking motion of a crescent-shaped knife when chopping fresh herbs. A hand-turned Mouli grinder comes in handy, especially for parsley, mint and oregano. And the food processor can be quite a gem for chopping copious amounts of herbs (there are now miniature food processors on the market specifically designed for chopping herbs and garlic). Make sure herbs are free of moisture (particularly if they have been rinsed first) or they will become soggy.

A fun way to introduce guests to herbs is to use several small pots or a basket of fresh herbs as the centerpiece at the dining table. Provide scissors or small clippers so guests may snip off small sprigs to flavor their meal. Or provide a tiny bouquet of herbs at each place setting, and tuck a few sprigs of herbs in the napkin rings.

Although fresh herbs from the garden may be dried or frozen, these are not my favorite ways to preserve them. Instead, I devote a chapter to making herb butters, whose lively flavors quickly enhance many dishes. The butters can be successfully frozen for later use. I also include a detailed chapter on making herbal vinegars. The versatility and burst of intense flavors they give to foods is quite exciting, and they make beautiful gifts as well. Pestos – herbs ground to a thick paste with garlic, olive oil, nuts, and often freshly grated Parmesan cheese – offer another delicious way to preserve the herb harvest; they freeze well and make thoughtful gifts.

Still, you may want to dry some herbs for winter use, especially thyme and oregano, which taste even more flavorful when dried. Many herbs (especially mints, Mexican marigold mint, Mexican oreganos, sage, thyme, lemon verbena, epazote, estafiate, and lemon balm) may be tied up in bunches and hung upside down to dry in a well-ventilated, dark, dry room. Rinse them lightly first, removing any damaged leaves, and shake out excess moisture (high humidity will cause them to mold). They look so picturesque hanging that it's hard to take them down; however, as soon as they are dried, they should be stored in airtight containers because prolonged hanging turns them brown and dusty and impairs their flavor. Dark-colored glass jars help dried herbs retain their green color and fresh flavor. I often place dried herbs in labeled, tightly sealed plastic freezer bags or jars and store them in a place with little exposure to light.

Smaller-leafed herbs dry well on screens or drying racks. You can improvise by placing an old window screen on two bricks, which keep it raised to allow air circulation, and place in a dark, well-ventilated room, turning the leaves occasionally. Larger-leafed herbs such as basil may be removed from their stems, but smaller-leafed herbs such as savory and thyme may be dried on their stems. (Always remove rosemary from its stem.) I use an electric dehydrator with five plastic racks stacked above one another, and I especially like to dry fragrant herbs for their use in potpourri. Others extol the virtues of the microwave oven for drying herbs. Spread them on a paper towel and heat them on low for about 2 minutes. Turn them over and heat another minute or two. (Basil's high moisture content makes it difficult to dry in this manner.)

Dry seeds from coriander, dill, parsley, and fennel by hanging the umbrella-shaped ripened seed heads upside down in brown paper bags in a well-ventilated room away from direct light. Shaking the bag will cause the seeds to fall. Store them in airtight containers or freeze them.

Basil, dill, fennel, chives, sorrel, oregano, parsley, lemon grass, Mexican marigold mint, and marjoram may be frozen in freezer-proof plastic bags (squeeze out excess air). They may be frozen first on a baking sheet, then stored in the bags to prevent their sticking together. Because herbs flourish in Southwestern gardens almost year round, and because fresh herbs are now readily available neatly sealed in plastic bags or tiny bouquets in supermarkets throughout the country, I rarely bother with this method. Instead I freeze herbs in butters, pestos, and sauces.

USING THIS BOOK

I have written this book primarily to encourage the use of fresh herbs: how to grow them and what to do with them. Twenty popular herbs that grow well in the Southwest are included in the following chapters, as are a variety of more unusual Mexican and Oriental herbs. Each chapter is filled with pertinent growing and cooking information about the herbs, followed by several recipes in which they figure prominently. The chapters on herb vinegars, herb butters, and cooking tips provide further information. Menu suggestions and mail-order sources are found at the end of the book.

FOLLOWING THE RECIPES

How a recipe tastes depends on many factors: the ripeness of tomatoes, the potency of garlic and onions, the piquancy of chiles, and the freshness of herbs, spices, and other crucial ingredients. Treat yourself to flavorful extra-virgin olive oil, freshly grated Parmesan cheese, pine nuts, and freshly made pastas. After all, your homegrown herbs deserve the best! Keep on hand the best quality whole spices: white and black peppercorns, cloves, allspice, coriander, cumin (*comino*), and a variety of dried chile peppers to grind in a spice grinder. Combining them with fresh herbs tantalizes your tastebuds with exciting new pleasure. Try making a variety of herbal vinegars. You will be amazed at the flavor they impart. Have fun discovering ethnic markets, farmer's markets, and speciality food stores in your area. At these places, you can discover unusual and tasty products and meet new friends – and they often have a good variety of fresh herbs to offer.

But most of all, when cooking, rely on your sense of smell and taste instead of merely following written words. Often, a pinch of sugar provides a delicate balance; a dash of vinegar, citrus juice, or wine gives that extra sparkle; and fresh herbs bring incredible nuances to food. Innovation is crucial. Allowing substitutions or altering a recipe to suit your taste or ingredients at hand makes cooking fun. My tastebuds are accustomed to a hearty barrage of flavors. I adore spicy and spirited foods and no longer have to tell the waitress at my favorite Thai and Vietnamese restaurants to "make it extra spicy." So don't be surprised to find garlic and chile peppers in most of my recipes; after all, they are as inherent to the Southwest as is the sunshine. If you don't share my enthusiasm, however, reduce the amount of these ingredients or omit them.

Throughout the chapters, you will find simple suggestions for using herbs in cooking and many recipe ideas for everyday fare. But many of my recipes are suitable for celebrations and festivities. I love beautiful food: vivid colors and varied textures offer visual delight, and garnishes and presentation can transform the simplest meal into a memorarable occasion. Naturally, this takes more time, but the final presentation is worth it, pleasing the eye as well as the palate.

None of my recipes are very complicated, although I often use many ingredients. Don't let this fact intimidate you; it is the complementary flavors that make these recipes unusual and delicious. Preceding the ingredients, I offer a brief description of each dish, along with serving suggestions, and at the end of each recipe you will find additional tips as well as suggestions for substitutions and variations. Many of the recipes take on a totally different character when a different herb is substituted; I give you choices so that you may use whichever herb is on hand.

Without a doubt, once fresh herbs have graced your garden and filled your kitchen with their persuasive aroma, you, too, will never want to be without them.

COOKING TIPS
Helpful hints and procedures used throughout this book

GARLIC CROUTONS

French baguette
Olive oil
Butter
Garlic

Cut day-old bread into ½-inch slices. Heat 1 part olive oil to 2 parts butter with 2–4 cloves mashed garlic. Add bread slices, turning quickly on both sides to coat. Sauté until golden, replacing garlic cloves as they turn brown and adding more oil and butter if needed. Bake sautéed bread in 325-degree oven until crisp and golden. If desired, shake in a paper bag with freshly grated Parmesan and crushed red pepper.

TOSTADA CHIPS

To make your own fresh tostada chips, quarter corn tortillas, then cut into triangular chip shapes. Fry in ¼ inch hot oil until crisp (turning once), and drain on paper towels. Salt to taste if desired.

ROASTED PEPPERS (RAJAS)

This procedure applies to bell peppers as well as Anaheim or poblano peppers. Poke peppers with a fork to keep them from bursting, then place them directly on the flame of a gas burner, turning them until they are evenly blistered; or place peppers on a foil-lined baking sheet in a preheated oven about 4 inches from the flame. Peppers also can be charred over the open flame of a barbecue grill.

After roasting, place the chiles in a plastic bag or damp dish towel and leave them to steam for about 15 minutes. Peel by removing the charred skin. Do not rinse under water, as this will wash away the flavor. The chiles may be frozen in their charred skins, which are easily peeled when thawed.

To make chile *rajas*, or strips, peel the roasted chiles. Remove the stems, scoop away the seeds and veins, and cut into 3-by-⅜-inch strips. These may be tossed with minced garlic and used in salsas, quesadillas, chile on queso, stews, soups, and marinated salads, and to top steaks or hamburgers, or grilled chicken.

ROASTING TOMATOES

Line a baking pan with foil and place tomatoes in it about 4–6 inches from a preheated broiler. Broil 15–20 minutes, or until skin is evenly charred and blistered, turning tomatoes occasionally. Remove only badly charred areas from skins, as the charring is what gives the special flavor. Purée tomatoes in a blender, and use according to recipe.

PEELING TOMATOES

Plunge whole tomatoes in boiling water for 20–30 seconds; remove with a fork and dunk in cold water. Skin will slip off easily. Remove core and gently squeeze out seeds.

TOASTED NUTS

To toast nuts, place about 1 cup (pine nuts, almonds, pecans) in a pie pan, and bake in a preheated 325-degree oven, turning occasionally, until nuts are golden brown (about 5 minutes). Do not burn! The same procedure may be used for toasting sesame seeds.

COOKING PASTA

To cook fresh or dried pasta, bring salted water to boil in a 4–5-quart pot. (A teaspoon of olive oil and a pinch of crushed dried red chile pepper may be added.) When water is at a rolling boil, add the pasta; return to boil and cook 2–3 minutes for fresh pasta, 10–12 minutes for dried pasta. Drain but do not rinse.

FESTIVE HERBAL ICE CUBES

Making festive ice cubes is well worth the effort; you will be rewarded with enthusiastic comments from guests. Artistically arrange any combination of the following in ice cube trays: small slices of oranges, limes, lemons, kumquats; small sprigs of mint, lemon balm, lemon verbena, pineapple sage, salad burnet, rosemary leaves; and marigolds, Mexican marigold mint flowers, rose petals, pansies, Johnny jump-ups, and violets. Cover with water and freeze. Store ice cubes in tightly sealed plastic bags to use as needed.

HERB CHIFFONADES

To make a chiffonade of herbs (for large-leafed herbs such as basil, sorrel, and arugula, as well as spinach, lettuce, and cabbage), stack several leaves, roll up tightly (like a cigar), and slice into thin strips, crosswise. Use as a garnish or add to soups, salads, and sauces for texture and flavor.

CHOPPING HERBS IN A FOOD PROCESSOR

To chop fresh herbs in your food processor, they must not be moist as they get soggy when chopped. Remove stems from woodier herbs and process with brief on/off touches.

USING A SPICE GRINDER

The combination of fresh herbs and freshly ground spices gives delightful nuances to food. Purchase whole spices (cloves, coriander, pepper, allspice, *comino* or cumin) and dried chile peppers, and grind in a small electric coffee grinder (or with mortar and pestle) as needed.

BROILING FISH

Broil fish approximately 8–10 minutes per inch of thickness, or until it flakes with a fork, 4–6 inches from broiler flame.

BASIC CHICKEN STOCK

A rich and flavorful chicken stock is a must for soups; it can make all the difference in their flavor. Although necks and backs give the most flavor, I often use whole chickens, which may be cooked, then removed from the bone and reserved for other dishes (soups, salads, casseroles). The large bones are then returned to the pot and simmered for 40–60 minutes, strained, and refrigerated or frozen.

1 whole fryer, 3–3½ pounds (plus 1 pound necks, backs, and/or chicken bones if desired)

1 large onion, quartered and studded with 2 whole cloves

4–6 cloves garlic, lightly mashed

2 stalks celery, quartered

2 carrots, halved

2 bay leaves

½ teaspoon whole coriander seeds (optional)

½ teaspoon whole peppercorns, freshly ground

1 large handful fresh herbs (parsley, cilantro, marjoram, etc., depending on recipe)

Water to cover (preferably ½ chicken stock), about 3 quarts

Salt and pepper to taste

Best quality chicken bouillon cubes or granules (to taste) for a more full-bodied stock

Place all ingredients except fresh herbs and salt in a large (4–6-quart) stock pot. Slowly bring to boil, skimming off any accumulating foam; reduce to simmer and cook until chicken is tender (about 45 minutes). Remove chicken and allow to cool. Pull chicken meat from the bones, discard skin, and return bones to stock pot. Simmer 40–60 minutes, covered, adding fresh herbs the last 10 minutes. Cool, then strain, pressing hard to extract all juice. Chill overnight; skim off congealed fat and proceed with recipe, or leave fat and freeze in labeled container, discarding fat when thawed.

NOTE: Sometimes in a pinch, it may be necessary to use canned broth; if so, be aware that canned broth is now available without added salt, preservatives, or monosodium glutamate. Simmer canned stock with a piece of onion studded with clove, celery, carrot, fresh herbs, and a teaspoon vinegar or lemon juice. When cooking chicken for other purposes, remember to reserve bones and freeze, to add to stock as needed later. If the stock is not used within 3–4 days, reboil it.

ARUGULA
Eruca vesicara subspecies *sativa*
Brassicaceae (Cruciferae) family

Arugula's oak-shaped leaves.

Common Names:
arugula, roquette, rocket; rucola (Northern Italy); rugula (Southern Italy)

Characteristics:
wavy green leaves resembling oak-leaf lettuce and radish; peppery and nutty taste; 4-petaled white flowers streaked with crimson when plant is about 2 feet tall; readily re-seeds; annual

Conditions:
rich, moist, well-draining soil in full sunshine; grows best in fall and winter gardens in the Southwest; heat causes plant to bolt

Size:
about 2 feet tall and 1 foot wide

Propagation:
successive plantings of seeds from early September through April; thin to 1 foot apart; 6–8 plants per garden suggested

Fertilizer:
occasional feedings of fish emulsion and compost

Pests:
harlequin bugs, flat red insects with distinct black markings, are especially destructive in warm weather–pick bugs off or pull up plants; caterpillars may also cause damage–use bacillus thuringiensis; flea beetles leave numerous tiny holes on leaves–use rotenone, a natural pesticide

Companions:
none noted

Several years ago, Sol Meltzer, "the herb man" of Houston, plucked a few leaves from an oversized looking radish plant that he called arugula and said to me, "Taste this." I was as quickly overcome with passion as a rabbit in a carrot patch. I simply could not get enough of it! So there I stood in the middle of his herb garden, barely brushing off the sandy grit from the leaves and devouring handfuls of this newly discovered treat. (To this day, I am convinced that arugula contains a nutrient that my body craves.)

For centuries, arugula plants have dotted the rocky hillsides of the Mediterranean. Known in Italy as *rucola* and in France as *roquette*, this tasty plant in the mustard family has long been used as a salad green. Obviously, I adore the flavor: crunchy leaves with a peppery taste that piques tastebuds with nutty undertones redolent of sesame oil. Others apparently share my zeal, as it is currently one of the popular herbs (sometimes called rocket) touted on chic menus throughout the United States and Europe. But I must admit,

not everyone is a fan; in fact, many actually detest it.

But I could eat arugula with anything! A handful of the dark green, wavy, oak-like leaves thrown into a salad makes a sassy complement to the more subtle lettuce. I love the leaves tossed with a light vinaigrette or in salads with orange slices. Strips of freshly roasted peppers and pungent goat cheese are perfect partners for this salad green. Or combine fresh spinach and arugula leaves, crisp crumbled bacon, hard-boiled egg slices, red pepper slices, and garlic croutons in a creamy Dijon mustard dressing.

In Italy and Sicily, arugula is collected in the wild and, being free for the taking, makes a favorite "poor man's salad." Italians toss the leaves with vine-ripened plum tomatoes, olive oil, and vinegar. The more affluent may try adding marinated artichoke hearts and ripe olives with gorgonzola cheese crumbled on top.

Arugula leaves also may be tucked inside a Sunday omelet with bacon, grilled onions, and sour cream. And the leaves certainly lend themselves to wrapping around bite-sized pieces of grilled or broiled fish, chicken, pork, or beef, then dunked into spicy dipping sauces. Arugula also is good simply stir-fried in sesame oil and garlic.

The versatile leaves make a peppery chiffonade for soups and sauces, and they may replace lettuce in sandwiches. (I especially love arugula with roasted red peppers on Italian bread spread with homemade garlic mayonnaise.) A handful of the leaves may be added to the blender when making a favorite dip, or ground with olive oil, garlic, and freshly minced parsley for a unique pesto. And arugula may even be eaten as dessert. Simply wrap a leaf around a fresh pear slice spread with rich mascarpone cheese and sprinkled with toasted pine nuts.

The added joy of this herb is that it is relatively easy to grow. It fares especially well in the cooler months in the Southwestern climate, unscathed by mild freezes. And what a spicy, welcomed salad green it makes in the middle of winter! On the other hand, warm weather causes the plant to bolt and to taste fiery and bitter. As arugula bolts, it soon bursts into clusters of small, 4-petaled white flowers streaked with crimson. By then, the leaves of this 2-foot plant are tough and hot, but the flowers may be sprinkled on soups or used for perky garnishes.

Arugula is as easy to grow from seed as are radishes and the seeds germinate in a few days. I generally make successive plantings from September through April, avoiding the coldest months and then thin seedlings to 1 foot apart. This plant likes a rich, moist, well-draining soil and plenty of sunshine. As you thin the seedlings, you may save them for salads if you have not already popped them into your mouth. The plant's leaves may be eaten at various stages except during flowering. I cut off as many leaves as needed instead of pulling up the whole plant. The new, small leaves are especially tender and delicious; even my 9-year-old cat thinks so! Remember that arugula tastes especially flavorful when freshly picked from the garden to the salad bowl.

One note of caution: in the warmer months, I have unmerciful competition for the tasty leaves. Harlequin bugs (red with distinct black markings) chomp holes in the leaves when they're not prolifically mating. Although they can be picked off in early morning or at dusk when their metabolism is low, they can be invasive. As the plants will bolt soon anyway, I usually pull them up to dissuade the hungry marauders from other plants in my garden. Arugula's family name, *Eruca*, means caterpillar in Latin; hence, beware of the wrinkled creatures who love to devour the "caterpillar green."

Inevitably, once you have tasted this flavor-packed green, you will understand why French and Italians have eaten it for years!

SPRING GREENS SALAD

Arugula is at its best in fall or early spring, before summer's heat turns it tough and fiery. Combined with oranges, red onion rings, and toasted pine nuts, this colorful salad makes a stunning presentation.

1 generous handful per person (approximately 1½ cups) tender young spring greens, mostly arugula with some red-leafed or bibb lettuce and/or spinach (sorrel is good in this, but use only a small amount because of its tartness)

3 navel oranges, peeled and thinly sliced

1 small red onion, cut into thin rings

Zesty Vinaigrette (recipe follows)

1 tablespoon toasted pine nuts per salad

2 teaspoons crisp, crumbled bacon per salad (optional)

Freshly ground pepper

Arrange the crisp greens attractively on chilled salad plates (I like to leave some greens whole and tear some into bite-size pieces). Top with orange slices and onion rings. Drizzle with Zesty Vinaigrette and sprinkle with toasted pine nuts and crumbled bacon if desired. This salad also looks lovely composed on a large platter. Serves 8.

ZESTY VINAIGRETTE

4 tablespoons Mexican marigold mint vinegar or tarragon vinegar [*see chapter on herb vinegars*]

2 tablespoons sherry vinegar

2 cloves garlic, minced

1 tablespoon small capers, drained

2 teaspoons Dijon mustard

½ teaspoon brown sugar

½ teaspoon sweet paprika

1 tablespoon freshly chopped arugula

½ cup best quality olive oil

Mix ingredients together, slowly whisking in olive oil. It will be a rich orange color. Shake well before drizzling over salad. Yields about 1 cup.

NOTE: Sorrel may be substituted for arugula in the vinaigrette recipe. For instructions on toasting pine nuts, see Cooking Tips chapter.

EMERALD ARUGULA PESTO

The creamy texture of this bright green and garlicky sauce partners perfectly with grilled or broiled fish or chicken.   Or serve it on crackers or crudités. Arugula's peppy flavor certainly shines, and unlike traditional basil pestos, this one retains its bright green color. You can even freeze it.

5 slices (¾-inch) day-old baguette, crusts removed, torn into 1-inch pieces
    (about 1 cup)
5 tablespoons Lovely Lemon vinegar, bouquet garni vinegar, dill vinegar,
    or white wine vinegar [*see chapter on herb vinegars*]
3 tablespoons water
3 cloves garlic
1½ cups tender arugula leaves, tightly packed
½ cup Italian parsley, tightly packed
2 teaspoons Dijon mustard
½ cup (or more) best quality olive oil
1 pinch brown sugar (optional)
Freshly ground white pepper to taste

In a small bowl, soak the bread pieces in the vinegar and water (this will thicken the sauce). Grind the garlic with the arugula and parsley in a food processor or blender. Add the mustard and the soaked bread, and continue to grind until well mixed. With the motor running, slowly add the olive oil in a continuous stream until mixture forms a thick purée, adding more oil if necessary. If desired, add a pinch of brown sugar and a generous sprinkling of freshly ground white pepper. Serve immediately, or refrigerate and serve at room temperature later. This sauce keeps its vivid green color for up to a week and freezes beautifully.

NOTE: For a milder sauce, decrease arugula and increase parsley accordingly.

▼▼▼▼▼▼▼▼▼▼▼▼▼▼▼▼▼▼▼▼▼▼▼▼▼▼▼▼

▲▲▲▲▲▲▲▲▲▲▲▲▲▲▲▲▲▲▲▲▲▲▲▲

SESAME CRUSTED FISH IN ARUGULA WRAPPERS WITH SPICY DIPPING SAUCES

▼▼▼▼▼▼▼▼▼▼▼▼▼▼▼▼▼▼▼▼▼▼▼▼

This makes festive finger food for a party. Bite-size pieces of fish are dipped in black and white sesame seeds and gently fried, wrapped in crunchy arugula leaves, then dunked in a choice of two spicy dipping sauces.

½ pound firm fish (halibut or mahi mahi), rinsed and patted dry
Light cooking oil (such as safflower)
Oriental sesame oil
1 egg, lightly beaten in a small bowl
¼ cup white sesame seeds on a plate
¼ cup black sesame seeds on a plate
20 fresh arugula leaves

SPICY MUSTARD DIPPING SAUCE

▼▼▼▼▼▼▼▼▼▼▼▼▼▼▼▼▼▼

2 teaspoons Chinese hot dried mustard
2 tablespoons Chinese 5 vinegar or rice wine vinegar [*see chapter on herb vinegars*]
2 garlic cloves, minced
4 tablespoons fresh lime juice
2 teaspoons honey
1 tablespoon green tops of scallions, minced
½–1 serrano pepper (preferably red), minced

Dissolve the Chinese mustard in the vinegar, mixing well. Cover with plastic wrap while chopping other ingredients. Add the garlic, lime juice, honey, scallions, and serrano. Allow to set before tasting; additional lime juice or honey may be added. Makes ½ cup, approximately.

SPICY ORIENTAL DIPPING SAUCE

2 cloves garlic, minced

4 tablespoons fresh lime juice

2 tablespoons soy sauce or tamari

2 tablespoons Chinese 5 vinegar or rice wine vinegar [*see chapter on herb vinegars*]

1 tablespoon sesame oil

¼ teaspoon crushed dried red chile pepper

1 tablespoon green onion, minced

1 teaspoon brown sugar

½–1 serrano chile, minced

Combine all ingredients in a small bowl (keeps several days). Makes approximately ½ cup.

Prepare the dipping sauces; place in small bowls, and set aside.

Cut the fish into bite-size pieces, approximately 1¼ inches by 2 inches. Quickly dip half the fish pieces, one piece at a time, in the egg then in the white sesame seeds, coating both sides.

Heat 2–3 tablespoons oil in a medium-size frying pan, and drizzle in 1 teaspoon sesame oil to give extra flavor.

Sauté on medium-high heat until seeds are golden and fish is tender. Drain on paper towels and keep warm in low oven.

Wipe out the pan (to prevent burning of sesame seeds); add fresh oil and fry the rest of the fish (coated with black sesame seeds) in the same manner.

Serve on a plate surrounded with fresh arugula leaves and the dipping sauces. Have guests wrap the fish with the arugula leaves, then dunk in the spicy dipping sauces.

NOTE: Oriental sesame oil, black sesame seeds, and Chinese hot mustard are available at Oriental markets. Mustard greens or cilantro may be substituted for arugula. Both sauces may be used as marinades for fish or chicken, or drizzled over Oriental salads.

BASIL

Ocimum species
Lamiaceae (Labiatae) family

Basil beginning to blossom.

Common Names:

basil; varieties often named after their scent or physical characteristics

Characteristics:

leaves range in colors from dark purple to pale green and may be serrated
or smooth, glossy or crinkly; highly aromatic, spicy fragrance; flowers grow
in whorls ranging from white to purple; annual

Conditions:

rich, slightly moist soil and plenty of sunshine

Size:

most common varieties range from 1–3 feet tall and 1–2 feet wide

Propagation:

grows well from seeds planted when soil and air temperatures are warm; transplant to 1 foot apart; purchase nursery transplants; root cuttings in water

Fertilizer:

fish emulsion to get plants started and after heavy harvest

Pests:

worms cause some damage—treat with bacillus thuringiensis

Companions:

grows well next to tomatoes and other sun-loving plants

I will never forget a leisurely trip through the wine country north of San Francisco. Driving down the sleepy country roads in Sonoma County, we often stopped to sample the local vineyards' offerings. Although the crisp California chardonnays delighted me, it was my first nibble from a bunch of fresh basil that made the afternoon so memorable.

A crudely painted sign promising *Fresh Vegetables* tempted us to pull into a dirt driveway leading to a small farmhouse. A plump, amiable woman greeted us and pointed proudly to baskets of freshly picked samples from her garden. She pinched off a few leaves from a large bunch of basil for us to taste, and I was immediately impressed by its fresh and spicy flavor. Then, with a thick Italian accent, she instructed us how to make pesto—a thick sauce made by pounding basil, garlic, pine nuts, freshly grated Parmesan, and olive oil with a mortar and pestle. We bought several big bouquets, and with the car redolent of basil's clove-like fragrance, we merrily made our way across the Golden Gate Bridge, eager to try our hand at pesto making.

This initiation occurred 15 years ago, and the ritual of spreading the green, garlicky sauce on almost everything edible has become an addiction for me and most people who have ever eaten pesto. Because of its current popularity, you'll find it featured on chic restaurant menus and packaged with fancy labels on gourmet shelves. But despite pesto's trendy reputation, varying its ingredients and its uses can produce exciting possibilities for the creative cook.

My love for pesto led me to experiment with growing basil, and I discovered innumerable varieties, each with a unique aroma and taste, adding subtle nuances to pesto. Fortunately, basil grows as well basking in the Southwestern sunshine as it does in the Mediterranean.

The most common basil, sweet basil (*Ocimum basilicum*), has bright green, shiny, slightly serrated leaves and whorls of white blossoms. The plant usually attains about 3 feet in height with leaves that are 2½ inches long. Its flavor is robust and spicy —clove-like with minty undertones. A larger leafed Japanese variety called lettuce leaf basil (*O. basilicum* var. *crispum*) has curly, puckered leaves resembling those of curly leafed lettuce. Its flavor is more mild than sweet basil, although it may be used interchangeably. Add the leaves to salads or use as wrappers for savory fillings—grilled or boiled shrimp, spicy shredded chicken or pork, chopped vegetables (cellophane noodles may be added)—and dunk into lively sauces. Or wrap the large leaves around tabbouleh.

Smaller leafed basils also are culinary staples. Provençal cooks especially favor French fine leaf basil (*O. basilicum* 'Minimum'), whose numerous ¼-inch leaves have an enticing sweetness. This 1½-foot tall, bushy plant grows well in pots. A similar plant, bush basil, reaches about 12 inches in height with small, slightly rounded, clove-scented leaves; tiny bouquets of these leaves make dainty garnishes. Spicy globe basil grows about 1 foot tall in a uniquely round shape, and its prolific white blossoms make it a valuable ornamental plant. Italian cooks prefer *picolo verde fino*, a basil with narrow dark green leaves, and many agree that its sweet and spicy flavor is best for making pesto. This is a tall plant (2½ feet) that likes some elbow room.

An absolutely delightful herb, lemon basil (*O. basilicum* 'Citriodorum') has pale green, pointed leaves (approximately 1 inch long and 1 inch wide) that are slightly hairy with a prominent and delicious lemon scent; in fact, its lemony aroma actually masks that of basil. What a burst freshness these leaves impart to salads and steamed vegetables! I often add large handfuls to rice or pasta dishes and stuff the leaves in the cavities of fish, turkey, or chicken. (Stuff under the skin of chicken breasts as well.) A pesto flavored with lemon basil and ground almonds is quite extraordinary tasting. This variety of basil seems to seed very quickly—keep seed heads pinched continually.

Another aromatic basil, cinnamon basil (*O. basilicum*) has deep-green, glossy leaves (generally 2½–3 inches long) redolent of spicy cinnamon when crushed. In the summer, this 2-foot-tall plant bursts forth in whorls of purplish flowers, which make lovely garnishes and bouquets. Cinnamon basil's leaves may be rubbed on beef and cooked with pot roast or pork tenderloin stuffed with apples. Use it in pesto flavored with ground walnuts. Apple and pear salads especially benefit from this flavorful herb; try adding toasted pine nuts or walnuts and a vinaigrette made with port and lemon juice. Apple and cranberry juice and fruit nectars benefit from sprigs of cinnamon basil, as do fruit jellies and chutneys.

Licorice basil (*Ocimum* species) has 2½-inch-long bright-green leaves with a subtle licorice scent. This rather lanky (2½ feet) plant has purple flowers whose delicate scent enhances bouquets. Garnish cold fruit drinks and iced tea with this herb, and toss some of the leaves in salads, steamed vegetables, and fruit dishes or sorbets. Its smooth anise flavor lends itself to fish, pork, and veal dishes as well.

The deep purple color of dark opal basil (*O. basilicum* 'Purpurascens') gives good contrast in the garden as well as in food. Most notable, however, is the rich ruby color it gives to vinegar. The sweetly perfumed leaves make colorful additions to salads and look quite appealing sprinkled over slices of ripe tomatoes. A delicious and colorful pesto made with dark opal basil and sun-dried tomatoes may be used with pasta or in a layered cheese torta. Dark opal basil usually reaches about 1 foot in height with leaves that are 2½ inches long and 1½ inches wide. It has serrated leaves and lovely lavender flowers tinged with deeper purple.

Although the top leaves remain purple, the lower leaves often become mottled with green variegation. As with most variegated plants, they are weaker and more prone to fungus disease and root rot. A new basil cultivar, 'Purple Ruffles,' an All American Selections winner, retains its deep and true purple color without fading. Its crinkly and serrated leaves resemble perilla [*see chapter on Oriental herbs*], providing color and texture in the garden and making unusual garnishes and bouquets.

▼▼▼▼▼▼▼▼▼▼▼▼▼▼▼▼▼▼▼▼▼▼▼▼▼

'Purple Ruffles' may be used similarly to dark opal basil in cooking.

Basil is as popular in the cuisines of Southeast Asia (especially Thai and Vietnamese cuisines) as in those of Italy. Several other varieties exist [*see chapter on Oriental herbs*]. Because of basil's popularity, it seems that new varieties are always being introduced. Shepherd's Garden Seeds in California added three new basils to their 1987 catalog: basil *napoletano*, with a buttery soft flavor; basil *Genova profumatissima*, with its intensely perfumed flavor; and basil *fino verde compatto*, with its small leaves packed with sweet flavor. The catalog also boasts a scented basil collection of five fragrant basils. Marilyn Hampstead, author of *The Basil Book*, offers more than 20 varieties of basil in her mail-order catalog (several are her own hybrids), as well as freshly cut basil from her Fox Hill Farm in Michigan.

Despite the many varieties of basils, they all require basically the same growing conditions. Plenty of warm sunshine is imperative for these sun worshippers. Although they like a slightly moist and rich soil, it is essential that it drains well. Basil is an herb that I highly recommend growing from seed since it germinates in a few days; however, do not attempt to plant seeds during a cold, damp spring. Wait until warm soil and air temperatures allow the seeds to germinate properly; cool temperatures stunt the plants. If desired, plant seeds in flats indoors and set them out once their true set of leaves has emerged, spacing the seedlings about 1 foot apart.

Although I use light applications of fish emulsion to get the plants started, and perhaps again after heavy harvesting, too much fertilization will produce lush leaves at the sacrifice of flavor. Applications of compost mulch during the hot summers help the soil retain moisture, and a drip irrigation system can be quite valuable. My best advice is to pinch back the plants continually – besides, the verdant tips taste the best – to encourage new growth.

Insects have never been a serious threat to my basil patch; worms can be pests but are easily controlled with bacillus thuringiensis. Bothersome, however, are the ugly black spots that sometimes discolor the leaves. Gertrude B. Foster and Rosemary Louden in *Park's Success with Herbs* say that droplets of cold water that collect on the plant toward the end of the season cause black spots on the leaves, and they advise against spraying with cold hose water in the late afternoon. My plants seem to be the most distressed by these spots in August, however, when I think the high heat and humidity steam the plant, thereby causing the unattractive dark spots. Take caution to water the roots and not the leaves to help prevent the problem. The main damage is, fortunately, only aesthetic.

Basil bruises and darkens easily when harvested, so only pick just the amount you need. Overzealous gardeners too often cram the kitchen sink full of basil, bruising tender leaves or allowing them to stand too long in water. To their dismay, many of the leaves blacken. My advice for harvesting basil (and in fact, most herbs) is to spray the leaves gently with the hose in the early morning to remove any debris, then allow them to dry naturally in the sunshine. After harvesting, take them to the kitchen, discard any damaged leaves, and proceed with your favorite recipe.

Basil is a prolific grower, so frequent harvests are necessary to keep the plants from going to seed. Because the flavor of the leaves is diminished when the plant puts its energy into flowering, the emerging flower stalks should be pinched continually to encourage new growth and discourage cross-pollination. Toward the end of the growing season, allow some plants to set seed for next year's crop.

Although in areas with very mild winters basil can be treated as a tender perennial (if kept pinched back), it is generally treated as an annual. In fact, a near frost darkens the leaves and withers the plant. As basil's branches become woody in the late summer and fall (by which point I have harvested many times), I usually pull up the plant, making use of any remaining leaves.

Throughout the season, I make gallons of basil vinegar, often flavored with lots of garlic and dried red chile peppers, to give as Christmas presents. My freezer is packed with jars of pesto to toss with pasta on a chilly winter eve, and I have dried some basil for winter use. Larger leafed basils dry best taken off their stems and placed on a screen with plenty of air circulation (but not light, which causes discoloration). The smaller leafed basils may be tied in small bundles and hung upside down. During times of high humidity, alternative methods – such as a very low oven, microwave, or dehydrator – must be used to prevent darkening.

Many cooks prefer freezing basil. Take the leaves off the stem, place in freezer-proof plastic bags, pressing out excess air before sealing, or purée the herb in a food processor or blender with enough water to blend. Pour purée into ice cube trays, adding more water if needed; once frozen, remove from the tray and freeze in air-tight containers. Add these cubes to soups or stews, or to water when steaming vegetables and cooking rice or pasta.

Another way to preserve basil is in olive oil. Simply layer clean, dry leaves with olive oil and slightly mashed cloves of garlic in a glass jar, pressing down well between the layers. Or grind the basil leaves, put them in a jar, and cover them with olive oil. Store in a cool place, shaking daily for about 2 weeks. Many English herbalists recommend setting the jar in a sunny window to let basil's fragrance permeate the oil, but Southwestern sun is generally too strong for this method and actually can damage the flavor of the oil.

To me, the best way to eat basil is fresh from the garden – or in the garden! Pop a cherry tomato in your mouth followed by a bite of basil. After all, where there are tomatoes, there should be basil. Not only are tomatoes and basil companions in the garden (requiring the same growing conditions and mutually benefiting one another),

but they are fine companions in the kitchen as well.

Whether sprinkled on vine-ripened tomato slices drizzled with basil vinegar and olive oil, or simmered in a rich and lusty tomato sauce, or stuffed in chicken breasts with sun-dried tomatoes before baking, basil is the tomato herb *par excellence*. Use it on homemade pizza, in spaghetti and lasagna, in tomato soup and gazpacho. A simple garden sandwich (or appetizer) can be made by spreading pesto (or basil-garlic-Parmesan butter) on slices of baguette and topping with a slice of roma tomato, a sprinkling of freshly grated Parmesan, and a fresh basil sprig.

Basil also complements other sun-loving vegetables of the Southwest: corn, eggplant, squash, and green beans. Try rolling steaming corn on the cob in basil-garlic-Parmesan butter and freshly grated Parmesan. Or add plenty of basil leaves to a spicy spinach casserole. Basil leaves enhance garden salads, both to the eye and to the palate. Experiment with the many basil varieties for color and taste.

Shepherd's Garden Seeds recommends laying fish fillets on a bed of anise basil before baking, or tying a bunch of basil together to use as a brush when basting fish. Lemon basil especially enhances chicken or fish marinades, and chicken breasts taste delicious with chopped basil and garlic stuffed under the skin before baking or grilling.

And of course, there is pesto, Italy's answer to Mexico's salsa picante – a spunky condiment that enhances innumerable dishes. Traditionally, it is added to bowls of minestrone and tossed with pasta. It makes a fabulous stuffing for mushrooms or chicken breasts and tastes wonderful over fish. Grilled shrimp and steamed artichoke leaves dunked into melted butter mixed with pesto and a squeeze of fresh lemon juice are my favorites. I love to melt pesto over corn on the cob, steamed new potatoes, or sautéed vegetables, and it certainly gives pep to vinaigrettes and sour cream-based salad dressings. Pesto is espe-

▼▼▼▼▼▼▼▼▼▼▼▼▼▼▼▼▼▼▼▼▼▼▼▼▼▼

cially wonderful on pasta with lots of fresh-ly grated Parmesan, and part of the fun of making it is experimenting with different varieties of basil.

My summer garden is full of basils, ranging in color from the deepest purple to the palest green, and in texture from smooth and glossy to crinkled, providing culinary as well as ornamental pleasure. The spicy, complex aromas fill the garden with splendid and alluring fragrance, and the leaves almost beckon to be picked. After picking, new sprigs quickly appear, offering another gift. Indeed, this prima-donna of herbs reigns in my garden.

PESTO TIPS

Use only the freshest ingredients.

Make sure basil is free of moisture before grinding with a mortar and pestle, a mezzaluna (Italian crescent-bladed chop-ping knife), food processor, or blender. Don't skimp on the basil!

Select top-grade imported Parmesan and Pecorino Romano cheese, and grate them yourself.

Use a good quality olive oil; if using a food processor, slowly add it last with the motor running.

Make sure that the pine nuts are fresh, as they have a tendency to become rancid if improperly stored.

Try substituting walnuts, pecans, or almonds for the pine nuts. Lightly toasting the nuts beforehand gives a nice flavor.

Pour a ⅛-inch layer of melted butter or olive oil over pesto before storing to prevent its darkening. (Also make sure there are no air bubbles in the jar.)

Add a few tablespoons of the water used to cook the pasta when tossing hot pasta with pesto; allow 1 cup pesto per pound of pasta (you may also add butter).

Serve pesto at the last minute, as exposure to air causes it to oxidize and darken; once some pesto has been used from a jar, the top layer will darken but may be mixed in with the rest.

GARDEN PESTO

3 cups fresh basil (tightly packed), gently rinsed and dried (experiment
  with various kinds of basil)

4–6 cloves garlic

½ cup pine nuts (or walnuts or pecans)

½–¾ cup freshly grated Parmesan

2–3 tablespoons freshly grated Romano cheese

⅔ cup olive oil, or more

Grind basil and garlic. Add nuts and cheeses, then slowly add the olive oil. Blend to the desired consistency, adding more olive oil if desired. Spoon into small jars and seal with melted butter. (Try substituting cinnamon basil and pecans or walnuts.) Yields approximately 2 cups. Freeze half if desired.

LUSCIOUS LEMON BASIL PESTO

2 cups fresh lemon basil, gently rinsed and dried
2–3 cloves garlic
⅓ cup blanched almonds, lightly toasted
½ cup freshly grated Parmesan cheese
½ cup olive oil

Make according to recipe for garden pesto. This is especially delightful over grilled fish, shrimp, or chicken and is wonderful with rice, pasta, or steamed green beans or other vegetables as well. Yields approximately 1 generous cup.

PURPLE PESTO . . . ALMOST

2 cups fresh dark opal or 'Purple Ruffles' basil

3–4 cloves garlic (or more, chopped)

¼ generous cup minced sun-dried tomatoes packed in olive oil

¼ cup pine nuts

½ cup freshly grated Parmesan cheese

¾ cup olive oil

2 teaspoons freshly minced rosemary

½ teaspoon crushed dried red chile

Grind the basil, garlic, tomatoes, cheese, and pine nuts. Slowly add the oil (using some of the oil from the sun-dried tomatoes); add the peppers, and blend to desired consistency. I like to stuff this under the skin of chicken breasts and melt it over grilled fish or chicken. It tastes fabulous tossed with fettuccine with more sun-dried tomatoes or used in a cheese torta garnished with additional purple basil sprigs. Yields approximately 1½ cups.

BASIL CHEESE TORTA WITH RED BELL PEPPER STRIPS AND TOASTED PINE NUTS

This Italian-inspired appetizer features sweet basil that flourishes in Southwestern gardens in the summertime. Strips of roasted red bell pepper strips, sun-dried tomatoes, and toasted pine nuts alternate between layers of green pesto and provolone. Serve on slices of baguettes or on homemade garlic croutons with a glass of chilled white wine.

½ pound cream cheese, softened

4 tablespoons butter, softened

¾ cup basil pesto

½ pound provolone, thinly sliced

¼ cup toasted pine nuts

1 red bell pepper, roasted, peeled, seeded and cut into 3-by-⅜-inch strips
  [*see Cooking Tips chapter*]

1 small jar sun-dried tomatoes packed in olive oil

Fresh basil for garnish

Mix cream cheese and butter with a fork; add pesto and mix well.

Line a small (3-cup) loaf pan or bowl with plastic wrap, leaving several inches of overhang on each side. Make a thin layer of provolone slices on the bottom and partially up the sides. Spread ⅓ of the pesto mixture over the cheese; artistically arrange 2 or 3 sun-dried tomatoes, 4–6 bell pepper strips, and about 1 tablespoon toasted pine nuts over the pesto. Repeat layers until all ingredients are used (reserving some of the pine nuts to sprinkle on top), pressing down well between layers. Chill overnight or for several days. Serve at room temper-ature on a platter wreathed with fresh basil sprigs. Additional toasted pine nuts, sun-dried tomatoes cut into flowers, red bell pepper strips, and fresh basil sprigs may be used as garnish.

NOTE: Torta may be presented inverted or not. Keeps several weeks refrigerated. Although best served at room temperature, it slices best chilled. I like to serve it on a platter adorned with grape leaves and small clusters of red and white grapes.

VARIATIONS

Use lemon pesto; substitute slivered toasted almonds for the pine nuts; omit the sun-dried tomatoes and add 1 teaspoon lemon zest to the cream cheese mixture.

Use purple pesto; omit the red pepper if desired and increase the sun-dried tomatoes.

Use cinnamon basil pesto; omit the sun-dried tomatoes and the red peppers if desired, and use pecans instead of pine nuts.

CITY GRILL'S GULF REDFISH WITH SPICY SZECHUAN SAUCE

No wonder this is the most popular item on the menu at City Grill in Austin! Exemplary of the Oriental influence on the Texas Gulf coast, Spicy Szechuan Sauce partners with marinated mesquite-grilled redfish, garnished with an exquisite purple-flowering Thai basil sprig.

6 redfish fillets, ⅓–½ pound each, *or* fillets of swordfish, tuna, Mahi Mahi, or shark
Garnish: 6 Thai basil sprigs, lime wedges, and slivered scallion

SZECHUAN MARINADE

1 8-ounce can Szechuan chile paste
1 cup dark honey
2 tablespoons rice wine vinegar
3 tablespoons Oriental sesame oil
3 tablespoons peanut oil
Juice of 1–2 fresh limes

SPICY SZECHUAN SAUCE

1 cup mayonnaise
2 tablespoons rice wine vinegar
1 tablespoon Oriental sesame oil
¼ cup Szechuan marinade
3–4 tablespoons Thai basil, chopped

Prepare the marinade by mixing all of the ingredients, blending well.

Mix together the ingredients for the Spicy Szechuan Sauce and chill.

Dip the fillets in the marinade, and place presentation-side down on the grill over red-hot coals. Grill until well marked by the grill, turning once (approximately 8 minutes per inch of thickness of fish).

Serve with a generous dollop of Spicy Szechuan Sauce, either on the side or melted on the fish, and garnished with a sprig of Thai basil, several lime wedges, and slivered scallion. Serves 6.

NOTE: Try this recipe with grilled chicken breasts as well. Spicy Szechuan Sauce makes a zesty dressing for chicken salad, especially when made with cold leftover chicken that has been grilled with Szechuan marinade.

▼▲▼▲▼▲▼▲▼▲▼▲▼▲▼▲▼▲▼▲▼▲▼▲▼▲▼▲▼

BALKAN BASIL AND TOMATO SAUCE

▼▲▼▲▼▲▼▲▼▲▼▲▼▲▼▲▼▲▼

This sauce, adapted from a recipe by Slavik food specialist Rosa Rajkovic', is a perfect way to preserve vine-ripened tomatoes and basil from the garden. It keeps for weeks in the refrigerator, readily available for making quick and refreshing summertime meals. Spread crusty whole grain peasant bread with a creamy feta cheese mixture (recipe follows), and top with the tomato sauce and fresh basil sprigs. I like to dunk boiled shrimp in it, toss it with pasta, or serve it over chicken or fish.

12–14 medium-size fresh ripe tomatoes

5 tablespoons olive oil

6–8 cloves garlic, minced

½ teaspoon freshly ground pepper

¼–½ teaspoon crushed dried red chile pepper

4 tablespoons (or more) basil-chile-garlic vinegar or red wine vinegar [*see chapter on herb vinegars*]

1–2 teaspoons brown sugar

6 tablespoons chopped fresh basil

2 green onions with tops, chopped

Salt to taste

Peel, core, seed, and chop tomatoes. [*For instructions, see Cooking Tips chapter.*]

In a large enamel saucepan, heat the oil; add the garlic, coating well with oil. Add the tomatoes and bring to boil; add pepper, reduce heat to low, and simmer, uncovered, until it cooks down to a thick sauce (about 1 hour), stirring frequently toward the end to prevent sticking.

Add the vinegar and sugar to taste the last 5 minutes of cooking. Remove from heat, allow to cool slightly, and adjust seasonings (adding more sugar or vinegar if needed). Add the chopped basil, green onions, and salt to taste. Let sit several hours before serving. If refrigerated, serve at room temperature sprinkled with minced green onions and fresh basil sprigs. Yields about 4 cups. Keeps several weeks.

CREAMY FETA SPREAD

6 ounces feta cheese
8 ounces cream cheese, softened
1½ sticks butter, softened

Combine feta, cream cheese, and butter in a food processor or blender and mix until slightly creamy (some feta should be apparent). Do not overprocess. Keeps several weeks tightly covered in refrigerator. Serve at room temperature with marinated bell peppers or Balkan Basil and Tomato Sauce and crusty peasant bread. Yields 2 cups.

NOTE: I like to spread this cheese on slices of baguette, followed by the tomato sauce and a fresh basil sprig, and serve as appetizers with wine.

LEMONY RICE WITH TOASTED ALMONDS

Lemon basil's fresh flavor and aroma make this rice a delicious and lovely accompaniment to fish, chicken, or lamb. Green flecks of herbs, toasted almonds, and thin lemon slices further the elegance.

1 tablespoon olive oil

2 tablespoons butter

1 cup long-grain white rice

½ medium-size onion, chopped

2 cloves garlic, chopped

1½ cup chicken broth [*for recipe, see Cooking Tips chapter*]

¼ cup dry white wine

3 tablespoons fresh lemon juice

4 medium-size green onions with tops, chopped

⅓ cup toasted almonds, crushed [*for instructions on toasting nuts, see Cooking Tips chapter*]

Salt and pepper

½ cup lemon basil, finely chopped and tightly packed

2 tablespoons butter

6 thin slices lemon

In a medium-size flameproof casserole, heat the olive oil and butter. Add the rice, and sauté on medium heat, stirring frequently, until rice is golden (5 minutes). Add the onion and garlic, and sauté about 4 minutes. Add the chicken broth, wine, and lemon juice, and bring to a boil; reduce heat and simmer covered 15–16 minutes.

Quickly add the green onions, almonds, salt and pepper, lemon basil, and butter, lightly mixing to melt the butter. Place 6 lemon slices on top and allow to stand, covered, for 10 minutes. Before serving, mix well, arranging the lemon slices on top. Garnish with lemon basil sprigs. Serves 6.

NOTE: Parsley, lemon thyme, lemon verbena, or any combination of these herbs may be substituted for, or used along with, lemon basil. To crush toasted almonds, place in a clean dishtowel and lightly crush with rolling pin or back of a heavy wooden spoon.

CHIVES

Allium species
Liliaceae family

Garlic chives in bloom.

Common Names:

onion chives; garlic chives, Oriental garlic or Chinese chives; Egyptian topping onion or tree onions; rocambole; society garlic

Characteristics:

onion chives have dark green tubular leaves 10–15 inches tall with distinct onion aroma; attractive pompom flowers ranging from white to vivid pink; garlic chives have lighter green, flat reed-like leaves with distinct garlic aroma; star-like white flowers bloom on long stems; perennial

Conditions:

rich, moist, well-draining soil; full sun (some afternoon shade tolerated)

Size:

onion chives grow in clump 10–12 inches tall; garlic chives grow in clumps 2 feet tall

Propagation:

sow seeds in the fall; divide clumps in the fall and early spring; purchase nursery transplants; several varieties of each per garden suggested for ornamental and culinary purposes

Fertilizer:

regular feedings of manure, fish emulsion, and/or compost to supply necessary nitrogen; coffee grounds may be applied as mulch

Pests:

too damp a soil causes root disease; some slug and snail damage; may attract aphids, distracting them from roses

Companions:

grow around roses and carrots; deters detrimental insects from the garden (a natural insecticide can be made by grinding garlic, chiles, and chives with water and spraying on plants); plant near nitrogen-giving comfrey

Garlic. Shallots. Chives. Scallions. Leeks. Elephant garlic. I was deliberating about how to write one chapter about all these indispensable members of the lily family; after all, they could merit an entire book. And indeed, they did. "It's time the lilies of the kitchen received starring roles and the applause they so richly and deliciously deserve," says Barbara Batcheller in her book *Lilies of the Kitchen: Recipes Celebrating Garlic, Onions, Leeks, Shallots, Scallions, and Chives.*

"They are," says Batcheller, "each one, distinctive. Highly compatible, they mingle easily with each other and are mostly interchangeable." And even more important, these bulbous plants have been noted for centuries in peasant cultures for their ability to safeguard health by preventing disease with their antibiotic qualities.

For the sake of simplicity, I will concentrate on chives, plants that are easy to grow and give a burst of fresh, zesty flavor to many foods. An added bonus is their beautiful cluster of star-like flowers that bloom in shades of pink and white. Chives may be planted as ornamental borders and as edgings around the vegetable garden, or dispersed among flowers. Their strong aroma deters insects when randomly planted among vegetables and flowers.

When onion chives (*Allium schoenoprasum*) first emerge from the ground, they resemble long stalks of grass, but as they grow, they become tall and tubular with the familiar onion aroma. Although they have small bulbs at their base, chives are grown for their leaves, which may be harvested frequently to encourage new growth. Don't snip the leaves straight across, however, or you will quickly diminish the plant. Instead, pinch off the desired stems from the base. If you harvest too heavily from the plant, it will not set

A Spicy Southwestern Supper

Queso Fundido with Warm Tortillas

Tomatoes Rellenos

Flank Steak in Cilantro, Citrus, and Gold Tequila Marinade

Velvety Lemon Verbena Flan

Mexican Peer/Fiesta Tequila/Sangría

QUESO FUNDIDO (Spicy Broiled Cheese)

1½ pounds cheese (Cheddar, Monterey Jack, and/or Muenster), grated or thinly sliced
3-4 cloves garlic, minced
4-6 Anaheim or poblano chiles, cut into *rajas* (strips) [See Cooking Tips chapter]
1-2 jalapeños, chopped (optional)
3 green onions, chopped
1 tomato, chopped
1 bunch fresh cilantro; chop 2 tablespoons; use remainder for garnish
Optional condiments: additional chopped onions and tomatoes, cilantro sprigs, red and/or green salsa picante, avocado wedges, chorizo

In a 9-by-12-inch earthenware serving dish, mix grated cheese, garlic, peppers, and half the onions. Cook at 450 degrees until bubbly, stirring occasionally. Add the tomato and broil until golden brown. Sprinkle with remaining onions and 2 tablespoons of the chopped cilantro. Garnish with avocado slices, cilantro sprigs, and your favorite hot sauce. Scoop the melted cheese into warm tortillas or tostada chips. Pass small bowls of your

NOTE: Sometimes I fry Mexican chorizo sausage and crumble it on top of the cheese as it broils. Or add sautéed squash, mushrooms, or squash blossoms with peppers. Substitute epazote for cilantro when white cheese is used, but use it sparingly if serving to those unaccustomed to its taste.

flower, but if allowed to flower, the chive's flavor will decrease. (Keep the flowers pinched off to flavor and color vinegar a rosy hue.) Because the cheerful pink pompom-like flowers are a welcome sight in the garden in spring and summer, I make sure to grow enough clumps so that some may flower and some may be harvested.

My mother always grows a pot of chives outside her kitchen door to snip and sprinkle over baked potatoes and garlic bread. My grandmother did the same, favoring a smaller, thinner-leafed variety that sported small white flowers. (Actually, the flower head of chives is comprised of a round clump of individual florets.) Chives fare well in pots – sometimes mixed with parsley, basil, or summer savory – as long as the soil is rich and well draining and as long as they are fed at regular intervals. Whether you grow chives in a pot or in the ground, yellowing of their leaves signifies lack of nutrients. Because they are nitrogen-loving plants, light applications of fish emulsion, manure, and/or compost help. English herbalist Dorothy Hall says that growing comfrey (*Symphytum officinale*) benefits chives because it releases nitrogen into the soil. Others recommend coffee grounds, which serve as a mulch and slightly acidify the soil.

Chives may be grown from seed sown in the fall, but they are much easier and quicker to grow by dividing existing clumps (found as nursery transplants or given by a friend). Plant 2–3-inch clumps about 1 foot apart in a rich, light, moist soil in full sun (some afternoon shade is tolerable). Chive clumps will eventually attain about 10–15 inches in height. As with potted chives, regular feedings are beneficial, and the plants cannot be allowed to dry out. During hot summers, chives may die back to reappear with renewed vigor in fall, when they may be divided. During mild winters, chives may remain green, but they usually die back. Remember to mark their location so as not to disturb them while they are dormant. They also may be divided when they reappear in the spring. Because chives eventually rob the soil of nutrients and because the clump will die out if allowed to get too big, I divide it every few years, moving the small clumps to other spots in the garden.

While giving their spunky flavor to foods, chives also give nutrients to the body, being rich with calcium, phosphorus, sulfur (a natural antibiotic), iron, Vitamins A and C, and pectin. The flavor and nutrients, however, are diminished by cooking, so it is best to sprinkle the chopped leaves over foods at the last minute. Yet there are more uses for chives than garnishing garlic bread and baked potatoes. They are a crucial ingredient in *fines herbes*, a blend of herbs that are finely chopped and used to season soups and stocks, sauces, egg dishes, fish, and poultry. Add fresh chives to salad dressings, homemade mayonnaise, herb butters, dips, and cheeseballs or spreads, as well as potato, chicken, tuna, and marinated vegetable salads. In fact, use chives whenever a mild onion flavor is desired. Sometimes I tie up bundles of steamed green beans or asparagus with slender chive stems, tucking in a chive blossom.

And remember to use the delicate flowers which bloom throughout the late spring and summer. They look lovely tossed in a salad, used as a garnish, and added to flavor and color herb vinegars. They make colorful additions to bouquets as well.

Garlic chives (*Allium tuberosum*), also known as Oriental garlic or Chinese chives (*gow choy*), are another kind of chives. Growing taller than onion chives (about 2 feet) with flat, light green, reed-like leaves boasting delicate clusters of starry white flowers, they give color to the garden throughout the late spring and well into the fall. This is truly a beautiful plant that remains green year round. When allowed to remain on the plant, the white flowers dry to rice-paper opaqueness, hosting small, black seeds (in this dried form they look attractive on wreaths), which drop to the ground to grow. The emerging seed-

▼▼▼▼▼▼▼▼▼▼▼▼▼▼▼▼▼▼▼▼▼▼▼▼▼▼

lings can become quite thick—quickly spreading from rhizomes and being invasive if not controlled.

Graceful and elegant, especially when their delicate white flowers contrast with other blooming flowers, garlic chives are a must for the herb gardener; their tender new leaves have a tasty mild garlic flavor and may be used as you would onion chives. One of my favorite Vietnamese restaurants rolls up boiled shrimp, grilled pork, mung bean sprouts, mint, and garlic chives in a rice paper wrapping, neatly tucking in the ends so it is sealed; the cook always leaves one wispy stem of garlic chives poking out from one end to make an attractive presentation. These tightly rolled delicacies are then dunked into a pungent *hoisin* (fermented bean) sauce sprinkled with peanuts, or into a fiery fish sauce.

I especially like using the flowers of garlic chives as garnish. They have a mild, sweet aroma and a pleasant flavor. Toss them in salads, add them to stir-frys at the last minute, or add them to sautéed or steamed vegetables or baked potatoes. Use them to garnish herb butters or sauces and to garnish plates. To make a simple yet spectacular party platter, arrange fresh garden greens (try kale, arugula, savoy cabbage, and assorted lettuces) on a wicker tray, adding attractively sliced raw vegetables adorned with groupings of chive blossoms. Serve with a lively dip garnished with freshly chopped chives.

Another allium worthy of mention—and fun to grow—is the Egyptian topping onion, sometimes called tree onions (*Allium cepa* var. *proliferum*). Its leaves are more onion-like—thick and round with hollow stems. The unusual thing about this plant is that it produces clumps of "bulblets" instead of seeds at the top of the plant. The weight of the bulblets causes the stem to fall over, and the bulblets often start rooting in mid air, creating a whimsical appearance. As soon as the bulblets hit the ground, they take root and become invasive if not thinned. They are quite flavorful and may be used like green scallions,

while the tender stems may be chopped like chives. And they are available in the garden year round. Propagate this plant by dividing the clump or simply letting the bulblets grow.

Similarly, rocambole (*Allium sativum* v. *ophioscorodon*) is a topping garlic with purple-skinned bulblets developing in showy coils at the top of the stems; hence its nickname "serpent garlic." Its flat, reed-like leaves resemble those of garlic chives except they are wider. As they grow, stems shoot up, often looping, before forming the mild, garlic-tasting bulblet. In their book *Park's Success with Herbs*, Gertrude B. Foster and Rosemary F. Louden accurately describe it as perching on the stem at an angle suggestive of a crane's bill. The bulblets may be used as one would Egyptian onions—slightly mashing them as one would garlic with the back of a knife to release their flavor. The fresh, new leaves may be chopped like chives. Once established in the garden, rocambole continually reproduces.

Another of my favorites, society garlic (*Tulbaghia violacea*), is grown especially for its ornamental effect, although its leaves are tasty when chopped like chives. Its flowers are lovely, blooming throughout the summer and fall in star shapes of lilac hue. These flowers grace the garden as well as platters when used as garnish. Try serving an emerald-colored fresh pea soup contrasted with the vivid pink blossoms. Or toss some of the flowers among marinated cucumber slices and paper-thin slices of red onion.

The leaves of this 1–1½-foot-tall plant are flat and reed-like; they grow in a nice, round clump while the stems with the flowers shoot up taller. Tricolor society garlic has delicately variegated leaves in shades of green, white, and pink. Divide individual bulblets from the mother plant in the fall or early spring. Society garlic looks good planted as a border or planted randomly among flower and vegetable beds.

Although commercial freeze-dried chives remain green, when dried at home, chives often turn yellow and unappealing, but they can be successfully frozen. Chop them and freeze in small packets, or freeze them in herb butters. The best and most nutritious way to use them, though, is fresh. And as there are usually several varieties to choose from in the garden almost year round, I don't bother with freezing or drying them.

I could go on to extol the virtues of the other alliums – garlic's assertiveness, leek's subtlety, elephant garlic's mild and inoffensive flavor, shallot's unrivaled perfection, and the freshness of scallions. But Barbara Batcheller said it best. Indeed, alliums are the lilies of the kitchen!

▼▼▼▼▼▼▼▼▼▼▼▼▼▼▼▼▼▼▼▼

BOURSIN WITH FRESH HERBS

I like to divide a batch of this homemade cheese spread into 4 parts, flavoring each with different herbs. Serve with crudités, crackers, thin slices of baguette, as a spread for sandwiches, or stuffed under chicken breasts. You can create an attractive party platter of open-faced sandwiches by using the following variations and placing different fresh herb sprigs on each variation.

BASIC BOURSIN

1 pound farmers cheese *or* ½ pound cottage cheese and ½ pound ricotta

8 ounces cream cheese, softened

1 stick butter, softened

4 large cloves garlic, minced

2 medium shallots, minced

½ cup finely minced parsley, tightly packed

3 tablespoons minced chives

1 teaspoon freshly ground pepper

¼ teaspoon cayenne

Salt (optional)

In a medium-size bowl, blend the cheeses and butter; mix in the other ingredients. Divide cheese mixture into 4 small bowls or ramekins and make the following variations.

BOURSIN AU POIVRE (PEPPER BOURSIN)

½–1 teaspoon freshly cracked pepper (white and black)

¼ teaspoon crushed dried red chile pepper (optional)

Mix peppers with the basic boursin.
Serve with cold cuts and/or roast beef.
Meat may be rolled around cheese.

DANISH BOURSIN

3 tablespoons chopped fresh dill

2 teaspoons chopped fresh chives

Mix ingredients with the basic boursin. Serve on dark bread with cucumber slices, caviar or smoked salmon, and fresh dill sprigs.

ITALIAN BOURSIN

3 tablespoons chopped fresh basil

¼–½ teaspoon crushed dried red chile pepper

2 teaspoons chopped garlic chives (can substitute onion chives)

2 tablespoons freshly grated Parmesan cheese

Mix ingredients with the basic boursin. Serve with crudités, in stuffed broiled mushroom caps, or on garlic baguette croutons with roasted red bell pepper strips.

FRENCH BOURSIN

2 tablespoons chopped fresh thyme (part lemon thyme preferable)

2 teaspoons chopped fresh chives

Mix ingredients with the basic boursin. Serve with crudités or stuffed under skin of chicken breasts.

NOTE: All the above variations may be served from four 1-cup ramekins, or line the ramekins with plastic wrap and fill with mixture, then chill overnight. Turn out on a platter lined with ornamental greens such as grape leaves, and garnish with complementary herbs. Adorn the platter with chive blossoms if available.

If cheese mixture is not divided into 4 parts, add approximately ½ cup chopped fresh herbs and additional freshly ground pepper.

▼▼▼▼▼▼▼▼▼▼▼▼▼▼▼▼▼▼▼▼▼▼▼▼▼▼▼▼▼▼▼▼

SALAD SAMPLER

Simple! Use your imagination to decorate the platter, and let guests assemble their own salads, sampling a variety of fresh herbs. Although a vinaigrette or creamy dressing may be passed at the table, the flavorful herbs and herbal vinegar speak for themselves. Choose from among the following suggested ingredients.

Cucumbers, tined with a fork and sliced with sprigs of dill, salad burnet, or lemon basil

Carrots, cut into sticks and sprinkled with minced tarragon, Mexican marigold mint, mint, or parsley

Firm roma tomatoes, sliced with small sprigs of basil or coriander

Squash, crookneck and/or zucchini, sliced and barely steamed with fresh oregano or marjoram

Green beans, barely steamed with sprigs of savory

Radishes, sliced with minced chives

Jicama, cut into sticks with minced parsley or sprigs of coriander

Arrange chilled vegetables in overlapping vertical rows on a large platter. (Carrot sticks, green beans, and jicama sticks may be arranged horizontally.) Drizzle vegetables generously with chive vinegar or other complementary herb vinegar (or lime juice). Tuck fresh herb sprigs among some vegetables; sprinkle others with minced herbs. Arrange colorful chive blossoms randomly along platter.

NOTE: Vegetables may be chopped in advance and kept chilled. Garnish at the last minute before serving. After steaming squash and green beans, plunge them in ice water to keep them crisp.

▼▼▼▼▼▼▼▼▼▼▼▼▼▼▼▼▼▼▼▼▼▼▼▼▼▼▼▼▼▼▼▼▼

CHICKEN BREASTS STUFFED WITH CHIVES AND FRESH HERBS

Simple but savory, this chicken may be grilled or broiled. It can be served cold the next day, or shredded or sliced for chicken salad. Great for a picnic!

4 split chicken breasts with skin

4 cloves garlic, minced

8 teaspoons chopped fresh chives

8 generous tablespoons chopped fresh herbs (suggestions follow)

½ cup complementary vinegar or dry white wine

1 teaspoon dried mustard

1 teaspoon honey

¼ teaspoon crushed dried red chile pepper

3 tablespoons olive oil

Salt, freshly ground pepper, and paprika to taste

Rinse chicken breasts and pat dry. Gently lift up skin of each and rub each with a clove of minced garlic and 2 teaspoons chopped chives. Stuff about 2 tablespoons of the fresh herbs beneath skin of each breast. Set aside.

Mix herb vinegar or wine with mustard, honey, crushed red pepper, and any herbs that did not fit into chicken, and whisk in the olive oil. Marinate chicken in this mixture for 2 hours or more, turning occasionally. Sprinkle with salt, pepper, and paprika, and grill over hot coals or under broiler (about 6 inches from flame), skin-side down, for approximately 7–8 minutes. Turn skin-side up and cook another 6–8 minutes, basting occasionally with marinade. Do not burn!

SUGGESTED HERBS (per chicken breast)
▼▼▼▼▼▼▼▼▼▼▼▼▼

Lemony Herbs:

1 tablespoon lemon thyme

1 tablespoon lemon balm or lemon verbena

⅛ teaspoon lemon zest

Lovely Lemon vinegar

French:

Substitute shallots for garlic

1 tablespoon chopped thyme (try lemon thyme)

1 tablespoon chopped parsley or marjoram

Bouquet garni vinegar

Southwestern:

1 tablespoon chopped cilantro

1 tablespoon chopped oregano

2–4 chile *rajas* [*see Cooking Tips chapter*]

Oregano-chile-garlic vinegar

Italiano:

1 tablespoon chopped basil

½ tablespoon chopped oregano

½ tablespoon chopped parsley

1 small sprig rosemary

Mediterranean marinade vinegar

Note: For vinegar recipes, see chapter on herb vinegars.

CILANTRO

Coriandrum sativum
Apiaceae (Umbelliferae) family

Bright green leaves of cilantro.

Tricia Shire

Common Names:

cilantro, Chinese parsley, coriander

Characteristics:

original leaves are flat and green, resembling Italian parsley; strongly pungent odor; leaves become spindly and lacy as white or mauve flowers appear; umbrella-shaped cluster of round seeds; annual

Conditions:

loose, rich, well-draining soil; full sun

Size:

2–2½ feet tall and 1½ feet wide

Propagation:

sow seeds in fall ½ inch deep, thin seedlings to 1 foot apart; taproot difficult to transplant once established; 2 or more plants per garden suggested

Fertilizer:

light application of fish emulsion when plant is small; occasional applications of compost

Pests:

attracts beneficial insects and deters harmful ones with its strong odor; weevils may attack dried seeds

Companions:

avoid planting near other Apiaceae such as fennel

Most people seem to find the flavor of fresh coriander leaves (better known as cilantro in the Southwest) either most appealing or absolutely appalling! Its unique aroma and pungence often demand an acquired taste; however, once you acquire the taste for it, cilantro can be addicting! I quickly learned that my pot of frijoles and my salsa picante lacked that distinct fresh flavor when cilantro was omitted.

Consequently, I eagerly planted coriander seeds in my spring garden as various herb books instructed. Unfortunately, this untimely planting caused my plants to bolt prematurely as soon as May's 90-degree weather arrived. I found that sowing seeds in the fall assured me of healthy plants by early spring. Successive plantings may be done from September through February, although the last seeds planted will be the first to bolt. Cilantro tolerates freezing temperatures (in moderation); in fact, it has even withstood mild snowstorms in my garden.

I have but one dismay in growing this plant: cilantro has already gone to seed in late summer when its culinary partners, tomatoes, squash, eggplant, and jalapeños flourish in the garden. Fortunately, the increased popularity of Mexican, Chinese, Southeast Asian, and Indian cuisines (which rely on this fresh herb) gives cilantro a permanent place on the produce shelf.

Coriander's flat and gently serrated dark green leaves, resembling Italian parsley, are best used when the plant is about 6 inches high, and they must always be used fresh. Do not even attempt to dry the leaves, because the flavor will be lost. You can store a bunch of cilantro for a week in the refrigerator in a jar of water loosely covered with a plastic bag. (Remember to change the water every few days.) This potent herb has a subtle cooling effect and complements spicy foods: fiery Indian curries and chutneys; garlicky Thai and Vietnamese dipping sauces, salads and soups; wok-fried Chinese food; and spirited Mexican chile sauces. Mediterranean cooks use the tasty leaves in salads and with fish, and Middle Eastern food favors it as well in salads and lamb dishes.

I like to use cilantro in curried deviled eggs, and on beef-and-tomato or chicken-and-avocado sandwiches. Thick grilled pork chops smothered in a tart tomatillo-and-cilantro sauce taste wonderful. And fresh fish marinated in a tangy marinade of cilantro, ginger, garlic, and lime is simply delicious!

Surprisingly, as the coriander plant begins to grow tall (ultimately reaching 2–2½ feet), it changes form. It no longer resembles the bouquet we buy at the grocery store. Instead, the plant begins to look spindly with sparse and lacy secondary leaves. Soon, umbrella-shaped clusters of whitish-mauve flowers bloom in abundance, providing a beautiful contrast to spring's colorful bulbs and flowers. These delicate flowers attract bees and butterflies and a host of other beneficial insects into the garden. Equally important, they make lovely additions to spring bouquets and create attractive edible garnishes for soups, salads, and crudité platters.

Shiny seeds resembling small green peppercorns result from the profusion of flowers. Their potent smell, offensive to some, mimics that of a small stinkbug. I find, however, that the clean, strong, citrus taste of the unripened seeds gives a burst of freshness when sprinkled on salads and deviled eggs. Sometimes I pickle them in a jar of herb vinegar with a few pinches of salt and use them as I would capers–in seafood salads, homemade mayonnaise, and other sauces.

Generally, these seeds ripen to a toasty color in June. Because they dry out quickly in the hot sun, watch them carefully and harvest them just as they begin to turn brown. Then hang the plants upside down in large bunches in a dark, well-ventilated room in a large paper bag. The seeds will fall off the stalks when gently shaken; store them in an airtight container. By this time, the seeds have a perfumy and mellow citrus taste, which has flavored pastries and breads throughout Northern Europe for centuries. Try adding two teaspoons of slightly crushed seeds to your favorite apple, pear, or peach pie or strudel. Gingerbread and other baked goods can be similarly enhanced.

The aromatic coriander seeds are an essential ingredient in chile powder, curry powder, and pickling spice. Slightly toasting the seeds on a griddle before grinding them releases more flavor. I usually add a teaspoon of whole seeds to chicken or beef stock for soups, and they also make a lively addition to marinades.

The early monks incorporated coriander seeds into various liqueurs and medicines because of their digestive properties. Two such liqueurs, still popular today, are Benedictine and Chartreuse, made by secret recipes of French monks. The bittersweet coriander seeds are also crucial ingredients in flavoring gin.

Today, many people still chew the seeds after a meal to aid in digestion and to sweeten the breath. Mexican children slowly savor pastel-colored round "jawbreaker" candies, delighted by the whole coriander seeds hidden within. These *colaciónes* colorfully adorn platters of *capirotada*, a fruit-filled bread pudding that is traditionally served at Easter throughout Southern Mexico.

And through the centuries, coriander has been renowned as an aphrodisiac. I remember walking down the narrow and dimly lit halls of a covered bazaar in Istanbul. A vendor enticed me into his stall with steaming coffee, which he served in a small, clear glass. With a mortar and pestle, he crushed several coriander seeds and added them to the glass. Then he poured thick, dark coffee over it, generously sweetening the brew with sugar and handing it to me with an expression of anticipation. To his dismay, I sipped the marvelous concoction and resumed my shopping. Today, I still serve this Turkish coffee after a heavy meal, adding a twist of lemon peel.

Remember, whole or powdered coriander seeds cannot be interchanged with the fresh leaves of the same plant; they have distinct flavors and different uses.

But because coriander so readily reseeds itself once established in your garden, you will find its versatility a culinary treasure!

NOTE: For further information, see Mexican herbs chapter.

QUESO FUNDIDO (SPICY BROILED CHEESE)

Fiesta food! This broiled cheese specialty of Northern Mexico may be assembled ahead of time, then broiled at the last minute. Have ready attractive bowls of condiments and warm tortillas (corn or flour) or tostada chips, so that guests may assemble their own creations.

1½ pounds cheese (Cheddar, Monterey Jack, and/or Muenster), grated or thinly sliced

3–4 cloves garlic, minced

4–6 Anaheim or poblano chiles, cut into *rajas* (strips) [*See Cooking Tips chapter*]

1–2 jalapeños, chopped (optional)

3 green onions, chopped

1 tomato, chopped

1 bunch fresh cilantro; chop 2 tablespoons; use remainder for garnish

Optional condiments: additional chopped onions and tomatoes, cilantro sprigs, red and/or green salsa picante, avocado wedges, chorizo

In a 9-by-12-inch earthenware serving dish, mix grated cheese, garlic, peppers, and half the onions. Cook at 450 degrees until bubbly, stirring occasionally. Add the tomato and broil until golden brown. Sprinkle with remaining onions and 2 tablespoons of the chopped cilantro. Garnish with avocado slices, cilantro sprigs, and your favorite hot sauce. Scoop the melted cheese into warm tortillas or tostada chips. Pass small bowls of your choice of condiments.

NOTE: Sometimes I fry Mexican chorizo sausage and crumble it on top of the cheese as it broils. Or add sautéed squash, mushrooms, or squash blossoms with peppers. Substitute epazote for cilantro when white cheese is used, but use it sparingly if serving to those unaccustomed to its taste.

▼▼▼▼▼▼▼▼▼▼▼▼▼▼▼▼▼▼▼▼▼▼▼▼▼▼▼▼▼
▲▲▲▲▲▲▲▲▲▲▲▲▲▲▲▲▲▲▲▲▲▲▲▲▲▲

SWEET POTATO RELISH WITH FRESH CILANTRO AND TOASTED PEANUTS

▼▼▼▼▼▼▼▼▼▼▼▼▼▼▼▼▼▼

This festive dish vividly captures all: color, texture, and flavor. It makes a zippy condiment for turkey, quail, or wild game, and may be served as a salad on crisp greens. Try it for a Thanksgiving relish. Best made in a wok.

2 teaspoons peanut oil

1 cup raw peanuts, skins removed

2–3 sweet potatoes (approximately 2¼ pounds), cut into matchstick julienne strips (about 6 cups julienne)

2 tablespoons peanut oil

½ teaspoon crushed dried red chile pepper

3 teaspoons finely chopped fresh ginger

1 teaspoon orange zest

½ teaspoon lime zest

¼ cup freshly squeezed orange juice

3 tablespoons fresh lime juice

2 teaspoons Chinese Five vinegar *or* rice wine vinegar [*see chapter on herb vinegars*]

1 teaspoon Dijon mustard

½ teaspoon honey

Salt and freshly ground white pepper to taste

3 medium-size scallions, chopped

3 tablespoons chopped fresh cilantro

Additional cilantro sprigs for garnish

Heat 2 teaspoons peanut oil in a wok. Toast the peanuts by tossing them briefly; do not allow to burn! Set aside.

Briefly steam the julienned sweet potatoes in 2 batches until crisp-tender (about 1½ minutes per batch); do not overcook! Drain well in a colander, then place in a clean dishtowel and squeeze out excess moisture.

Wipe the wok clean; heat 2 tablespoons peanut oil. Add the ginger and crushed red chile to flavor the oil, taking care not to burn. Add the julienned sweet potatoes and toss well over medium heat until well coated and fragrant.

Place the sweet potatoes in a ceramic dish, about 9 by 10 inches. In a small bowl, mix the citrus zests and juice, vinegar, mustard, and honey; drizzle over sweet potatoes, then toss well. Mix in the chopped scallions and cilantro. Before serving, garnish liberally with half the toasted peanuts and fresh cilantro sprigs. Pass remaining peanuts in small bowl. Serves 10–12 as side dish.

NOTE: Using the julienne blade of a food processor certainly facilitates this recipe.

If serving as a salad, serve in "cups" made from savoy cabbage or purple cabbage.

▼▼▼▼▼▼▼▼▼▼▼▼▼▼▼▼▼▼▼▼▼▼▼▼▼▼▼▼

FETTUCCINE MARTINI

It all started with jalapeño-stuffed olives, which led me to think, "Hmmm....Martini pasta?" Coriander seeds, a crucial ingredient in gin, in turn flavor a creamy and peppery pasta sauce enhanced by tomatoes, sweet red pepper, and chopped cilantro.

3 tablespoons butter
1 tablespoon olive oil
2 shallots, minced
4 cloves garlic (or more)
1 jalapeño pepper, seeded and chopped
2 medium-sized tomatoes, chopped
4 ounces gin
3 tablespoons dry vermouth
2 tablespoons fresh lime juice
2 teaspoons best quality tomato paste
½ teaspoon freshly ground white pepper
¼ teaspoon freshly ground whole coriander
1 teaspoon salt
1 red bell pepper, chopped
1½ cups heavy cream
⅓–½ cup chopped fresh cilantro
3 tablespoons freshly grated Parmesan
3 tablespoons minced parsley
1 pound fresh fettuccine, cooked *al dente* [*for instructions on cooking fresh pasta, see Cooking Tips chapter*]
Jalapeño- or pimento-stuffed green olives
6 sprigs fresh cilantro

Heat butter and oil over medium heat in large saucepan. Add shallots and garlic, and sauté about 2 minutes. Add the jalapeños, and sauté 30 seconds. Add the tomatoes, gin, vermouth, lime juice, tomato paste, white pepper, ground coriander, and salt; raise the heat and reduce, stirring frequently, for about 3 minutes. Add the pepper and continue to simmer for 2–3 minutes. Add the cream, and reduce (10–12 minutes); when nearly the desired consistency, add the fresh cilantro, followed by the Parmesan, and simmer another minute. Add the chopped parsley and stir in. Keep mixture warm until served.

Serve pasta in warmed individual bowls and top generously with sauce, freshly grated Parmesan, olives, and a cilantro sprig. (Crushed red pepper is optional.) Serves 6.

NOTE: Make sure that the pasta is cooked in time for the sauce. This dish is delicious made with cayenne-flavored pasta.

FAJITAS OR FLANK STEAK IN CILANTRO, CITRUS, AND GOLD TEQUILA MARINADE

The flavor of fresh citrus mingles with cilantro and gold tequila in a robust marinade for flank steak or fajitas. After grilling or broiling the meat, slice it across the grain and serve with warm tortillas, avocado wedges, grilled scallions (lightly basted in oil until slightly charred), lime wedges, cilantro sprigs, and your favorite salsa picante.

1 pound fajita meat (preferably outer skirt) or flank steak

4 large cloves garlic, minced

3 tablespoons gold tequila

2 tablespoons fresh lime juice

2 tablespoons fresh orange juice

2 tablespoons oregano-chile-garlic vinegar *or* red wine vinegar [*see chapter on herb vinegars*]

1½ teaspoons freshly grated orange zest

¼–½ teaspoon crushed dried red chile pepper

½ teaspoon freshly ground black pepper

½ teaspoon brown sugar

3 tablespoons olive oil

3 tablespoons chopped fresh cilantro

Rub the meat with the garlic and place in a shallow dish. Mix the tequila, lime juice, orange juice, vinegar, orange zest, red and black pepper, and brown sugar; add the oil and mix well. Pour over meat, basting well. Add the cilantro to both sides of the meat. Cover and marinate overnight, turning occasionally.

Broil marinated meat in a preheated oven 6 inches from the flame, or grill on hot coals approximately 3–4 minutes per side (slightly longer for flank steak). Let stand 5 minutes before serving. Serves 4–6.

NOTE: Festive Mexican-style appetizers called nachos can be made by spreading crisp tostada chips with refried beans (optional), grated cheese, and bite-size pieces of the grilled meat, then broiling under a preheated broiler, watching carefully, until cheese is melted and bubbly. Garnish each nacho with a cilantro sprig and jalapeño slices and serve with salsa picante and ice cold Mexican beer.

HOT MULLED SPICE MIX

Keeping a pot of mulled cider simmering on the stove during the winter holidays (or any chilly day) fills the house with spicy redolence and good cheer.

2 cups whole coriander seeds
2 cups whole allspice
1 cup whole cloves
½ cup whole anise seeds
1 cup dried mint *or* Mexican marigold mint (optional)
2 cups 3-inch cinnamon sticks
1 cup dried lemon grass leaves and stalks (optional)
1 cup dried orange peel
1 cup whole star anise (optional)
Bay leaves

Mix all the ingredients together except the bay. Keep tightly sealed.

HOT MULLED CIDER

1 gallon unfiltered apple juice

2 apples, thinly sliced

2 oranges, thinly sliced

2 tablespoons (or more) mulled spice mix

1–2 bay leaves

1 dash vanilla

Dark rum or brandy

Pour apple juice into large stainless steel or enamel pot. Add the sliced apples, oranges, mulled spice mix, and bay leaves. Bring to a boil; reduce heat and simmer 30 minutes. Add a dash of vanilla. Strain into cups with a splash of dark rum or brandy if desired. Stir with cinnamon sticks.

NOTE: Fresh slices of oranges and apples may be added prior to serving. To make hot mulled wine, substitute a mellow red wine for apple juice and add a few table-spoons brown sugar if desired. More juice or wine may be added as needed.

DILL

Anethum graveolens
Apiaceae (Umbelliferae) family

Lucinda Hutson

This swallowtail butterfly caterpillar can ravage a dill plant overnight.

Common Names:
dill

Characteristics:
feathery plumes of dark green (bluish-green when young), wispy leaves
growing from a hollow stalk; umbrella-shaped yellow flower heads produce
small oval-shaped seeds; annual

Conditions:
rich, moist, well-draining soil; sunshine

Size:
approximately 3 feet tall; a taller variety known as mammoth dill

Propagation:

seeds may be planted in early fall and in early spring in successive sowings; thin to 15 inches apart; reseeds once established; difficult to transplant after established because of taproot; 4 or more plants per garden suggested

Fertilizer:

applications of fish emulsion or manure tea; compost mulch helps retain moisture in the summer and gives some protection from cold in winter

Pests:

caterpillar of swallowtail butterfly causes damage if not controlled with bacillus thuringiensis

Companions:

known to aid in the growth of cabbages and cucumbers; avoid planting near others in the same Apiaceae family

It was not the rich Danish pastries that made me sneak into the kitchen late at night. Instead, a jar of herring marinated in mustard and curry with fresh sprigs of dill beckoned.

The summer I spent as a governess for a family outside of Copenhagen introduced me to the unforgettably gracious Danish hospitality. Fresh flowers and herbs always graced the dining tables, where innumerable courses seemed to be served. One custom especially impressed me: that of acknowledging another with a friendly nod and saying, "Skoal!" while making eye contact before sipping beer or the inebriating schnapps (aquavit). Another favorite custom was eating delectable open-faced sandwiches–sometimes before a meal and often at midnight with beer or ice cold schnapps.

Fresh dill, with its feathery and delicate leaves, was the prevalent herb used to garnish the artistically arranged sandwiches. Thin slices of whole grain breads were spread generously with sweet creamy butter, then layered with an assortment of sliced meats, fish, cooked potatoes, fried onions, hard-boiled eggs, or pâtés. Garnishes of tomatoes, onion rings, caviar, and dill followed. I still find these open-faced sandwiches a cheerful way to greet guests in the garden and to serve as appetizers or midnight snacks. They are especially delicious when spread with homemade herbal butter, mayonnaise, or cheese spreads.

On morning walks to the Danish beach, I noticed gardens brimming with yellow heads of dill dancing in the breeze. On close observation, I marveled at how the dill flower head looked like clusters of golden fireworks exploding from green stems. These flower stalks make impressive additions to garden bouquets. After the plant has flowered, the seeds form and should be left on the plant until they turn a toasty color. Make sure to collect them before they have dried out. In fact, they may be harvested and hung upside down over a newspaper or in a paper bag until they fall. Store in an airtight jar away from direct light.

Dill seeds are a chief ingredient in pickling spice and add a fresh taste to beet, carrot, sorrel, cucumber, or potato soups and fish chowders. And of course, dill seeds give that unique flavor to dilly bread, which is a delicious accompaniment to homemade soups and salads.

But even more delicious is the fresh herb; in fact, I believe it is a waste of time to dry it, although some do and call it dill weed. The fresh herb is so much better! And it is full of minerals and provides a lovely garnish as well. I remember silver platters of rosy Skandinavian salmon adorned with feathery sprigs of dill and lemon slices; the pairing of the delicate fish and pungent herb was perfect. Sometimes *gravlax*, paper-thin slices of fresh salmon cooked in a marinade of aquavit, sugar, salt, fresh dill, and cracked pepper are served at Danish dinners with a savory mustard-dill sauce. Dill similarly enhances most fish dishes; lemon-dill butter melted over grilled, baked, or sautéed fish is simply exquisite! Boiled shrimp marinated in a vinaigrette with plenty of freshly chopped dill or scallops sautéed in butter and wine and garnished with fresh dill are elegant and easy. Dill also complements salmon or caviar mousse.

Cucumbers coupled with fresh dill have been a longtime American favorite, whether pickled or eaten fresh. And new potatoes (served warm or cold in salads) as well as squash-and-cheese casserole lend themselves to flavoring with this fresh-tasting herb. Dilled carrots are tasty, and Greeks have often seasoned spinach with dill. Cauliflower is enhanced with a dill-cheese sauce, and cabbage and brussels sprouts also benefit from this herb.

Plenty of fresh dill makes a pleasant addition to homemade sauces, mayonnaise, and salad dressings, and it also enlivens cottage cheese and cream cheese spreads. And try sour cream blended with fiery horseradish and fresh dill to complement slices of roast beef.

Dill is a relatively easy herb to grow in the garden, although it has a tendency to wither in the summer's heat. It is one of the herbs that grows well from seeds, which may be sown in successive plantings in early spring and again in the fall. Once established in the garden, it often reseeds itself.

For an early start, you may germinate seeds indoors in late winter and place the young plants outdoors in early spring. (Their taproots make them difficult to transplant if allowed to get too big.) If dill seeds are planted too late in the spring, the heat will cause the plant to bolt. Unfortunately, hot weather sometimes causes dill to set flower long before cucumbers are ripe enough to pickle; consequently, I find that planting seeds in early fall produces healthier plants. But remember not to let the dill seeds dry out. Seedlings planted in August may look yellow and puny at first (keep them well watered), but when they begin to look green and vigorous, it is a sure sign of fall.

In areas subject to strong winds, the dill stalks may need some protection or staking. I find that staggering clumps of dill plants together, as opposed to planting them in rows, looks attractive and offers support as well. Plenty of sunshine is important, although dill can tolerate some afternoon shade during the hot summer. And it requires a moist and well-draining soil to flourish. I don't like to plant dill in the vicinity of other plants in the same Apiaceae family such as carrots, fennel, parsley, and anise, as they can deplete the soil and compete for available nutrients.

It's hard to believe that the wrinkled yellow-and-black striped caterpillar that emits a rank odor and protrudes two orange horns from its head when disturbed could turn into the beautiful swallowtail butterfly. Unfortunately, this hungry fellow can devour a small dill plant overnight. Because he is so visible, he may be simply picked off the plant or controlled with bacillus thuringiensis.

Dill should certainly find its home in a chef's garden, offering versatility in its various forms. The leaves may be eaten throughout its growth except during flowering, when they are sparse and somewhat bitter. The seeds – a sparkling combination of anise, caraway, and camphor – add a pronounced flavor to a variety of foods, making them more digestible as well. Also, chew a few seeds after a heavy meal to ease the full feeling. Because of its properties that cure colic, the word *dill* comes from the Nordic word *dilla* meaning "to lull."

It is no wonder that this delightful herb remains a favorite in America, Southern Russia, and Northern Europe. Go out in the garden and munch on a few of the leaves. You will certainly understand the ecstasy of the swallowtail caterpillar!

BOUGAINVILLEA BEET SOUP (Pickled Borscht)

The vivid magenta color of this soup reminds me of bougainvilleas in bloom. The festive chopped garnishes allow you to eat salad and soup in one dish. Credit for this recipe goes to my talented sister, Christopher Peabody, whose delicious meals and splendid presentations are inspiring.

½ stick butter

2 medium onions, chopped

2 leeks, white part only, chopped

1 bay leaf

10–12 medium beets, parboiled (do not overcook!), peeled, and grated

2 medium carrots, grated

2 stalks celery, chopped

6 cups rich chicken stock [*for recipe, see Cooking Tips chapter*]

½ cup dill vinegar, red wine vinegar, or other complementary vinegar [*see chapter on herb vinegars*]

2 teaspoons dill seed

¼ teaspoon allspice, freshly ground

1 tablespoon (or more) brown sugar

Salt and freshly ground white pepper to taste

4 generous tablespoons fresh dill

Suggested garnishes: dill butter [*see chapter on herb butters*]; lemon slices; fresh dill sprigs; cold, cooked, cubed potatoes; chopped cucumbers; shredded purple cabbage; black caviar; chives and sour cream

Heat butter in large pot; sauté onions and leeks for about 5 minutes. Add bay, beets, carrots, celery, about 3 cups stock, vinegar, and spices. Bring to boil; reduce heat and simmer about 30 minutes. Reserve 1 cup, and purée the rest in batches, adding more stock as needed. Return to pot and simmer another 10 minutes with remaining stock and reserved beet mixture, sugar, salt, and pepper (and some more vinegar if desired). Add fresh dill. Serve warm with dill butter and a lemon slice, or chilled with some or all of the suggested garnishes.

NOTE: This tastes best when made a day in advance. Thin with additional chicken stock if necessary before serving. Serve with pumpernickel bread and herb butter.

▼▼▼▼▼▼▼▼▼▼▼▼▼▼▼▼▼▼▼▼▼▼▼▼▼

▲▲▲▲▲▲▲▲▲▲

GRANDMOTHER'S CUCUMBER SALAD

▼▼▼▼▼▼▼▼▼▼

These crisp and refreshing cucumbers accompanied many summer meals at my grandmother's house. Especially good with grilled fish.

3 medium cucumbers, tined with a fork and sliced

3 teaspoons sugar (approximately)

Salt and freshly ground pepper to taste

1 white onion, sliced into thin rings

4–6 tablespoons chopped fresh dill

1½ cups dilly vinegar, salad burnet vinegar, chive vinegar, lovely lemon vinegar, or white wine vinegar [*see chapter on herb vinegars*]

Fresh dill sprigs

Several hours before serving, layer cucumbers in a medium-size ceramic bowl. Sprinkle lightly with sugar, salt and pepper; add a layer of onion rings and chopped dill. Repeat the layers until all ingredients are used, pouring in vinegar last. Tuck several ice cubes among the cucumbers (this makes them crisp), and refrigerate until serving time.

NOTE: Salad burnet may be used in place of or in addition to the dill. Fresh chives may be sprinkled over the cucumbers as well.

DILLY POTATO SALAD

Bland or full of mayonnaise it's not! Instead, this is a crunchy, flavorful salad in a tangy vinaigrette. Lovely served in small red bell pepper halves or on crisp salad greens with fresh dill sprigs.

2 pounds new potatoes

Salt to taste

5 tablespoons dill vinegar, Mexican marigold mint vinegar, or tarragon vinegar [*see chapter on herb vinegars*]

1 tablespoon minced shallots

2 tablespoons Dijon mustard

1½–2 teaspoons good quality Madras curry powder

4 tablespoons olive oil

2 tablespoons capers

Salt and freshly ground white pepper to taste

4 medium-size carrots, sliced

2 stalks celery, chopped

6–8 tablespoons chopped sweet gherkins

8–10 green scallions with tops, chopped

1 medium-size green bell pepper, chopped

1 medium-size red bell pepper, chopped

3 tablespoons fresh chopped parsley

4 generous tablespoons fresh chopped dill

Bring salted water to boil; add potatoes, and cook until barely tender (do not overcook!). Allow potatoes to cool; cut into quarters. In a small bowl, mix vinegar, shallots, mustard, and curry; slowly drizzle in the olive oil. Drizzle vinaigrette over potatoes; add capers, and sprinkle with salt and pepper. Cover and chill several hours, gently tossing occasionally. Before serving, mix with the remaining chopped vegetables and herbs. Adjust seasonings, adding more oil and vinegar if necessary. Serves 8–10.

NOTE: Sometimes I add 2 or more tablespoons of freshly chopped sorrel leaves for a lively spark, or slices of hard salami or crumbled fried bacon. Thin red onion rings and black olives may be used as garnish.

CREAMY DILL AND MUSTARD SAUCE

Rich and savory, this sauce is delicious over steamed broccoli, cauliflower, carrots, new potatoes, and asparagus. But don't stop with vegetables! Serve it over fish, chicken, and veal as well.

2 tablespoons freshly chopped shallots

½ cup dry white wine

1 tablespoon dilly vinegar, tarragon vinegar, or white wine vinegar [*see chapter on herb vinegars*]

½ teaspoon freshly ground white pepper

1 cup heavy cream

¼ pound (1 stick) unsalted butter, divided into 4 pieces

2 generous tablespoons chopped fresh dill

2 teaspoons chopped chives

3–4 teaspoons Dijon mustard

Salt to taste

In a medium-size saucepan, combine the shallots, wine, vinegar, and white pepper. Bring to a boil, uncovered, and reduce by half. Add the cream, and reduce again by half. (Sauce should be slightly thickened.) Lower heat and whisk in the butter, one piece at a time. Quickly add the dill, chives, and mustard, and salt to taste. Sauce will be rich and creamy. May be made 3–4 hours before serving and kept warm in a thermos (separates if reheated). Yields about 1 cup.

VARIATIONS

Substitute tarragon or Mexican marigold mint for dill (you may want to decrease the amount slightly) and tarragon vinegar or Mexican marigold mint vinegar for the vinegars in recipe.

NOTE: Garnish dishes with fresh herb sprigs.

EPAZOTE

Chenopodium ambrosioides
Chenopodiaceae family

Tenacious epazote pushing its way through a stone walk and garden bench.

Common Names:

Epazote, wormseed, goosefoot, Mexican tea, Jerusalum oak

Characteristics:

uniquely serrated leaves with strong camphor-like odor; deep red blotches
sometimes found on leaves and veins; drooping spikes loaded with tiny
round green seeds in fall; branching stems form at base, and a thick, trunk-
like stem may develop when plant pushes through a barrier; annual

Conditions:

thrives along streambeds with some afternoon shade, but can adapt to
poor, disturbed soil and full sun; seen along country highways and growing
out of cracks in city sidewalks

Size:

3–5 feet tall and 2 feet wide or more

Propagation:

sow seeds in fall (germination takes 3–4 weeks); thin to about 12 inches apart; readily reseeds self when established; stems root slowly in water; 1–2 plants per garden suggested

Fertilizer:

not necessary, but light applications of compost aid protection against drought

Pests:

insects repelled by its strong odor

Companions:

other plants benefit from its insect-repelling property

Epazote has a remarkable reputation. The socially embarrassing consequences of eating beans are thought by some to be prevented by cooking the beans (especially black beans) with this potent herb. Simply add a couple of 4-inch sprigs of the fresh herb or about 2 teaspoons of the dried herb to a pot of beans the last 15 minutes of cooking. This herb is rapidly gaining popularity, and seeds are now available from special mail-order catalogs.

While once visiting a bustling Oaxacan marketplace, I noticed bunches of freshly picked epazote hanging from rafters of the vendors' stalls. There I learned that women make tea and flavor food with this herb to rid the body of intestinal parasites. Because of this medicinal benefit, epazote's culinary virtues are tasted in traditional recipes throughout Southern and Central Mexico, especially in Oaxaca, Veracruz, and Yucatán; however, it is relatively unheard of among cooks along the Northern Mexican border because epazote does not tolerate the arid conditions there.

Epazote's pungence came as a surprise when I first tasted it tucked away in a *quesadilla* (a folded corn tortilla with various fillings, toasted or fried), which oozed melted Oaxacan white cheese. I have, however, since found it a pleasing contrast to rich pork or crabmeat dishes and fiery red chile and chicken soup. A few chopped epazote leaves make a peppy addition to sautéed squash, chile, corn, and tomato dishes. The distinctly serrated 2–3-inch leaves resemble a goose's foot; hence, the common name "goosefoot." These leaves make attractive garnishes and unique flavorings for hearty corn, squash, or bean soups. Paula Lambert of the Mozzarella Company in Dallas even adds it with ancho chiles in one of her extraordinary cheeses.

I first encountered epazote along a streambed in Southeast Texas while on a plant-identifying expedition led by Austin naturalist Scooter Cheatham. Its sawtoothed leaves and sharp odor – camphor with minty overtones – smelled like turpentine to me! Yet these particular qualities make this plant easily discernible in the wild. And epazote can indeed grow like a weed. Although a native to Mexico and Central America, this pungent herb has naturalized throughout the Southeastern United States. And its popular use among Latinos in New York City finds it poking its way out of sidewalks there as well as in Central Park. Many Californians often find it a nuisance weed in the garden.

Epazote is a very tenacious herb. Although it thrives in moist soil and partial shade, it can also tolerate the most adverse conditions (which may promote smaller leaves and premature bolting). Consequently, one sees epazote growing out of rock walls and along highways. One particularly enthusiastic plant pushed its way up through a stone walk in my garden and through the wooden slats of a nearby garden bench.

To assure the survival of the species, epazote plants produce an inconspicuous flower spike in early fall that produces thousands of tiny round green seeds. It is imperative to keep these seeds pinched back, or the plant will reseed all over your garden the following spring. Although epazote can look straggly when grown in a pot, keeping the center branch pinched will discourage height and encourage bushiness. Pinching is also a good way to keep the plant in check, but I generally grow the plant in somewhat neglected areas – often in a semishaded area along the back fence so that it will not take over valuable garden space. Remember, this plant grows quite large!

As epazote matures, I often cut large bunches and hang them upside down in a dark, well-ventilated room until they are thoroughly dried. Then I store the leaves in tightly covered jars in a dark cabinet to prevent their turning yellow. Remember to add the dried leaves the last 15 minutes of cooking so that the food will not become bitter, and remember to use the fresh herb sparingly, as its flavor must be acquired by most. In very large doses, toxicity may occur.

The availability of epazote growing in the wild, coupled with its pungence, which has long enhanced the otherwise common peasant fare, have made this herb a popular "poor man's" herb for centuries throughout Mexico. Because it is easy to grow, requiring no special care, and because it offers an exciting and unusual taste, it certainly should be at home in a Southwestern cook's garden. Besides, it may improve your social life!

NOTE: For further information see chapter on Mexican herbs.

CRAB CUSHIONS WITH EPAZOTE

Rich crab meat and epazote are often paired in Mexico. Chef Mark Miller of the Coyote Cafe in Santa Fe shares this delicious duo. Serve these appetizers with his tangy green tomatillo sauce.

¼ cup very finely diced white onion

1–2 tablespoons sweet butter

½ pound fresh crab meat (Dungeness, Maine, or Gulf)

2 tablespoons chopped fresh epazote

2 tablespoons heavy sweet cream *or* crème fraîche

2 egg yolks

Salt and pepper to taste

8 fresh, thin, high-quality flour tortillas

1 quart peanut oil

Deep-fry thermometer

Sauté the onion in the butter over low heat, making sure not to color the onions. Cook them until soft and sweet; let cool. Add the cooled onions to the crab meat and mix together in a bowl over ice.

Add the epazote, cream, 1 egg yolk, salt, and pepper; mix well. (If you are not going to make cushions immediately, keep the mixture in the refrigerator.)

Cut the flour tortillas into strips, 2½ by 5 inches, discarding leftover pieces. Add about 1 tablespoon of the crab mixture to each tortilla strip at the end, and roll them up so that they are 2½ inches long. On the last inch of the strip on the inside, brush the tortillas with the remaining egg yolk to make them stick. Place on a pan, seam-side down. Refrigerate if not used at once.

Heat the peanut oil to 350–375 degrees, and fry the crab cushions until they are lightly browned and puffed slightly. Serve with Tomatillo Salsa (recipe follows). Makes about 16 cushions.

NOTE: Fresh marjoram or oregano may replace the epazote.

TOMATILLO SALSA

1 pound fresh green tomatillos

3 tablespoons finely chopped sweet red onions

1 serrano chile, finely chopped

1 bunch fresh coriander (cilantro), roughly chopped

Juice of 1 lime

Sugar to taste (optional)

1–2 tablespoons virgin olive oil (optional)

Husk the tomatillos and wash them under very hot water. Cool under cold running water, and purée in food processor or blender. Add the onions, serrano chile, coriander, and lime juice. Add a touch of sugar if the tomatillos are too sour and a little olive oil if you wish.

▼▼▼▼▼▼▼▼▼▼▼▼▼▼▼▼▼▼▼▼▼▼▼▼▼▼▼▼

FRIJOLES NEGROS EN OLLA

One of my favorite meals is a big bowl of thick, dark black beans, some salsa picante, and warm corn tortillas. No wonder they have been a staple in Mexico for centuries!

1 pound dried black beans

Water or broth (½ beer may replace some liquid) to cover about 2 inches
   above beans in pot

3 tablespoons olive oil or bacon fat

1 whole onion, quartered and studded with 2 whole cloves

4–6 whole garlic cloves

½ teaspoons *comino* (cumin) seeds

1 bay leaf

1–2 whole dried red chile peppers (ancho or pasilla)

Salt to taste

1 teaspoon crumbled dried oregano

3 sprigs fresh epazote

Wash beans well to remove dirt and any stones. Cover with cold water, broth, or some beer (room temperature), and remove any beans that float. Add oil, onion, garlic, *comino*, and bay leaf. Bring to boil; immediately reduce heat to simmer, and cover. Add chiles, and cook for approximately 2½ hours. If necessary, add hot water to prevent beans from bursting. When almost tender, add salt, oregano, and epazote; uncover and cook another 15 minutes. When beans are tender, the liquid should just cover them. Too much liquid will give a "watery" broth. Serves 6–8, depending on size of servings.

NOTE: Once cooked down to a thick broth, beans may be served in bowls with chopped green onions, cilantro, sour cream, lime wedges, and/or salsa picante.

VARIATION: NEGRITOS Y GRINGOS

Cook black beans as directed (with ½ beer), using anise seeds instead of *comino* and omitting the dried red chiles. Fry 4 pieces of bacon until crisp–drain and crumble, reserving 1 tablespoon fat.

Sauté 2 poblano chiles (cut into *rajas*), 1 chopped jalapeño, 2 cloves minced garlic, and 1 chopped onion for about 5 minutes in bacon fat. Add 1½–2 cups *fresh* pineapple chunks and sauté until onions are translucent. Add to the beans and simmer 10–15 minutes with the epazote, adding a dash of sherry before serving. Garnish with crumbled bacon, green onions, and lime wedges.

NOTE: Mexican marigold mint may replace epazote.

REFRITOS (REFRIED BEANS)

This makes a colorful side dish when served in a pottery dish, topped with a wide band of crumbled goat cheese and a thinner band of the reserved chorizo, and garnished with epazote or cilantro.

¾ pound Mexican chorizo sausage (optional)
2 tablespoons oil or reserved oil from chorizo
1 large onion, chopped
3 garlic cloves, minced
1 large tomato, chopped
2–3 cups cooked black beans
4 ounces crumbled white goat cheese
Fresh epazote or cilantro for garnish

Fry the crumbled chorizo, drain and set aside. Fry the onion and garlic in the oil until translucent; add the tomato, and cook until it is limp. Add 2 cups of the cooked beans with some of the broth, and mash, adding more beans and broth as needed. Add half of the fried chorizo, reserving the other half for garnish. Serves 6 or more.

CAFE ANNIE'S BLACK BEAN TERRINE WITH GOAT CHEESE

Southwestern chef Robert Del Grande of Houston's Cafe Annie describes this tantalizing dish—

"The Black Bean Terrine offers a rich, earthy and rustic flavor offset by the tanginess of the goat cheese and the fresh spiciness of the salsa and relish. It is a colorful dish, the red tomato salsa and golden relish flanking the rectangle of dark beans with its bull's eye of white goat cheese."

TERRINE

1½ pounds dried black beans

3 garlic cloves

3 sprigs epazote

½ pound pork fat back

¼ pound bacon

1½ pounds chorizo (Mexican smoked pork sausage)

3 ounces dried ancho chiles, soaked in water until soft and puréed in blender until smooth

½ pound butter, cut into small pieces

1½ teaspoons Tabasco

1½ teaspoons kosher salt

1 9-ounce log Montrachet goat cheese

2 bunches cilantro or epazote for garnish

TOMATO SALSA

4 tomatoes

½ red onion

2 serrano peppers

2 bunches cilantro

1 lime

Salt and pepper

▼▼▼▼▼▼▼▼▼▼▼▼▼▼▼▼▼▼▼▼▼▼▼▼▼▼▼▼▼▼▼▼▼▼▼▼

CORN RELISH
▼▼▼▼▼

4 fresh ears of corn, kernels removed

8 ounces chorizo (sausage)

1 red bell pepper, chopped

1 green bell pepper, chopped

4 green onions, chopped

2 ancho chiles, seeded and chopped

2 bunches cilantro, chopped

Juice of 1 lime

2 tablespoons maple syrup

PREPARATION OF TERRINE

Cook the beans over low heat with garlic in approximately 1½ quarts water. Cover the pot so that the water does not evaporate too quickly. When the beans are tender, there should be just enough water to keep them moist. Add epazote the last ½ hour of cooking. If excess water is still in the pot when beans are done, remove the liquid and reduce. Allow the beans to cool in the liquid (this keeps them very black and flavorful). Purée ¾ of the beans in a food processor or blender until very smooth. Combine the purée with the whole beans.

Finely grind the fat back and bacon in a meat grinder. Sauté the fat back and bacon over medium heat until the fat is rendered. Pour off the fat and reserve; add 2 cups of the fat to the pan with the chorizo, and sauté chorizo until it is lightly caramelized. Add the ancho chile purée and sauté for a few minutes. Add the black bean mixture and work the purée into the fat and chorizo. Cook the purée over medium heat to evaporate the excess water until it is very thick and pulls away from the sides of the pan. (*This is a crucial step in the recipe. If the mixture is not thick enough—i.e., contains excess water—it will not set firmly in the terrine. It is better to overcook the mixture than undercook it.*) Work the butter into the bean purée until fully incorporated. Add the Tabasco and salt. Remove from heat.

Fill three quarters of a terrine mold with the warm bean mixture. Press the log of goat cheese into the center, and cover it with more of the bean mixture. Cover with plastic wrap and allow to chill overnight. When completely chilled, the terrine should be very firm. Keeps 1–2 weeks in the refrigerator.

PREPARATION OF TOMATO SALSA

Chop the tomatoes, onion, serrano peppers, and 1 bunch of the cilantro, and combine in a bowl. Add the juice of the lime, and salt and pepper to taste. Reserve the remaining cilantro for garnish.

▼▼▼▼▼▼▼▼▼▼▼▼▼▼▼▼▼▼▼▼▼▼▼▼▼▼▼

PREPARATION OF CORN RELISH

In a very hot pan, sauté the fresh corn kernels. Add the chorizo, and continue to sauté. (If the fat being rendered from the chorizo is not enough, add a little oil.) Add the remaining ingredients and briefly toss in the hot pan until well mixed. Do not overcook.

SERVING

Unmold the terrine by immersing the mold briefly in hot water. Run a knife around the edge, and unmold. Slice the terrine into ½-inch slices, and quickly sauté over high heat. For each serving, place a slice in the center of a dinner plate, and garnish with tomato salsa, corn relish, and cilantro or epazote leaves. Makes one 6-cup terrine, about 10 slices.

GOLDEN CORN SOUP WITH ROASTED PEPPER STRIPS AND EPAZOTE

Corn and epazote have a natural affiinity for one another. This creamy, colorful soup, garnished with roasted peppers and crumbled cheese, is a fall favorite of mine. Varying the peppers and the herbs produces exciting variations.

2 medium onions, chopped

4–6 cloves garlic, chopped

½ stick butter

1 large red or golden bell pepper, chopped

2 jalapeño peppers, seeded and chopped

2 large tomatoes, chopped and preferably roasted [*for instructions for roasting tomatoes, see Cooking Tips chapter*]

4½ cups corn (fresh or frozen)

5–6 cups rich chicken broth [*for recipe, see Cooking Tips chapter*]

½ teaspoon dried oregano

½ teaspoon sweet paprika

Salt to taste

½ teaspoon freshly ground pepper

3 sprigs epazote

1½ tablespoons (approximately) grated or crumbled cheese per bowl (queso fresco, Monterey Jack, Muenster)

6 corn tortillas, cut and fried to make tostada chips [*for instructions, see Cooking Tips chapter*]

½ poblano or Anaheim chile per bowl, roasted, peeled, and cut into *rajas*–4 or more strips [*for instructions, see Cooking Tips chapter*]

Avocado wedges for garnish (optional)

Sauté onions and garlic in butter. When slightly translucent, add jalapeño and sauté briefly. Add the bell pepper and sauté for a few minutes. Add the tomatoes and corn and about 3 cups chicken broth; bring to a boil, then lower heat and simmer 15 minutes. Purée in a blender in batches until velvety.

Return to pot with additional 2–3 cups broth, oregano, paprika, salt, and pepper. Simmer 15 minutes; add the epazote during the last 5 minutes. In each warmed bowl, place a handful of fried tortilla chips, about 4 *rajas*, and grated cheese, then ladle the piping hot soup over them. Garnish with additional *rajas* and fresh epazote sprigs. Serves 8.

▼▼▼▼▼▼▼▼▼▼▼▼▼▼▼▼▼▼▼▼▼▼▼▼▼▼▼▼▼▼

VARIATIONS

1. Omit jalapeños and epazote and add 4 tablespoons fresh basil the last 5 minutes of cooking. Serve in bowls with roasted red bell pepper strips and grated mozzarella cheese, garnished with fresh Parmesan and fresh basil sprigs.

2. Add 1 teaspoon freshly ground *comino* (cumin) to soup when you add the dried oregano. Omit epazote and add 4 tablespoons freshly chopped cilantro the last 5 minutes of cooking. Serve as recipe instructs, except garnish with fresh cilantro sprigs, and a dollop of salsa picante.

POLLO CON EPAZOTE

Javier Aviles, who helps tend my herb garden, taught me how to make this hearty peasant chicken soup from Central Mexico, flavored with a rich and warming chile-flavored broth. Serve with warm corn tortillas and lime wedges, and Mexican beer.

1 large whole fryer, 3½ pounds
½ teaspoon whole *comino* (cumin), freshly ground
8–10 guajillo or pasilla chiles, lightly toasted [*see chapter on Mexican herbs*]
2 cups boiling water
4 cloves garlic
½ teaspoon whole *comino* (cumin), freshly ground
½ teaspoon whole peppercorns, freshly ground
½ teaspoon dried and crumbled oregano
3 tablespoons cooking oil
1 onion, chopped
Salt and pepper to taste
3–5 sprigs fresh epazote

Cook the chicken (preferably 1 day in advance) according to recipe for basic chicken stock [*see Cooking Tips chapter*], adding ½ teaspoon freshly ground *comino* to the stock. Remove chicken from bones, tearing into large bite-size pieces. Chill stock and chicken separately. The following day, skim fat from broth (should be 6–7 cups). Remove stems, veins, and seeds from the dried chiles. Place in a small bowl and cover with boiling water; cover and allow to sit 15–20 minutes. Purée in a blender with the garlic, *comino*, pepper, and oregano, and enough of the soaking water to make a thick, smooth purée. Heat the oil in a heavy saucepan. Sauté the onion until translucent. Add the chile purée and about ½ cup stock, and simmer 10 minutes. Meanwhile, heat the stock, add the purée, and simmer 15 minutes. Add the chicken pieces, salt and pepper, and the epazote, and cook 5 minutes. Do not overcook, or epazote will turn bitter. Serves 6.

NOTE: Traditionally, a chicken is cut into individual serving pieces and cooked and served the same day; however, the preceding method makes a more attractive presentation with a more flavorful broth.

FENNEL

Foeniculum vulgare
Apiaceae (Umbelliferae) family

The bulbous base of Florence fennel prior to harvesting.

Common Names:
sweet or common fennel; Florence fennel, finocchio; bronze fennel

Characteristics:
resembles dill with bright green, feathery foliage and subtle anise scent; forms an umbrella-shaped golden seed head in summer; annual

Conditions:
rich, moist, well-draining soil; can tolerate some afternoon shade

Size:
sweet fennel grows taller (3–5 feet) than does Florence fennel (2–2½ feet)

Propagation:
grow from seeds planted in early fall or from small nursery transplants; thin to 1 foot apart; several of each variety per garden suggested

Fertilizer:

occasional light applications of manure, fish emulsion, or compost

Pests:

worms and the caterpillar of the swallowtail butterfly cause damage – treat with bacillus thuringiensis; treat aphids with insecticidal soap

Companions:

do not plant with other Apiaceae, especially coriander; avoid growing near tomatoes; may help deter fleas

Feathery plumes of bright green fennel sway in the sea breeze of San Francisco. Growing in thick clusters along the crooked streets, it releases its sweet anise scent when brushed against. It seems that all along the coast of Northern California this plant has naturalized, although it is really a native of the Mediterranean.

While living along the coast, I first tasted fennel in a hearty soup prepared by a Portuguese fisherman's wife. She simmered white beans and potatoes with onions, fennel, and spicy sausage to create this simple and delicious meal. I must admit, fennel was a new taste to me, as I had never seen it growing in Texas. Somehow, I had always mistakenly associated it with foods from Northern Europe. But I enjoyed the slight sweetness, the crunchy texture, and the subtle anise flavor that it imparted to the soup. Fortunately, fennel has now become a more popular herb, and both its foliage and bulbous base (which is eaten as a vegetable) may be found at local specialty markets, especially in late spring and fall.

Fennel is often confused with dill, although fennel is a taller plant with slightly shinier, longer, and less divided leaves, and its stems are not hollow as are those of dill. If you are at all in doubt, simply taste the leaves for certainty; fennel's delicate licorice flavor will be evident. There are, however, several varieties of this herb. The more common fennel (*Foeniculum vulgare*) is used primarily for its seeds and leaves, which are favored by the French in salads, *court bouillon* (for poaching fish), and for wrapping around fish before grilling. Provençal cooks prepare the renowned *grillade au fenouil* by drying fennel stalks and placing them under a grilled white sea bass and flambéing it with brandy, igniting the stalks and permeating the fish with flavor. I find that adding dried fennel stalks to the hot coals directly before barbecuing fish or shrimp gives a good flavor, as does enveloping the fish with damp leaves before placing on the grill.

Bronze fennel (*F.* var. *rubrum*) is rapidly gaining in popularity for the reddish-bronze contrast is provides in the garden. The leaves are both ornamental and edible. Another type of fennel that has long been a favorite of Italians is Florence fennel (*F. vulgare* var. *azoricum*), more commonly known as *finocchio*. Although the leaves may be used, it is grown primarily for its stems and bulbous celery-like base. This plant grows smaller then common fennel (approximately 2 feet) and is harvested as an annual, whereas common fennel is a perennial.

Florence fennel, often considered a vegetable, has exciting culinary possibilities. To cook with it, discard the pithy stalks and cut off the bottom of the bulb; trim off the feathery leaves and reserve, then slice the bulb vertically or horizontally in rings. It may be sautéed, then baked with tomatoes, onions, and freshly grated Parmesan. Or it may be sliced and brushed with olive oil, minced garlic, grated Parmesan and baked at 400 degrees for approximately 10 minutes per side, then served with lemon juice and salt and pepper, garnished with fresh fennel sprigs. The bulb may be eaten cooked or raw in a cold salad. It may be substituted for celery whenever a crisp and crunchy texture is desired, although the two flavors are dissimilar. Tender, raw fennel stems may be used with antipasto platters or to scoop up a tasty cheese dip. My favorite way to use fennel is with fish, nesting a fresh fillet on a bed of the feathery foliage with the sautéed bulb and slices of orange.

Fennel seeds offer further culinary possibilities. Italians frequently add them to rich tomato sauces and sausages, and they give a welcome surprise to pizza, whether used in the crust or the sauce. These aromatic seeds find their way into spice blends for baking, pickling, and seasoning fish, salads, soups, sauces, and cooked vegetables. Northern Europeans seem to delight in adding the plump and flavorful seeds to breads, pastries, and cookies. Orange zest, molasses, and fennel seeds complement one another in Swedish limpa, a dark rye bread that accompanies hearty soups and makes delicious sandwiches. Even American apple pie takes on a continental flair when the crust is augmented with sharp cheddar cheese and a few teaspoons of fennel seeds!

So how does this relatively unknown herb fare in Southwestern gardens? Surprisingly well if given proper conditions, especially when planted in the fall to prevent premature bolting during warm weather. It requires plenty of sunshine but can tolerate some afternoon shade. Florence fennel requires a richer and moister soil than the more common type, but both demand a well-draining soil. Seeds should be sown directly into the garden (early spring and early fall for the common fennel and early fall for Florence fennel) and should not be planted near plants in the same Apiaceae family. Because the common fennel grows quite tall (3–5 feet), plant it in the back of the garden so it won't shade other plants. Its lovely plumage is an added attraction to the garden.

Sometimes it is simply easier to purchase transplants of Florence fennel (as long as they are small, because the taproot is difficult to transplant) so that the new seedlings do not suffer heat stress when planted in August. These transplants can be put out in September. Cool weather causes the formation of the bulb; when it is about the size of a lime, cover the bulb with raised soil and keep it mounded so that the bulb is covered or "blanched." Within two weeks (keep any flower heads pinched off), the bulb will be ready for harvest; simply cut it from the roots.

Fennel seeds form after the yellow umbrella-shaped flower heads fade. They should be harvested similarly to dill. Sometimes, though, I like to sprinkle the still-green seeds on salads and fish. And these seeds have other beneficial properties: a tea made from them (infuse a teaspoon of slightly bruised seeds in a cup of water) aids in digestion and is thought to have "slimming" effects, although I have yet to see the results. Indian restaurants often give customers fennel seeds after dinner to freshen the breath.

Although the leaves of fennel can be frozen or dried for later use, as with dill, I find it a waste of time. Fortunately, this plant fares well in cold weather. A severe freeze may cause it to die back, but it often reappears. And although it may not survive the hot summer, it can be replanted in early fall. Fennel simply tastes best in its freshest form.

PORTUGUESE WHITE BEAN AND FENNEL SOUP WITH SAUSAGE

This hearty soup smells wonderful simmering on the stove in wintertime. I serve it with crusty bread, mellow wine, a light salad, and fond memories for the fisherman's wife who shared her recipe.

1 pound white beans

3 tablespoons olive oil

2 medium-size onions, chopped

4 cloves garlic, chopped

1 large fennel bulb (about 1 pound) with stems and foliage, chopped, reserving 4 tablespoons of the leaves and several sprigs for garnish

1 bay leaf

2 teaspoons fennel seeds

½ teaspoon crushed red pepper or more

7 cups rich chicken stock [*for recipe, see Cooking Tips chapter*]

1½ pounds white potatoes, cubed

¾ pound precooked sausage (such as kielbasa), sliced

½ cup medium dry (amontillado) sherry *or* ¼ cup Pernod

Salt and freshly ground pepper to taste

Rinse the beans, discarding any shriveled or discolored ones. In a large soup pot, heat the oil and sauté the onions, garlic, and fennel until slightly softened (about 10 minutes). Add the bay, fennel seeds, crushed red pepper, beans, and stock. Bring to a boil; turn off heat and allow to stand covered for 1 hour.

Return to boil; reduce heat and simmer 1½ hours. Add the potatoes and cook 10 minutes. Add the sausage and cook another 10 minutes, or until potatoes are tender. Add the sherry or Pernod and about 4 tablespoons chopped fennel leaves. Salt and pepper the beans to taste. Remove pot from heat and let stand, covered, for 5 minutes before serving. Serve garnished with fresh fennel sprigs. Serves 8.

PASTA SALAD WITH PEPPERONI AND FRESH FENNEL

This colorful and festive salad is very inviting. Pass freshly grated Parmesan and crushed red pepper, and serve with crusty garlic bread and a mellow red wine for a simple spring meal.

THE DRESSING

2 teaspoons orange zest

2 teaspoons Dijon mustard

¼ teaspoon crushed red chile pepper

¼ teaspoon fennel seeds

¼ teaspoon brown sugar

4 tablespoons sherry vinegar

4 tablespoons olive oil

Combine the zest, mustard, red pepper, fennel seeds, and sugar; add the vinegar and mix well. Slowly whisk in the oil, and set aside.

THE SALAD

1 pound fresh fusilli (corkscrew) pasta

1 teaspoon olive oil

Salt

¼ cup olive oil

1 medium-size fennel bulb with tender stalks, chopped (2½–3 cups), with foliage reserved

1 large onion, chopped (about 2 cups)

½ teaspoon fennel seeds

½ teaspoon crushed dried red chile pepper

2 medium-size red bell peppers, chopped (about 2 cups)

4 cloves garlic, minced

4 tablespoons chopped fresh Italian parsley

4 tablespoons chopped fresh fennel leaves

Salt and freshly ground pepper to taste

6 tablespoons freshly grated Parmesan

2 ounces thinly sliced pepperoni *or* Italian toscado salami

▼▼▼▼▼▼▼▼▼▼▼▼▼▼▼▼▼▼▼▼▼▼▼▼▼▼▼

Bring salted water to rolling boil with 1 teaspoon olive oil. Add pasta; return to boil and cook 2 minutes. Drain in colander and set aside.

Heat ¼ cup olive oil, and sauté the fennel bulb, onion, fennel seeds, and crushed red chile until onion pieces are slightly softened (about 5 minutes). Add the bell peppers and garlic; sauté briefly, just until peppers are slightly soft. (Do not overcook!)

Pour sautéed vegetables over the pasta and mix well with the fresh herbs, adding salt and freshly ground pepper to taste. Toss the pasta with the dressing. Add the freshly grated Parmesan and pepperoni; toss well. If made in advance, refrigerate and serve at room temperature. Serves 4–6.

NOTE: The dressing also makes a good marinade for fish, chicken, or steak.

FENNEL-MUSTARD SAUCE

This rich sauce makes an excellent accompaniment to poultry, veal, pork, or fish dishes. The recipe comes from Mick Vann and Chris Shirley of Clarksville Cafe, Austin.

1 medium-size fennel bulb, minced
1 teaspoon minced garlic
3 shallots, minced
1–2 tablespoons clarified butter
½ cup Chardonnay wine
1 cup chicken stock
1 cup heavy cream
3 tablespoons Dijon mustard
½ teaspoon lemon juice
Salt and white pepper to taste

Sauté fennel, garlic, and shallots in clarified butter over low heat until fennel begins to soften (approximately 10 minutes). Briefly raise heat to high and add the wine. Decrease heat slightly and reduce the liquid until it is absorbed (approximately 5 minutes). Add chicken stock and reduce by ½. Add cream and reduce by ¼. Purée this mixture in a food processor. Return to pot and add mustard and lemon juice. Season to taste with salt and pepper, and serve over meat, garnishing with sprigs of fresh fennel. Serves 4–6.

▼▼▼▼▼▼▼▼▼▼▼▼▼▼▼▼▼▼▼▼▼▼▼▼▼▼▼▼▼▼▼

FIESTA FISH

This festive multicolored dish is visually inviting with a sweet and alluring aroma. Fennel is at its best complementing fish smothered with a medley of vegetables and other herbs.

4 fish fillets, 6–8 ounces each (redfish, red snapper, Pacific snapper, or
  mahi mahi)
4 teaspoons olive oil
4 tablespoons fresh orange juice
Salt and pepper
Paprika
Crushed dried red chile pepper (optional)
1 orange, sliced
½ large red bell pepper, cut into rings

FIESTA SAUCE
▼▼▼▼▼▼▼▼

3 tablespoons olive oil
3 cloves garlic, minced
½ medium onion, chopped
½ teaspoon fennel seeds
1 fennel bulb, chopped (reserve feathery foliage)
½ red bell pepper, chopped
⅓ cup fresh orange juice
3 tablespoons dry vermouth
Salt and pepper
Crushed dried red chile pepper (optional)
3–4 tablespoons chopped fennel foliage

Lightly oil a broiler pan that will hold fish. Drizzle each fillet with olive oil and orange juice, and sprinkle both sides with salt and pepper, paprika, and crushed red chile pepper. Place the orange slices and red pepper slices on the bottom of the pan, reserving 4 of each for serving plates. Place fish skin-side down on top of the orange and red pepper slices.

To make the sauce: heat 3 tablespoons olive oil in a large sauté pan. Sauté the garlic, onion, fennel seeds, and chopped fennel bulb for about 4 minutes. Add the chopped red pepper, and sauté 3 minutes. Add the remaining ingredients and sauté another 3 minutes.

Place fish under the broiler 4 inches from heat. Broil approximately 5 minutes (do not turn) or until fish flakes when tested with a fork. Spoon some sauce over fish the last 2 minutes of broiling, and/or serve fish with sauce on the side. Serve each fillet with a slice of orange and red pepper ring. Serves 4.

NOTE: The sauce also makes a delicious stuffing for a whole baked red snapper marinated in olive oil, orange juice, and vermouth.

LEMON BALM

Melissa officinalis
Lamiaceae (Labiatae) family

Lemon balm leaves (above wooden clogs).

Common Names:
lemon balm, balm, sweet balm, Sweet Melissa

Characteristics:
grows in large clumps with slightly heart-shaped, crinkly, bright green mint-like leaves with scalloped edges; deliciously lemon-scented foliage; small, delicate white flowers grow in clusters along stems in summer; also a yellow and green variegated variety, golden lemon balm (*Mel. off. variegata*); perennial

Conditions:
can tolerate full sun but appreciates some afternoon shade; loose, well-draining soil; do not overwater

Size:
approximately 1–2 feet tall and 2 feet wide

Propagation:

seeds slow to germinate (soak overnight); divide the clump in spring; 1 or 2 clumps per garden suggested

Fertilizer:

occasional light feedings of fish emulsion and applications of compost; over-fertilization produces large leaves with little fragrance

Pests:

spider mites during hot and humid summers – treat with insecticidal soap; some worm and pill bug damage; aphids

Companions:

attracts bees into the garden with its lovely fragrance

Lemon balm was one of the first herbs that I ever grew. Upon smelling its luscious and lemony fragrance I was absolutely amazed that an herb could so duplicate the scent of another plant. And lemon balm indeed captures the essence of the sweetest lemon imaginable. No wonder bees deliriously gather nectar from the delicate white flowers that cluster along its stems in summertime! In fact, its name, *Melissa*, comes from the Latin word for bees, and the leaves from this fragrant plant are rubbed on hives to attract these honey-producers.

Lemon balm's leaves resemble mint leaves but are larger and more rough and crinkly in appearance. Their edges look as if they had been trimmed with pinking shears. Unlike the mints, which rapidly spread by rhizomes, lemon balm forms a clump that can become quite large. I divide this clump in early spring and keep the plant continually trimmed so as not to exhaust it.

Lemon balm seems a bit more drought resistant and requires less water than some of the other mints that grow in the Southwest. I have grown it both in full sun and in partial shade with good results. This plant likes a slightly rich and well-draining soil. Obviously, a rich moist soil produces a verdant, lush plant, whereas less than optimum conditions produce small and often yellowed leaves. Fortunately, however, it is quite adaptive. I planted a few clumps in a shady, neglected area in my back yard where I never watered, yet it thrived all spring. And although it died back in summer, it returned the following spring.

There are many places in the garden for this aromatic herb. It makes a particularly attractive border plant and looks pretty planted against limestone rocks or walls. Lemon balm lends itself to container growing because it grows in a full and upright clump. It is pleasant to grow along paths where one may brush against it, releasing its lemony freshness into the air.

During times of high heat stress and following flowering, the plant often looks pale and peaked with slightly bronze-colored woody stems. I find that cutting back the plant and applying some compost and fish emulsion benefit it. Lemon balm is also susceptible to a virus (generally caused by too-wet conditions) that causes the leaves to look rather burned and pale and chlorotic; when this happens, I also cut the plant back. During the hot summer, spider mites and aphids may be eradicated by light sprayings of insecticidal soap after the plant has been cut back.

It is fortunate for me that frequent cuttings from lemon balm, especially after flowering, promote new growth, because I am often snipping this flavorful herb. Guests to my garden are encouraged to pinch off a sprig and enjoy its sweet perfume. In Elizabethan England, lemon balm was a favorite herb in nosegays, and it remains a favorite in my springtime bouquets. I especially like to garnish drinks with it so that the nose tingles with its lemony aroma as one takes a sip. Lemon balm makes an attractive garnish for fruit bowls, soups, salads, and elegant custards, ice creams, sorbets, and cakes. I like to freeze the leaves in ice cube trays with slices of fruit (strawberries, oranges, lemons) or flowers (violas, roses, marigolds) to serve in iced tea and other cold drinks.

Lemon balm also makes a delightfully soothing tea long used to treat melancholy (indeed, its sweet freshness restores spirits!), and this calming tea is said to cure heat exhaustion as well. Simply infuse a handful in a ceramic teapot and let steep for about 8 minutes. Serve in a pretty cup with a sprig of the fresh herb. Slightly bruising a few leaves and putting them in a glass of white wine makes a similarly uplifting drink.

This delicately flavored herb may be used in many recipes. Adding a few chopped leaves to garden salads gives a refreshing citrus flavor. Steamed vegetables taste wonderful tossed with melted butter, a squeeze of lemon juice, and a few fragrant lemon balm leaves. Or try stuffing a handful of the leaves and some minced green onions under the skin of chicken breasts, then sprinkle with lemon pepper before baking or grilling. A pork tenderloin may be stuffed with apple slices and lemon balm. And baked or grilled fish are delicious when drizzled with melted lemon balm butter.

Almost any fruit is enhanced by a few chopped lemon balm leaves. Remember that chopping with a knife usually bruises the leaves, causing them to discolor; I tear the leaves into small pieces instead. Marinating fruit and lemon balm leaves in citrus or wine dressings also will cause the leaves to discolor (although they give good flavor), so you may want to replace the darkened leaves before serving. One of my favorite summer sandwiches is made by spreading cream cheese blended with a small amount of mayonnaise on slices of whole-grain bread, then adding lots of lemon balm leaves and generous slices of juicy nectarines, strawberries, or peaches. Lemon balm similarly enhances—both as garnish and flavoring—other open-faced sandwiches and hors d'oeuvres to be served at festive luncheons. Or try some of the leaves in an omelet with fresh strawberries and crème fraîche for a spectacular presentation!

Once you have tasted and smelled this delightful herb, you will not want to be without it, and you will welcome its return each spring. Do remember that it is easily frostbitten, so harvest it before the first freeze. Hang the bunches upside down to dry, or place stems on airy screens to use for teas and in potpourris. Also freeze it in ice cube trays for a burst of citrus freshness on a gloomy winter's day.

▼▼▼▼▼▼▼▼▼▼▼▼▼▼▼▼▼▼▼▼▼▼▼▼

LEMON BALM VINAIGRETTE

This refreshing lemony vinaigrette tastes wonderful on salads. Try it on crisp greens with thin rings of red onion and orange and melon slices; on sweet red pepper slices with golden day-lily petals; or on grilled or poached fish or chicken salads. Also use it as a marinade for fish or chicken, and drizzle some over each portion before serving.

1 tablespoon minced shallots (1 large clove)
2 generous tablespoons finely chopped lemon balm
½ teaspoon lemon zest
6 tablespoons fresh lemon juice (1 medium lemon)
4 tablespoons Lovely Lemon vinegar *or* white wine vinegar [*see chapter on herb vinegars*]
1 teaspoon Dijon mustard
½–1 teaspoon brown sugar
8 tablespoons safflower oil

Mix the first 7 ingredients together, then slowly whisk in the oil. Mix well before serving. Yields approximately ⅔ cup.

VARIATIONS

Substitute sorrel for lemon balm, and serve on crisp greens (including several sorrel leaves torn into bite-size pieces), with kiwi, melon, and/or orange slices, or with poached scallops, shrimp, or fish. Can be used as a marinade as well.

NOTES: The smooth, buttery texture of day lily petals is exquisite in spring salads. Gently pull the petals from the stems, removing the bitter-tasting reproductive parts. Randomly toss the petals among a variety of crisp salad greens (and sweet red pepper rings if desired). Johnny jump-ups or violets may be used instead.

VALENTINO

Serve this sweet creamy dip in a bowl surrounded by plump fresh strawberries and garnished with fresh lemon balm sprigs. Or serve it as a spread on pretty heart-shaped open-faced sandwiches on a sunny morning in the garden with tea or Mimosas.

2 ounces unsalted butter, softened

8 ounces cream cheese, softened

2 generous tablespoons best quality strawberry preserves *or* orange marmalade

1 teaspoon orange zest

1 tablespoon Grand Marnier *or* other orange liqueur *or* fresh orange juice

3 tablespoons chopped fresh lemon balm

Fresh strawberries (optional garnish)

Fresh lemon balm sprigs (optional garnish)

Blend the butter and cream cheese with a fork. Mix in the other ingredients. Best made a day in advance for flavors to mingle; chill overnight and serve at room temperature. Keeps for a week.

NOTE: To make Valentino sandwiches, cut out Swedish limpa or whole-grain bread with heart-shaped cookie cutters, and spread with the cream cheese mixture. Cut strawberries in vertical slices to resemble hearts; garnish each sandwich with one or two strawberry slices and a fresh sprig of lemon balm. (Lemon verbena or mint may be substituted.) Also: simply spread the mixture on sweet crackers or croissants, or use it as a cheesecake topping.

▼▼▼▼ ▼▼▼▼ ▼▼▼▼ ▼▼▼▼ ▼▼▼▼ ▼▼▼▼ ▼▼▼▼ ▼▼▼▼ ▼▼▼▼

GARDEN PUNCH

This punch is simple to make, yet people always rave about it. A delightful and refreshing drink to serve in the garden, especially when poured over ice cubes that have been frozen with lemon balm and mint sprigs, small lemon slices, and flower petals.

2 generous bunches of lemon balm sprigs, on long stems if possible, *plus*

2 generous bunches mild-flavored mints (also on long stems if possible) to loosely fill the pitcher

1 large can (46 ounces) unsweetened pineapple juice *or* equivalent pure unfiltered apple juice

Juice of two lemons

1 lemon, cut in thin slices

Sparkling water *or* champagne to taste

Gently wring the bunches of lemon balm and mint to release their flavor. Place in a large glass pitcher, cover with the juices and the lemon slices. Chill overnight, occasionally stirring and pressing down on the herbs with the back of a wooden spoon. Pour into iced glasses with a splash of sparkling water (or champagne) and a sprig of fresh lemon balm and/or mint. Serves 8–10.

NOTE: The best mints to use are varieties of spearmint, apple mint, Egyptian mint, or pineapple mint. Orange bergamot mint is usually too strong. Also, lemon verbena or pineapple sage may be used. For a special touch, add festive herbal ice cubes (see Cooking Tips chapter).

LEMON VERBENA

Aloysia triphylla syn. *Lippia citriodora*
Verbenaceae family

Tiny, delicate white blossoms of lemon verbena.

Common Names:
lemon verbena

Characteristics:
a shrub-like herb with woody stems; narrow and rough-textured pointed leaves from 1–3 inches long grow in whorls of 3 or 4 with an intense lemon scent; tiny white flowers blossom in late spring, summer and fall and are especially fragrant; deciduous or semi-evergreen; tender perennial

Conditions:
somewhat dry and well-draining soil; do not overwater; do not crowd in the garden; full sun or some afternoon shade; grow along a southern wall for winter protection

Size:
generally 3–6 feet tall, although it can attain 20 feet or more in climates with mild winters; somewhat straggly with long, leggy branches

▼▼▼▼▼▼▼▼▼▼▼▼▼▼▼▼▼▼▼▼▼▼▼▼▼▼

Propagation:

make cuttings when green stems begin to harden (usually in summer) and keep in greenhouse in winter (do not overwater); 1 or 2 plants per garden suggested

Fertilizer:

light application of fish emulsion in early spring and occasional applications of compost during summer and winter

Pests:

spider mites, aphids, and worms may do some damage

Companions:

attracts bees and butterflies

Mary was my grandmother's best friend, and she lived in a rather run-down wooden cottage on a cliff above the sea in Southern California. As a child, I loved to romp in her untended garden, playing hide-and-seek among the overgrown plants and flowers. One particular shrub, lemon verbena, was taller than I, with woody stems and scratchy leaves that enticed me with their delicious lemony scent. I loved to run my hands along the straggly branches until I, too, smelled as fresh as its citrus perfume. And during the summer, when the tips of its branches were graced with clusters of tiny white star-like flowers, I would twist the branches into regal wreaths for my hair. Years later, I was delighted to find the pure essential oil of lemon verbena in a French perfumery in Toronto, so I could again reminisce about my childhood afternoons in Mary's garden.

My only regret in growing lemon verbena is that it does not attain the size that it may in its native South America or similarly temperate climates, where it may reach a height of 20 feet or more! California gardeners often grow plants at least 6 feet tall, although 3–4 feet is the norm in areas with colder winters.

Lemon verbena is a semi-evergreen plant that generally loses some or all leaves during the winter. Although it usually withstands the freeze down to about 20 degrees (when kept well-mulched), I sometimes bury the plant in a pot in the spring so that I can lift it out and place it in the greenhouse in the winter. There, it loses its leaves, so I make sure not to overwater it, and I keep it in a dormant state. In any event, make sure to harvest the leaves before the first frost, and dry the branches so that you may use the aromatic leaves in potpourris, among linens, and as tea. Or freeze the leaves in ice cube trays as you would lemon balm to make decorative ice cubes.

Lemon verbena can tolerate full sun but seems to appreciate a bit of afternoon shade during our hot Southwestern summers. It actually fares better in rather loose, dry soil but likes rich, moist soil as well. Fertilizer may increase the size of the leaves but decrease the flavor. Please give this spindly plant ample space in the garden, as it does not like to be crowded. The leaves are so luscious and lemony that you will frequently snip them, thereby keeping the plant in shape. The rough-textured leaves are narrow and pointed and grow in whorls of 3 or 4. It is best propagated from 3–4-inch cuttings in late spring or early fall, although it is slow to root.

The captivating lemon scent attracts butterflies and bees into the garden; unfortunately, a few detrimental pests are beckoned as well. Aphids and spider mites can be eradicated with repeated sprayings of insecticidal soap. Hungry worms may be discouraged by bacillus thuringiensis.

Once you have smelled this herb, you, too, will be enthralled by its magic. It may be used similarly to lemon balm whenever a delicate lemon taste is desired in food and drinks. It is especially lovely as a garnish for iced drinks, ice creams, and sorbets and a few leaves gently bruised and added to a glass of chilled champagne or white wine is an unforgettable sensory experience. A branch of the lovely ambrosial leaves may border simple flan custard or a cake magnificently frosted with a rich buttercream. How exquisite a wedding cake would be

adorned with lemon verbena in fragrant flower!

Lemon verbena may be used alone or in combination with lemon balm in fruit bowls and punches and makes an attractive garnish for soups, salads, and dinner plates. A few sprigs may be slipped in napkin rings or used in finger bowls as well. The flavorful leaves may be stuffed under the skin of chicken breasts or wrapped around fish fillets before baking or grilling. Sometimes I simply take large handfuls of the branches and stuff them in the cavity of a roasting hen or turkey along with onion slices, dried fruit, and orange and lemon slices. Pork and veal are also enhanced by its lemony aroma.

This herb, so redolent of fresh lemons, makes the beloved tea known as *verveine* in France. (Infuse a generous handful in a china teapot filled with boiling water.) I also like to add a few lemon verbena leaves to peppermint or jasmine tea for a mellowing flavor. And the leaves also delightfully enhance jellies, honey, and fruit glazes.

Lemon verbena also partners well with other sweet-smelling herbs and flowers. Remember to mix it with rose and lemon geraniums, lemon balm, mints, violas, roses, and violets in lovely bouquets and as garnishes. Truly, lemon verbena is the "Queen of Herbs!"

▼▼▼▼▼▼▼▼▼▼▼▼▼▼▼▼▼▼▼▼▼▼▼▼▼▼▼▼

SANGRÍA

Sangría, Spain's sassy wine cooler, tastes refreshing whether made with red or white wine. Garnishing the pitcher with wispy sprigs of herbs makes it especially appealing.

2 oranges, thinly sliced

1 lemon, thinly sliced

1 lime, thinly sliced (optional)

Fresh seasonal fruits, such as seedless grapes, apple slices, pear slices (soft fruits such as strawberries, peaches, and kiwis should be added only prior to serving)

1 gallon dry red or white wine

1½–2 cups Grand Marnier *or* any orange-flavored liqueur

1½ cups brandy

2 bunches long-stemmed lemon verbena (mint and lemon balm may be added also)

Club soda or champagne

Place oranges, lemon, lime, and other desired fruits in a large container. Add wine, orange liqueur, brandy, and herbs. Cover and refrigerate at least overnight, or up to 3 days. Fill a clear glass pitcher with sangría, adding freshly sliced seasonal fruit and fresh long-stemmed herbs. Pour into wine glasses with a spash of club soda or champagne, a tiny cluster of grapes, and a fresh herb sprig.

NOTE: When using red wine, I often add a long stick of cinnamon. Fragrant and wispy sprigs of blooming lemon verbena or pineapple sage look especially exquisite garnishing the pitcher. You might like to add festive herbal ice cubes as well. For instructions, see Cooking Tips chapter.

VELVETY LEMON VERBENA FLAN

This heavenly golden custard is simply exquisite adorned with fragrant sprigs of lemon verbena and delicate flowers.

4 cups half-and-half

1 cup lemony herbs (lemon verbena and/or lemon balm), tightly packed

4 teaspoons lemon zest

2 cups white sugar

7 eggs *plus* 2 egg yolks

1 pinch salt

¼ teaspoon mace

½ teaspoon vanilla

Optional garnishes: fresh lemon slices, brandy, fresh lemon verbena sprigs
(with flowers, when in season)

Scald the half-and-half. Gently wring the herbs to release their flavor; add them to the scalded milk with 2 teaspoons of the lemon zest, pressing down gently with a wooden spoon. Let sit at least 30 minutes.

Carmelize 1 cup sugar by heating it in a small pan over medium heat. Swirl it gently and constantly, until sugar liquefies and turns golden, being careful not to let it burn. Immediately pour caramel into a 1½-quart baking dish, or into 12–14 small ramekins, working quickly, swirling it around the sides. Set aside.

Preheat oven to 325 degrees. Lightly beat eggs and extra yolks. Mix in the remaining cup of sugar and 2 teaspoons lemon zest. Meanwhile, slowly add the half-and-half mixture to the egg mixture, mixing gently. Add salt, mace, and vanilla. Pour into caramel-coated baking dish or ramekins.

Place baking dish (or ramekins) in a larger pan and carefully pour about an inch of hot water into the larger pan (this is sometimes called a *bain marie*). Bake for about 1 hour or until a knife inserted in center comes out clean. (Bake individual flans for approximately 25 minutes.)

To serve, gently run knife around edge of flan. Set dish in a pan of hot water for 30 seconds, then carefully invert onto a platter with a slightly curved lip, to ensure that the caramel does not run over. Garnish with lemon slices, and flambé with brandy or dark rum.

NOTE: To flambé, barely heat 6 tablespoons of brandy or dark rum. Pour over the flan and ignite for a beautiful spectacle!

LOVELY LEMON VERBENA POUNDCAKE

Sour cream poundcake, a family favorite, is even more delicious when accompanied by a tart lemon verbena-brandy glaze. Line the bottom of the baking pan with fresh sprigs of lemon verbena before adding the batter (when the cake is inverted, the leaves will bake in a wreath-like pattern on top). Serve on a platter wreathed with fresh lemon verbena sprigs, fresh strawberry or peach slices, and Johnny jump-ups. Pass the warm glaze in a small pitcher.

Butter and flour to prepare a 10-inch tube pan
3 6″ fresh, tender lemon verbena sprigs (optional)
1 cup unsalted butter, slightly softened
2¾ cups sugar
6 eggs
¼ teaspoon almond extract
½ teaspoon lemon extract
1 teaspoon vanilla
3 cups white flour
¼ teaspoon salt
¼ teaspoon baking soda
1 cup sour cream
2–3 teaspoons lemon zest

LEMON VERBENA GLAZE

1/4 stick butter
3 tablespoons honey
4 tablespoons fresh lemon juice
½ teaspoon lemon zest
2 tablespoons brandy or dark rum
1 tablespoon finely chopped lemon verbena

Preheat oven to 300 degrees. Butter and lightly flour a 10-inch tube pan, and place lemon verbena sprigs to cover the bottom of the pan with the underside of the leaves facing up. In a large bowl with an electric mixer, cream the butter with the sugar until light and fluffy. Add the eggs, one at a time, and beat well, incorporating the almond, lemon, and vanilla flavorings.

Sift the flour, salt, and soda 3 times. Add alternately with the sour cream to the butter/sugar mixture, stirring constantly. Add lemon zest last.

Spoon batter into prepared pan, taking

care to flatten the lemon verbena leaves. Bake at 300 degrees for 1½ hours, or until a wooden pick inserted into middle of cake tests dry.

Loosen edges with a knife, and let stand for 15 minutes in the pan; then invert on a wire rack to cool. Serves 16–18.

To make the glaze, melt the butter in a small saucepan. Add the honey, lemon juice, and zest, then bring to a gentle boil. Remove from heat. Add the brandy and chopped lemon verbena. If made earlier in the day, reheat before serving and drizzle over slices of the cake. Makes ½ cup glaze.

NOTE: Lemon balm and lemon thyme may be substituted for lemon verbena in the glaze. You also may substitute rose geranium or lemon geranium leaves for the lemon verbena sprigs in the cakepan; if you do, use 1–2 teaspoons rosewater in place of the almond extract. This cake gets better with age.

MARJORAM

Majorana hortensis
(formerly *Origanum majorana*)
Lamiaceae (Labiatae) family

Marjoram growing in a Mexican pot.

Common Names:

majoram, sweet marjoram, knotted marjoram, *mejorana* (Mexico)

Characteristics:

soft, velvety, light-green leaves are gray underneath with sweet perfume-like odor; flower buds form tight knots from which white flowers emerge in late spring and summer; tender perennial (annual in warm climates)

Conditions:

loose, well-draining soil; full sunshine and adequate watering

Size:

1 foot tall

Propagation:

sow seeds in early spring, or purchase as transplant at nursery; 1–2 plants per garden suggested

Fertilizer:

light applications of fish emulsion when first establishing; occasional applications of compost (especially during summer) and mulch in winter; do not fertilize after well established

Pests:

white fly, aphids, and spider mites may be treated with insecticidal soap

Companions:

none noted

Gently rubbing the soft, downy leaves of marjoram releases the most delicious perfume, which is both sweet and spicy. It is no wonder that "when in doubt, use marjoram" has become a motto among herb enthusiasts, for it delicately enhances most dishes, from simple salads to savory casseroles and stuffed pork tenderloin.

Marjoram has long been considered the cultivated form of oregano, and confusion still exists in distinguishing these two plants. In many places, especially England, oregano is called wild marjoram or winter marjoram. But the flavor of oregano and marjoram are unmistakably different. Marjoram's perfumed scent is a sure way to differentiate it from the more robust oregano. Another thing to take note of is that oregano is a perennial, while marjoram must be treated as an annual in the Northern United States or as a tender perennial in the South. Keeping it well mulched may be enough protection during mild freezes, but prolonged freezing weather will freeze its roots and cause it to perish.

Marjoram makes an attractive soft and bushy plant in the garden and fills the air with its enchanting fragrance when brushed against. It grows from 8 to 12 inches in height, and its small, oval, velvety green leaves are soft and gray underneath. It has another unique characteristic: its flower buds form tight overlapping "knots" (actually plaited bracts) from which graceful white flowers emerge in spring and summertime; hence, its common name, knotted marjoram. I remember by grandmother singing a favorite English nursery song to me when I was a child. Years later, I realized that one of the verses, "Here we go gathering knots in May so early in the morning," was about gathering the sweet marjoram knots. These flower bracts look lovely in summer bouquets and as garnishes for festive platters, especially when the small white flowers begin to poke out their heads. The leaves are especially flavorful just as the knots appear, prior to flowering, and should be harvested at this time. Woody branches and stems should be removed. I usually harvest again in October. Unlike some herbs, marjoram's flavor intensifies when dried, making it a useful year-round seasoning, and many people prefer its flavor in this form.

Marjoram germinates well in soil that has a constantly warm temperature; how − ever, the emerging stems are weak and susceptible to root rot and insect attack. Consequently, it is easier to purchase a few plants from a nursery. When planted in a pot or hanging basket, marjoram tends to cascade attractively; in the garden it will grow more upright. Look for the lovely and fast-spreading creeping golden marjoram (or oregano) (*Origanum vulgare* 'Aureum'), which makes an excellent ground cover, although it has little culinary value.

Like oregano, marjoram requires plenty of sunshine and a well-draining soil, but it also needs more water than oregano. In mild climates, where marjoram may be treated as a perennial, it is important to divide the plant by the roots every 2–3 years to prevent woodiness and to assure good flavor. As marjoram is in the mint family, it is sometimes troubled by some of the same insects that attack mints: white fly, mites, and aphids. Generally though, these pests manifest themselves when the herb is grown in less-than-favorable conditions.

It seems that in American kitchens, the heartier and more assertive oregano outshines the more demure marjoram. Too often forgotten, marjoram never overpowers; it simply complements foods with elegance. Marjoram mingles well with the sweet taste of freshly roasted red peppers doused in olive oil and wine vinegar and sprinkled with minced garlic. And a few sprigs tossed randomly on tomato slices drizzled with a delicate vinaigrette is sure to please. Marjoram's meadow-fresh flavor enhances cottage cheese and cheese spreads [see recipe for *boursin*] as well as scrambled eggs and omelets.

Stuffing a chicken or hen with marjoram and tiny leeks thinned from the garden makes an unforgettable dinner, as does filling a whole trout with small bunches of marjoram before grilling. (Remember to add fresh sprigs of marjoram to the hot coals.) During the Middles Ages, marjoram was renowned for its preservative and disinfectant qualities in cooking meats that had passed their prime. It remains a popular seasoning in preserved and aged meats, especially sausage. Pork and veal are always enhanced by marjoram, especially when they are presented on platters adorned with this graceful herb.

I love crumbling dried marjoram between my palms and generously sprinkling it over split pea, white bean, or lentil soup as wafts of its balmy delicacy fill the room. And I especially love marjoram with carrot soup − served chilled or warm. The subtle sweetness of the freshest carrots and marjoram do not mask one another's flavor; instead, they harmoniously complement each other. Almost any steamed or sautéed vegetable's flavor is improved with the addition of this aromatic herb.

Whenever I am feeling low, certain foods seem to soothe. Squash is my "soul food," steamed until it is soft, with slices of onions and lots of butter and freshly chopped (or dried and crumbled) marjoram. As soon as I raise the lid of the pan and the marjoram-scented steam escapes, my spirits are uplifted. It's no wonder that for centuries, this delightful herb has been known to restore peace and happiness.

▼▼▼▼▼▼▼▼▼▼▼▼▼▼▼▼▼▼▼▼▼▼▼▼▼▼▼▼▼▼▼▼

CALABACITAS

I adore calabacitas, the plump, sweet Mexican squash that resemble baby watermelons. Sautéed with onions, roasted chile strips, tomatoes, and fresh marjoram, they make a dish that is a sure crowd-pleaser.

3 medium-size calabacitas (about 2½ pounds), cut into 1-inch slices, then cut into large bite-size chunks

1 small handful fresh marjoram sprigs

Salt to taste

½ stick butter

3 cloves garlic, minced

1 medium-size onion, chopped

1 cup chopped tomatoes

4–6 Anaheim *or* poblano chiles, roasted, peeled, and cut into *rajas or* 2–4 chopped jalapeños [*for instructions on preparing* rajas, *see Cooking Tips chapter*]

3–4 tablespoons chopped fresh marjoram

Salt and freshly ground pepper to taste

1 cup grated cheese (optional), preferably

½ cup yellow Cheddar and

½ cup Monterey Jack or white Cheddar

Steam squash with the marjoram sprigs until crisp-tender; do not overcook! Drain in a colander and lightly sprinkle with salt; let sit while chopping other ingredients.

Heat butter; sauté garlic and onions. When slightly softened, add tomatoes and chile *rajas* or jalapeños, and cook for about 5 minutes. Add the steamed squash, chopped marjoram, salt, and pepper. Mix in the cheese, stirring well until melted. Serve immediately. Serves 8.

NOTES: If desired, roasted red bell pepper strips may replace the rajas, *or peppers may be omitted. Fresh oregano and/or cilantro may be substituted for the marjoram. This dish tastes delicious with or without the cheese. For a more substantial dish, add cooked shredded chicken, pork, or beef.*

TRICOLOR ROASTED PEPPERS IN GARLIC VINAIGRETTE

Marjoram mingles well with the sweet taste of freshly roasted bell peppers doused in olive oil, wine vinegar, and plenty of garlic. Serve in salads or on crisp, homemade croutons spread with garlicky Montrachet cheese and a mellow red wine.

2 each medium-size red, golden, and green bell peppers, roasted and peeled, and cut into ½-inch strips [*for instructions on roasting peppers (rajas), see Cooking Tips chapter*]

4 large cloves garlic, minced

½ cup extra virgin olive oil

4 tablespoons oregano-chile-garlic vinegar, *or* Mediterranean marinade vinegar, *or* red wine vinegar [*see chapter on herb vinegars*]

3 tablespoons sherry vinegar

1 pinch brown sugar

Salt to taste

Freshly ground white pepper to taste

2 generous tablespoons chopped fresh marjoram

Toss the roasted pepper strips with the minced garlic. Mix the oil, vinegar, and sugar, and heat in a small saucepan. When nearly boiling, remove from heat. Drizzle over the peppers. Sprinkle with salt and freshly ground pepper. Toss well with the freshly chopped marjoram. Serves 10–12.

NOTE: Keeps for weeks in refrigerator. Serve at room temperature. A more piquant version can be made with poblano chile strips and fresh oregano instead of marjoram. The remaining vinaigrette is good on salads. These peppers also are delicious on sandwiches spread lightly with homemade mayonnaise and arugula leaves, or served with Mardi Gras Montrachet.

▼▼▼▼▼▼▼▼▼▼▼▼▼▼▼▼▼▼▼▼▼▼▼▼▼▼▼▼
▲▲▲▲▲▲▲▲▲▲▲▲▲▲▲▲▲▲▲▲▲▲▲▲

PORK TENDERLOIN MEDALLIONS WITH FRESH MARJORAM

▼▼▼▼▼▼▼▼▼▼▼▼▼▼▼▼▼▼▼▼▼▼▼▼▼▼

Sweet, roasted red bell peppers, fresh marjoram sprigs, minced garlic, and toasted pine nuts are rolled up inside a succulent pork tenderloin to show a medley of color when sliced. Serve warm as an entrée or chilled on open-faced sandwiches and in salads.

¾–1 pound pork tenderloin, butterflied and lightly pounded

Salt and freshly ground pepper to taste

3–4 cloves garlic, minced

1 medium-size sweet red bell pepper, roasted, peeled, and cut into strips, 3–4 inches long by ⅜ inch wide [*for instructions on preparing* rajas, *see Cooking Tips chapter*]

1 teaspoon whole fennel seeds

1 tablespoon chopped fresh marjoram

6 tender sprigs fresh marjoram, each about 6 inches long

2 generous tablespoons pine nuts, toasted [*for instructions on toasting nuts, see Cooking Tips chapter*]

1 tablespoon olive oil

Paprika to taste

4 tablespoons sweet red vermouth

Sprinkle meat with salt and pepper, and rub with minced garlic. Arrange the roasted pepper strips vertically to cover the meat, and sprinkle with fennel seeds and chopped marjoram. Lay the fresh marjoram sprigs vertically, sprinkle with pine nuts, then tightly roll up the meat from end to end; place seam-side down in a baking dish. Rub the olive oil into the meat; sprinkle it generously with sweet paprika, and rub it into the meat. Sprinkle with more salt and pepper if desired.

Place in a preheated 450-degree oven for approximately 6–8 minutes. Remove from oven and reduce temperature to 300 degrees. Drizzle 2 tablespoons sweet vermouth over meat and return immediately to oven. Cook approximately 30 minutes, basting with the remaining vermouth the last 5 minutes. Do not overcook; the red peppers may stain the meat somewhat pink, so do not mistake this for uncooked pork. Serves 2–4.

VARIATIONS

Substitute fresh sage for marjoram; or substitute poblano pepper *rajas* for the bell pepper strips and oregano for the marjoram. Omit fennel seeds.

NOTES: Ask your butcher to butterfly the pork for you. The pork also may be drizzled with vermouth and cooked at 350 degrees for 40–45 minutes, which makes it succulent without a crusty top.

▼▼▼▼▼▼▼▼▼▼▼▼▼▼▼▼▼▼▼▼▼▼▼▼▼▼▼

DUCK CONFIT

Marjoram has long been known for its properties of cutting fat in duck and preserving meats. The addition of thyme, bay, allspice, peppercorns, and juniper further the flavor of this scrumptious duck confit. Amy Ferguson, executive chef at Baby Routh in Dallas serves her creation with pasta or in elegant salads. Since it keeps well, it's convenient for last minute occasions.

1 duck, quartered
1 cup kosher salt
½ cup fresh thyme leaves
½ cup fresh marjoram
¼ cup crumbled fresh bay leaves
1 tablespoon peppercorns, crushed
½ tablespoon juniper berries, crushed
2 sprigs fresh thyme with bay leaves
8 cups solid unrendered duck fat

Rinse the duck and pat dry. Mix salt, herbs, and crushed spices (except for 2 sprigs fresh thyme with 2 bay leaves) in a bowl. Coat each piece of duck thoroughly with this mixture; put the duck in a dish, sprinkle with more of the salt mixture. Refrigerate for 24 hours, turning every six hours.

To render the duckfat, put the solid fat in a pot with 5 times the volume of water as duckfat. Bring to a boil and simmer for 2 hours. Do not let the water boil away. Strain and chill the fat and water until the fat is hard. Lift off the fat and discard the water.

Wipe the duck pieces free of salt. Melt the rendered duck fat and put the pieces in it, fitting tightly so that the duck is covered with the fat. Simmer very gently until the duck is tender when pierced with a skewer, about 1 hour. The breast pieces will be done first. Take the cooked pieces out and set aside.

Strain the fat and let set until the juices fall to the bottom. Carefully remove the fat so as not to get any juices in the fat. Put the duck in a clean jar or crock along with the 2 springs of fresh thyme with 2 bay leaves. Pour the fat over the duck. Let cool in the refrigerator; then cover.

The duck *must* be covered with fat–it will then keep up to 2 months in the refrigerator. It has only to be heated in 1 tablespoon of its fat in a 400° over for 15 minutes before serving.

NOTE: This is a recipe for 1 duck, but it is better to cook about 4, once you have decided to do the work. Save up the duck fat and freeze it until there is enough to make confit. If necessary supplement it with chicken fat.

MEXICAN MARIGOLD MINT

Tagetes lucida syn. *T. florida*
Asteraceae (Compositae) family

Brilliant golden flowers of Mexican marigold mint bloom throughout the fall.

Common Names:

Mexican marigold mint, mint marigold, Texas tarragon, sweet marigold, cloud plant; *yerbanís, hierba anís, coronilla, pericón, hierba de las nubes* (Mexico); winter tarragon (England)

Characteristics:

glossy lance-shaped leaves, finely serrated; strong anise scent; brilliant golden marigold-like flowers in fall; perennial

Conditions:

loose, well-draining soil; full sun

Size:

1½–2½ feet tall

Propagation:

reseeds in late fall; roots in water; or plant seeds in flats (germinate in a few days) approximately 6 weeks before planting, and set out in early spring; plant 1 foot or more apart; 1–2 plants per garden suggested

Fertilizer:

none required

Pests:

some spider mite damage possible during hot months; spittlebugs, which may burrow in emerging leaves during high humidity, should be picked off

Companions:

none noted

Today, I can look back with humor on some of the trials and errors I have experienced in herb gardening. Once, while passing a deserted herb plot at our local community gardens, I noticed a plant that I could not identify. Picking off a few of the lance-shaped leaves and bruising them gently released a sharp but pleasant sweet anise scent. I thought I had found French tarragon! (I had never seen it growing and was accustomed to tasting it only in its dried form.) "What a find!" I thought, carefully uprooting a small clump to transplant to my own garden. And so for a few months, I happily grew my "Texas tarragon."

One day, however, a fellow herbalist informed me that my cherished plant was not tarragon, but a somewhat similar herb commonly called Mexican marigold mint. Tarragon (an artemisia) has difficulty tolerating our hot and dry summers; in fact, it requires a cold winter during its dormancy to produce healthy spring growth. Because of this, and because tarragon does not set seed and must be propagated by cuttings,

it is difficult to grow in the Southwest.

On the other hand, Mexican marigold mint flourishes in our region and can even be weed-like if not kept in check. And this plant offers an extra bonus: throughout October and November, it prolifically produces marigold-like flowers to grace the garden. (In cases of drought, it also may try to flower in the summer to preserve the species). You can make a breathtaking bouquet by combining Mexican marigold mint's brilliant golden flowers with scarlet spikes of pineapple sage and violet-colored blossoms of Mexican sage (*Salvia leucantha*). The flowers of marigold mint also make attractive edible garnishes, and the petals may be sprinkled on salads or pasta dishes and used in vinegars and potpourris. I love to adorn the turkey platter at Thanksgiving with them.

The leaves also offer exciting culinary possibilities. Although French chefs would scoff at Mexican marigold mint replacing their beloved tarragon, I find it the best available substitute. *Estragon*, the French word for tarragon, literally means "little dragon," and there is indeed an assertive and fiery taste to tarragon that Mexican marigold mint lacks. And Mexican marigold mint's anise flavor is definitely more pronounced. But use Mexican marigold mint as you would tarragon; in fact, it gives tarragon some competition as a flavoring herb for vinegar. Vinaigrettes made with it enliven mixed spring greens and chicken, tuna, or shellfish salads. (Toss about a tablespoon of the chopped fresh herb into the salad as well.)

Sauces, from the classic French *béarnaise* to homemade mayonnaise, take on a new flair when marigold mint replaces tarragon. A tablespoon of the freshly chopped herb added to a melting stick of butter with minced garlic gives steamed artichoke leaves a tasty dunk. It makes a fabulous herbal butter blended with orange zest and minced green onions and tastes delicious tossed with pasta in a creamy tomato sauce. It enhances dips for vegetables, and the sprigs make an attractive garnish.

Because this herb grows so plentifully in my garden, I have devised innumerable ways to use it. I add a tablespoon of whole, fresh leaves to a quart jar of pickled beets, and a few teaspoons of minced leaves to crunchy carrots sautéed in butter. A simple entrée can be prepared by stuffing minced garlic and marigold mint leaves under the skin of chicken before baking or grilling it.

Others also extol the versatility of this flavorful herb. Mexican marigold mint has recently become the darling of renowned Southwestern chefs such as Stephan Pyles (Routh Street Cafe in Dallas), who partners it with catfish and smoked tomatoes. Anne Greer (author of several Southwestern cuisine books) uses it with pecans to make a unique pesto. Robert Del Grande (Cafe Annie in Houston), uses the flowers in his spectacular salads and various fish dishes. And the Mozzarella Company in Dallas adds it to *caciotta* cheese, giving it a uniquely delicious flavor.

Mexican marigold mint makes a pleasant flavoring for hot and cold beverages alike. As a tea, it is slightly sweet and refreshing. I also add it to fruit punches and sangría. Hot mulled apple cider warmly welcomes guests in the fall, filling the house with its spicy redolence. As marigold mint is at its peak at this time, I add a few large sprigs to the simmering cider and garnish each mug with a sprig of the cheerful golden flowers, evoking enthusiastic comments.

Germans traditionally drink May Wine to celebrate winter's passing into spring, serving it from ornate crystal punch bowls adorned with garlands of the season's freshest flowers and strawberries. May Wine is customarily flavored with sweet woodruff, an herb with a woodsy nutmeg flavor that simply cannot abide the heat of the Southwest. Consequently, I have adapted May Wine to our part of the country by replacing sweet woodruff with marigold mint and calling it Mexican May Wine. This makes a festive drink to serve on the Mexican holiday often celebrated in the Southwest, *Cinco de Mayo*. Remember to decorate the base of the serving bowl with long stems of marigold mint and the garden's finest flowers (float them as well) and fruits.

Fortunately, Mexican marigold mint is now available from several seed catalogs, but unless you plan to grow it for an ornamental border, I recommend buying one or two plants the first year. Believe me, by the following year it will have readily reseeded! Or take a few cuttings from a friend, as they root in water. Plants should be spaced about 1½ feet apart because they will grow a few feet wide and approximately 2 feet tall with long, spindly branches abundantly covered with finely-serrated lanceolate leaves. A well-draining soil and plenty of sunshine are necessary to produce the brilliant golden flowers.

Although I always cook with this herb in its fresh form, I also hang large bunches of it to dry in a well-ventilated room and then store it in jars to use as a tea or as a spicy and fragrant addition to potpourri. Actually, some chefs prefer it in its dried form, as its taste is more mellow. One note of caution: some find marigold mint's flavor overpowering, especially those who dislike the taste of anise; therefore, you may want to use it judiciously at first. Fortunately, I find its perky flavor and versatility an attribute.

NOTE: For further information, see chapter on Mexican herbs.

TOMATOES RELLENOS

(TOMATOES STUFFED WITH CORN AND SQUASH IN MARIGOLD MINT DRESSING)

Golden corn and zucchini nest in a ripe tomato shell. Delicious served with grilled fish, chicken, or steak.

4 medium-size tomatoes

Salt

3 cloves garlic, minced

4 tablespoons fresh lime juice

3 tablespoons Mexican marigold mint vinegar *or* tarragon vinegar [*see chapter on herb vinegars*]

¼ cup olive oil

½ teaspoon dried mustard

1 tablespoon tomato paste

1 teaspoon brown sugar

½ teaspoon crushed dried red chile pepper

3 tablespoons marigold mint, finely chopped

2 tablespoons fresh parsley, minced

1½ cups cooked corn kernels, chilled

2 small zucchinis, chopped

4–6 green onions, chopped

1 green or red bell pepper, chopped

Salt and freshly ground black pepper to taste

Garnish: bibb lettuce and marigold mint sprigs (and flowers)

Peel tomatoes (if desired) by plunging them in boiling water for 30 seconds, then immediately immersing them in cold water. Cut tops off tomatoes and remove some of the pulp. Lightly salt the shells and invert on paper towels to drain.

Make the vinaigrette by combining garlic, lime juice, vinegar, olive oil, dried mustard, tomato paste, brown sugar, and half of the fresh herbs. Dribble a small amount of vinaigrette (reserving half) into each tomato shell, and chill.

Combine corn, zucchini, green onion, bell pepper, salt, pepper, and the remaining fresh herbs. Mix with remaining vinaigrette, and chill for several hours. Line chilled salad plates with bibb lettuce and sprigs and flowers of marigold mint. Generously stuff each tomato with the corn/squash mixture, and drizzle any remaining vinaigrette over the tops. Serves 4.

NOTE: Fresh mint and mint vinegar or fresh basil and basil vinegar may be substituted for marigold mint and marigold mint vinegar.

MARIGOLD MINT VINAIGRETTE

Try this tangy golden dressing on chicken, seafood, cold beef, or pasta salads, or with zesty greens such as arugula. It also tastes lively drizzled over grilled fish, chicken, and flank steak, or a chilled salad made with steamed slices of golden-orange sweet potatoes and chopped pecans.

1 egg yolk
1 large clove garlic, minced
2½ teaspoons Dijon mustard
¼ teaspoon freshly ground pepper
1 teaspoon (or more) honey
¼ cup Mexican marigold mint vinegar *or* tarragon vinegar [*see chapter on herb vinegars*]
1 tablespoon chopped marigold mint *or* chopped tarragon
½ cup best quality olive oil
Pinch of salt and cayenne

Blend the egg yolk, garlic, mustard, pepper, and honey with a fork. Add the vinegar and chopped herbs; mix well. Slowly whisk in the oil in a steady stream until thickened. Adjust seasonings. Makes about 1 cup.

NOTE: 3 tablespoons fresh dill may be substituted for the marigold mint in this recipe. Use dill vinegar or bouquet garni vinegar as well.

MUSTARD AND MARIGOLD MINT CHICKEN

In this dish, Mexican marigold mint gives tarragon some competition! Served warm or cold, this chicken makes lively picnic fare when sliced into medallions and served on baguette slices spread with honey-mustard. Garnish with fresh sprigs of marigold mint.

4 boneless chicken breasts, split, with skin
Salt and freshly ground pepper to taste
3 green onions, with tops
2–3 cloves garlic, minced
2–3 tablespoons chopped fresh marigold mint
3 tablespoons Dijon mustard
2 teaspoons honey
2 tablespoons butter, softened
1 tablespoon dry vermouth *or* white wine

Slightly flatten breasts and trim excess fat. Sprinkle with salt and pepper. Set aside.

Combine the remaining ingredients to make a thick paste. Place approximately 1½ tablespoons of the paste on each breast (skin-side down), and roll up tightly from end to end, starting with wider end. Place seam-side down on a lightly oiled baking dish, and dot breasts with any remaining herb mixture. Bake in preheated 350-degree oven for about 30 minutes. Serves 4.

NOTE: Fresh tarragon or dill may be substituted for Mexican marigold mint. Sliced into medallions, chicken may be served warm or cold in salads with crisp greens. Allow 3–4 slices per salad and dress with marigold mint vinaigrette (see chapter on herb vinegars).

GRILLED CATFISH WITH SMOKED PEPPERS AND MEXICAN MARIGOLD MINT

Celebrated Southwestern chef Stephan Pyles of Routh Street Cafe in Dallas, well known for his magic at the grill, created this special recipe.

½ red bell pepper, seeded and deribbed
½ yellow bell pepper, seeded and deribbed
¼ cup white wine vinegar
1 shallot, finely diced
1 clove garlic, finely diced
8 ounces (1 cup) butter, room temperature
1 tablespoon finely chopped fresh marigold mint leaves
4 6–8-ounce catfish fillets
1 tablespoon oil or clarified butter
Salt to taste

TO PREPARE PEPPERS AND SMOKER

Soak 6–8 chunks of aromatic wood (such as almond, hickory, cherry, apple, or orange) in water for 20 minutes. Build fire in smoker with hardwood charcoal briquettes and electric starter. (Avoid chemical starters, as they impart unpleasant flavors to the smoke.) When briquettes are still glowing but somewhat gray (about 20 minutes after starting fire), add soaked wood chunks. Let burn for 5 minutes.

Place peppers on grill over water pan and cover with top of smoker. Smoke peppers for 20–30 minutes. Remove from smoker and roast in preheated 400-degree oven for 10–15 minutes. Peel peppers and chop. Set aside.

TO MAKE SAUCE

Place vinegar, wine, shallot, and garlic in a medium-size saucepan. Over high heat, reduce liquid to 2 tablespoons. Over medium-low heat, begin whisking in butter, a piece at a time, until all butter is incorporated. Remove from heat.

Add chopped peppers and marigold mint. Season with salt and keep warm in pan set over barely simmering water while grilling catfish.

Salt catfish fillets to taste, and grill 3–4 minutes per side, basting with oil or butter. When fillets are done, place each on a plate and cover generously with sauce. Serves 4.

NOTE: Garnish with marigold mint sprigs and/or flowers.

MINT

Mentha species
Lamiatae (Labiatae) family

A variety of mints adorn a basket and enhance a delicious fruit punch.

Common Names:

mint; assorted varieties often named after scent

Characteristics:

highly aromatic leaves may be roundish, oval, or slightly pointed, smooth or wrinkly, and have slightly serrated edges; square stems; whorls of small flowers bloom throughout summer in shades from white to lavender; perennial

Conditions:

loose, well-draining soil; full sun to afternoon shade; frequent and consistent moisture

Size:

1–3 feet tall according to variety; may be rampant spreaders if not restricted

▼▼▼▼▼▼▼▼▼▼▼▼▼▼▼▼▼▼▼▼▼▼▼▼▼▼▼▼

Propagation:
cuttings (roots readily in water); root division; nursery transplants; seed; several varieties per garden recommended

Fertilizer:
not recommended; compost-mulch in summer and winter beneficial

Pests:
susceptible to rust when kept too damp; aphids, white flies, and spider mites may be controlled with insecticidal soap

Companions:
repels fleas and sometimes aphids, as well as rodents; dried mint in drawers may repel moths and cockroaches

When I was young, roasted leg of lamb, fresh green beans, and golden ears of buttery corn comprised my favorite summertime meal. Just before dinner, my grandmother would send me out to her mint patch to gather a large handful of the fragrant leaves to use in a sauce – a simple concoction made by simmering vinegar, sugar, and the freshly chopped mint. I would drizzle spoonfuls of it over the tender slices of lamb, infatuated by its tangy sweet, sour, and minty flavor.

To me, the alluring aroma of garden mint always evokes pleasant memories: sitting in the garden with friends sipping frosty mint juleps; guzzling icy glasses of mint tea at family picnics; or discovering a clump of "this wonderful-smelling stuff" growing around a leaky drainage pipe at my secret childhood hiding place.

Like many people, I grew up believing that mint needed to grow in the shade by a leaky faucet, a myth I can now dispel. Granted, mint requires a frequent and consistent moisture level and appreciates afternoon shade during hot summers, but this Mediterranean native also likes the sun, so I make certain that it gets at least a full morning's worth. I have even found that using a drip irrigation system enables me to grow mint in full sun.

Those who attempt to grow mint in the deep shade of their backyard, in poor, unworked and soggy soil, often are faced with unhealthy plants susceptible to "rust," a fungal disease that gives the leaves a rusty color. Should rust invade, the diseased plants must be dug up and burned. One especially rainy and humid summer had many local gardeners lamenting this problem, but ideal growing conditions may prevent it, including a loose, moist, and well-draining soil. (Compacted soil dwarfs the plant and eventually causes it to die out.)

There are many varieties of mint and, like many other herbs, their botanical nomenclature gets rather confusing. Everyone seems to have his own idea about what is what, and dissident common names abound. To further confuse the issue, there are at least 25 main species of mint and hundreds of hybrids and variants. Generally speaking, mint leaves may be rounded, oval, or slightly pointed; smooth or wrinkly; and have slightly toothed or serrated edges. The most distinguishable characteristic is that the stems are always square. Whorls of tiny flowers bloom in luscious pastel shades of pink, lavender, and white throughout the summer; unfortunately, they should be kept cut off and the stems kept about 6 inches from the ground to discourage straggliness and to encourage new growth and robust flavor. If you grow several varieties of mint and allow them to flower, they will quickly cross-pollinate, producing variants (often weaker) of the original varieties.

One drawback in growing mint is that it is a rampant spreader and must be restricted. Never attempt to grow it in the vegetable garden or you will be gathering baskets of mint instead of tomatoes. Although divisions in beds may be made by burying metal or plastic edging or using bricks, stones, or wood for barriers (some herbalists even bury mint in large containers), the elusive mint roots usually push their way through, making the spade the only truly effective control. Dig up these trespassing clumps and share them with friends.

An excellent solution to the problem is to build specific mint beds, isolating them from other parts of the garden. I recently purchased several 1-by-4-foot landscape timbers with flexible galvanized metal backings, which allowed me to shape the desired beds. I filled them with a well-draining soil and planted a few different varieties of mint in each one. You also can grow mint in large clay pots, barrels, or other containers.

Unfortunately, mint tastes as good to aphids, white flies, and nasty little spider mites as it does to us. Of course, the insect problem is exacerbated when mint is grown under adverse conditions. Spraying them down with the hose and applying insecticidal soap should remedy the problem.

Although exotic varieties of mint such as ginger mint, grapefruit mint, variegated golden mint, orange bergamot mint, lime mint, and eau de cologne mint are fun to grow, the 3 species (and their many varieties) best used for culinary purposes are: *Mentha spicata* (spearmint), *Mentha piperita* (peppermint), and *Mentha suaveolens* (apple and pineapple mint).

People are most familiar with spearmint – the bright green, crinkly mint whose oval, serrated leaves often tickle their noses when they're drinking iced tea. Spearmint grows about 2 feet tall with reddish purple stems and pale pink or white flowers; it can be quite invasive. One may also find a smaller and smoother-leafed variety whose inviting smell is like unwrapping a stick of spearmint gum. Or try the narrow-leafed spearmint. Curly mint (*M. aquatica* v. *crispa*), with its light green curly leaves, or Kentucky colonel, with broader leaves, make exquisite juleps. A Lebanese friend of mine shared her favorite spearmint with me, claiming it to be the best for *tabbouleh* and other Middle Eastern dishes. Its leaves are quite wrinkled, tinged with purple, and highly aromatic. Spearmint's refreshing taste and smell make it the most favored for food and drink; it makes an attractive garnish as well. And, especially with mild winters, it is available in the Southwest almost year round.

Although the flavor of peppermint is generally too strong for uncooked foods, the leaves can enhance cooked foods, especially hearty soups, sauces, jellies and lamb. I feel that every garden must have a patch of black-stem peppermint. This particular variety has small, smooth, slightly pointed dark green leaves, purplish-black stems, and pale purple flowers. This makes the most refreshing herbal tea. I especially enjoy it in the summer – a light and refreshing substitute for coffee. Simply place a very generous handful of the freshly picked leaves into a china teapot, and cover with boiling water. Allow to steep about 6-7 minutes and serve in a cup with a fresh leaf. I must admit, the color is rather strange – quite yellow – but the cooling menthol flavor will certainly perk up your day. This tea is excellent for queasy or over-stuffed tummies, and it also soothes colds.

The mints associated with *Mentha suaveolens* include apple mint (sometimes called wooly mint) and pineapple mint (*Mentha suaveolens* cv. 'Variegata'). These are discernible from other mints because of their large fuzzy leaves and stems and their delicate fruity aroma. The fragrance and taste of these herbs often vary depending on growing conditions. Sometimes they are quite fruity and other times quite faint. Apple mint is one of the tallest mints, often reaching three feet high, while pineapple mint attains about 1 foot with smaller variegated green and cream-colored leaves. Both produce white flowers in the summer. I particularly enjoy growing apple mint because of its tolerance of full sun. It also makes an attractive ornamental plant when restricted by a border.

Similarly, Egyptian mint (*Mentha x niliaca*) is lanky (3–4 feet tall) with large, pale green fuzzy leaves and tolerates full sun. It also makes an appealing ornamental plant; in fact, I grow it in small beds against the front of the house, confining it with limestone rocks. As it is a fast grower, it quickly fills the bed with graceful stems, looking lush all summer. Its delicate white blossoms also attract bees. Like apple and pineapple mint, Egyptian mint may be finely chopped (it loses its fuzzy texture) for salads, sauces, and fruit dishes, although it lacks the peppy flavor of spearmint. I find that these fuzzy mints make good vinegar and mint sauce.

It's too bad that most people only remember to use mint in cold drinks and as a garnish because its culinary uses are limitless. Mexican women often add a few leaves toward the end of cooking their chicken soup, thereby uplifting the flavor. And one of the finest Mexican soups I ever tasted was in a picturesque kitchen in Pátzcuaro, Michoacán, where a handful of fresh mint was added to a pot of rich tomato soup before it was ladled into bowls with strips of fried tortillas, toasted chiles, and crumbled cheese. You will find fresh mint a delightful addition to many soups—from simple chicken broth to chilled cucumber or green pea soup to hearty lamb stew.

Vegetables are similarly enhanced. For instance, try barely steaming fresh peas and carrots, then sautéeing them in butter slightly sweetened with honey, adding a teaspoon of grated orange rind and a few tablespoons of chopped mint. Or try some of the chopped leaves with buttered new potatoes, or squash, tomato, and eggplant dishes.

I especially like the assertive flavor of mint in salads—whether it's just a few torn leaves tossed in a garden salad or small, skinned tomatoes marinated in a tangy vinaigrette and then rolled in chopped mint. And using flavorful mint vinegar in the vinaigrette is quite complementary. Grilled fish and shellfish salads take on more pizazz with the addition of fresh mint, and of course, fruit salads and compotes are equally enhanced. But it's impossible to mention salads without including the traditional Middle Eastern *tabbouleh*, a marvelous meal-in-itself salad made with cracked wheat, tomatoes, onions, and lots of fresh mint, marinated in a zesty dressing.

Mint also finds its way into numerous condiments and sauces, often providing a cooling respite from spicy foods or serving as a palate cleanser. For example, Indians often make *raita* by combining yogurt with chopped cucumber and fresh mint, serving it with their fiery curries. Mint jelly, tangy mint sauce, and mint sorbet are also popular ways to use this versatile herb.

Mint's ability to temper spicy foods is especially visible in the increasingly popular Thai and Vietnamese foods. I love visiting Vietnamese restaurants, where a platter is brought to the table piled high with fresh herbs—cilantro, basil, and of course, mint. These may be wrapped around the delicately fried spring rolls, and added to the soups or noodle dishes to cool the fiery bite of peppers.

And mint and lamb make naturally perfect partners. Leg of lamb or lamb chops may be studded with thin slices of garlic and crushed mint leaves. For a special treat, try making jalapeño jelly flavored with mint leaves instead of using the overly sweet and colored commercial ones. This jelly may be melted in a saucepan and used as a delicious glaze for meat or game. And do try stuffing a trout with minced garlic and mint or substituting mint for dill when preparing salmon.

Mint even finds its way into desserts; almost any fruit is enhanced by it. For a special treat, drizzle Grand Marnier or champagne over a medley of sliced fruits, and sprinkle it with finely chopped mint. Fanciful confections may be made by painting mint leaves with a lightly beaten egg white, then sprinkling them with extra fine sugar and allowing them to dry. And a rich chocolate mousse or a fruity sorbet may be garnished with a perky sprig of fresh mint.

Mint dries reasonably well – especially peppermint. In this form it may be used for tea and seasoning, although the fresh leaves are still the best. Hang small bunches upside down to dry, or dry the leaves on a screen. Also remember to freeze mint leaves in ice cube trays – along with flowers (violets, violas, pansies, borage, marigolds) or small slices of oranges, lemons, limes, or strawberry halves. Guests will be delighted, and the punch bowl will never look prettier!

Once you begin experimenting with this friendly herb, you will no longer want to be without it. Fortunately, its growing habits make sure of that! If you are not careful, one harmless-looking cutting can rapidly take over. Still, mint's varied uses and its delightful aroma make it indispensible. No wonder the Mexicans call it *yerba buena*, the good herb!

TORTILLA SOUP FROM PÁTZCUARO

A meal in itself, this rich amber colored soup is a much heartier version of the popular tortilla soup found throughout Mexico. A Tarascan Indian cook at a small hotel in Pátzcuaro, Mexico shared her recipe with me. Vary the chiles according to the piquancy desired, balancing them with cooling sprigs of fresh mint.

2–3 dried guajillo *or* pasilla chiles

2 dried ancho chiles

3 tablespoons light cooking oil

1½ medium white onions, finely chopped

4–6 cloves garlic, minced

3½ cups roasted tomatoes *or* one 29-ounce can whole tomatoes, peeled and
　　crushed or lightly blended [*for instructions on roasting tomatoes, see
　　Cooking Tips chapter*]

3 tablespoons best quality tomato paste

1 bay leaf

6 cups very rich homemade chicken stock

1 teaspoon dried oregano, crumbled between palms

1 teaspoon dried thyme, crumbled between palms

Salt and pepper to taste

1 handful fresh mint sprigs

2 large avocados

Fresh lime juice

6 corn tortillas

Cooking oil to fill skillet ½ inch

½–¾ cup crumbled *queso fresco* or grated Monterey Jack cheese

Garnishes: 4 dried pasilla chiles (optional); fresh mint and cilantro sprigs

Lime wedges

Remove the stems and seeds (and the midrib veins for less piquancy) from the dried chiles, and lightly toast on a hot, ungreased griddle for about 30 seconds; do not burn, or they will taste bitter. Heat the oil; sauté the onions and the garlic until translucent. Add the tomatoes and the tomato paste, bay leaf, chiles, and chicken broth, and bring to a boil. Reduce heat and simmer for 25 minutes.

Add the oregano and thyme, and simmer another 15 minutes. Season with salt and pepper, and add fresh mint. Simmer a final 5 minutes.

While soup is simmering, cut the avocados into bite-size chunks and sprinkle with fresh lime juice; set aside. Quarter the tortillas, then cut each into 16 triangular chips. Fry in hot oil until crisp; drain on paper towels. Quickly fry the 3 pasilla chiles in the remaining hot oil; they will puff up slightly. Do not burn! After they have cooled, crumble and set aside.

Divide the fried tortillas among the bowls. Ladle in the piping hot soup, and quickly add the avocado chunks and grated cheese; garnish with crumbled chiles and mint and cilantro sprigs. Serve with lime wedges. Serves 6–8.

NOTE: 3 sprigs of epazote may replace the fresh mint and be used as garnish as well. See chapter on Mexican herbs for more information about mint and using dried chiles. Soup may be made ahead, allowed to sit, then heated just before serving; the next day, it may be thinned with additional broth. See Cooking Tips chapter for instructions on roasting fresh tomatoes.

▼▲▼▲▼▲▼▲▼▲▼▲▼▲▼▲▼▲▼▲▼▲▼▲▼

ENSALADA FAVORITA

Freshly roasted green chiles and squash mingle in a tangy garlic and mint marinade. The cream cheese melts into the marinade, adding a rich and creamy smoothness. This makes an attractive summer luncheon salad when served with crusty garlic bread and may accompany grilled chicken, fish, or steak.

3 medium zucchinis, tined with a fork and cut into ⅜-inch slices

4 green Anaheim peppers, roasted, peeled, and seeded, and cut into *rajas*
   [*for instructions on preparing* rajas, *see Cooking Tips chapter*]

4–6 green onions with most of their green tops, chopped

4 ounces cream cheese, torn into ½-inch pieces

2 tablespoons chopped fresh mint

1 tablespoon chopped cilantro or parsley

Salt and pepper

2 ripe avocados, cubed and sprinkled with lime juice

1 head red-tipped lettuce

Fresh mint sprigs and cilantro sprigs (optional)

Lime wedges

MARINADE
▼▼▼▼▼

¼ cup mint vinegar or white wine vinegar [*see chapter on herb vinegars*]

4 tablespoons fresh lime juice

3 cloves garlic, minced

½ teaspoon brown sugar

Salt and freshly ground white pepper to taste

¼ teaspoon crushed red pepper (optional)

2 tablespoons fresh mint, finely chopped

6 tablespoons best quality olive oil

Bring water to boil; steam zucchini for about 2½ minutes or until crisp-tender (do not overcook!). Dunk immediately into ice water; drain in colander. Lightly sprinkle with salt and allow to drain for 15 minutes in colander.

Meanwhile, make the marinade by combining the vinegar, lime juice, garlic, sugar, salt, pepper, and mint; slowly whisk in the olive oil.

Pat the zucchini dry and place in a shallow glass dish. Add the green chile *rajas*, green onions, cream cheese pieces, chopped mint and cilantro, and sprinkle with salt and freshly ground white pepper. Drizzle the marinade over the squash mixture, gently mixing well. Marinate several hours or overnight, mixing occasionally. Before serving, add the avocados and mix well. Serve on chilled plates with crisp lettuce, mint and cilantro sprigs, and lime wedges. Serves 6–8.

NOTE: I once ruined this salad by using chiles that were too picoso *(hot), masking* the other flavors. Sometimes I make this salad by omitting the green chile strips, then serving each portion in a whole roasted and peeled green chile. Simply slit the chile down the middle, leaving the stem intact, and fill with the squash mixture. Serve on a lettuce bed with a mint sprig, drizzling any remaining marinade over the chile.*

▼▼▼▼▼▼▼▼▼▼▼▼▼▼▼▼▼▼▼▼▼▼▼▼▼▼▼

GRANDMA'S SUMMER MINT SAUCE

Use this sweet and savory sauce to drizzle over leg of lamb or lamb chops. When there are leftovers, I add a little bit of olive oil and minced garlic to the sauce and use it as a vinaigrette for a cold lamb salad. Sometimes I drizzle the sauce over cooked carrots or peas.

½ cup garden mint vinegar *or* white wine vinegar [*see chapter on herb vinegars*]

3 tablespoons brown sugar

⅓ cup fresh mint, chopped

1 tablespoon water

Bring the vinegar and sugar to a boil, stirring constantly. Reduce heat to simmer and add the water and the mint leaves; remove from the stove and allow to stand at least an hour before serving. Serve warm. Yields about 1 cup.

NOTE: I often add about ½ teaspoon crushed red pepper or a seeded, slivered serrano when I add the mint. Sometimes I add a few leaves of fresh rosemary as well.

TABBOULEH

This tangy and refreshing Middle Eastern cracked wheat salad makes a light summer meal and may be served with grilled chicken or shish kebabs. Traditionally, tabbouleh is scooped up and eaten with romaine lettuce or ruby-stemmed chard. It lends itself to attractive presentation; mound the tabbouleh on a platter lined with crisp greens and surround it with chopped or cherry tomatoes, chopped cucumbers, mint sprigs, lemon slices, and marinated black olives.

1¼ cup bulgur

1½ teaspoon whole coriander seeds

½ teaspoon whole allspice

2 tomatoes, chopped

1 cucumber, peeled, seeded, and chopped

Salt

3 cloves garlic, minced

1 small red onion, chopped

⅓ cup chopped green onions with tops

2 cups finely chopped fresh parsley, tightly packed

½ cup finely chopped fresh mint, tightly packed

½ teaspoon white pepper

¼–½ teaspoon crushed dried red chile pepper (optional)

½ cup fresh lemon juice *or* ¼ cup lemon juice and ¼ cup mint vinegar *or* ½
   cup Lovely Lemon vinegar [*see chapter on herb vinegars*]

⅓ cup best quality olive oil

Salt and pepper to taste

Romaine or ruby-stemmed chard

Rinse the bulgur and place in a bowl covered by 1 inch of water. Allow to soak for about an hour.

Meanwhile, on a hot, ungreased skillet, carefully toast the coriander and allspice seeds; grind and set aside. Chop the tomatoes, sprinkle lightly with salt, and allow to drain in a colander. Do the same to the cucumbers. (This step prevents the salad's becoming soggy.) Set aside for 15–20 minutes.

When the bulgar has absorbed the water, drain in a colander, then squeeze out any remaining moisture with your hands to prevent sogginess.

Add the chopped garlic, onions, parsley, mint, peppers, and toasted seeds. Toss in the chopped tomatoes and cucumbers. Drizzle with lemon juice and olive oil, tossing well. Cover and refrigerate for several hours or overnight. Allow to stand at room temperature for ½ hour, adjust the seasonings, adding more oil, lemon juice, or herbs if needed, and serve. Serves 6–8.

DAVID LORD'S MINT JULEPS

I first sipped a mint julep made with dark rum in the beautiful courtyard of Las Mañanitas Restaurant in Cuernavaca, Mexico. My friend David Lord's version may be even better. Remember to chill the glasses—preferably silver or pewter julep cups—and to sip from a silver straw . . . Sigh!

1 teaspoon superfine sugar
4 large fresh mint leaves
1 teaspoon water
1 handful of ice cubes
2 ounces best quality dark rum (such as Mount Gay) *or* bourbon

Chill glasses in freezer at least 30 minutes. Muddle the mint leaves by gently bruising them with the sugar and water (with the back of a spoon) in the chilled glass. Fill glass with cracked ice (crack ice with the back of a spoon). Pour dark rum or bourbon over ice; stir until glass becomes frosted. Fill glass with additional cracked ice. Garnish with a fresh mint sprig, gently bruised to release its flavor as it is sipped. Serves 1.

NOTE: a small squeeze of fresh lime juice may be added when using dark rum.

SANGRÍA SORBET

The refreshing, fruity flavors of sangría are blended in a summer sorbet. Serve garnished with mint sprigs and small clusters of grapes (or other seasonal fruit).

MINT SYRUP

2 cups sugar

2 cups water

1½ cups loosely chopped mint, tightly packed (preferably a combination of mints such as spearmint, lemon balm, and curly mint)

Make a syrup by slowly bringing sugar and water to boil; reduce and add mint; simmer 6 minutes. Set aside for at least an hour, or overnight.

SORBET

The mint syrup

2 cups Spanish dry red wine

1½ cups freshly squeezed orange juice

¾ cup fresh lime juice

¼ cup fresh lemon juice

3 teaspoons grated orange zest

Mix the ingredients together; taste, and add more citrus if desired. Freeze in an ice cream machine according to manufacturer's directions. Serve in crystal champagne glasses garnished with fresh mint sprigs and a small cluster of grapes. Serves 6-8.

OREGANO
Origanum species
Lamiaceae (Labiatae) family

An oregano plant ready for harvest.

Common Names:
oregano; Greek, Italian and Mexican oregano; wild marjoram; winter marjoram; pot marjoram

Characteristics:
slightly woody stems; leaves that are oval to elliptical in shape and generally slightly hairy underneath with a robust and aromatic scent; flowers in summer range from white to mauvish-purple; creeping roots; perennial

Conditions:
loose, well-draining soil (preferably alkaline) and full sunshine imperative; best flavor usually comes from arid conditions

Size:
10–24 inches high; some erect and some more prostrate

Propagation:

nursery transplants suggested to select the desired flavor; cuttings and root division in spring; 1 or 2 of each of several varieties per garden suggested

Fertilizer:

none suggested, although light applications of fish emulsion may be used to get plant established

Pests:

some spider mite damage during high heat and humidity – use insecticidal soap; leaf miners chew serpentine patterns in leaves

Companions:

seems to deter insects (away from other plants as well) with its strong odor

Oregano's spicy and peppery flavor enhances many cuisines. Greeks sprinkle it over *souvalaki*, tender chunks of marinated beef. Spaniards smother grilled fish with a thick green oregano sauce. Middle Easterners flavor eggplant and other vegetables distinctly with this pungent herb, while Mexicans add it to their spicy chile sauces and stews. Of course, Italians adore oregano, using it in hearty tomato sauces and pasta dishes. And in the United States it is the beloved pizza herb.

Unfortunately, despite oregano's popularity, the variety most frequently available at nurseries is *Origanum vulgare*, an attractive and fast-spreading plant but one with little culinary value. I learned this fact the hard way after buying a nursery transplant years ago. Since then, I have been in search of the perfect culinary oregano, a rather difficult task because there are so many varieties, and they are often mislabeled.

When selecting an oregano plant, my rule of thumb is to pinch off a few leaves, rubbing them gently to release their aroma and tasting them as well. A tantalizing peppery pungence is what I look for. The best cooking oreganos – labeled Greek, Italian, or Mexican – often have smaller and paler leaves than the more common *Origanum vulgare*, which I reserve to use as an ornamental border along limestone rocks.

Still, *Origanum* is a confusing genus, especially because there are so many species. To add to the confusion, marjoram, its sister plant, used to be classified as an oregano as well (*Origanum majorana*) but has been reclassified as *Majorana hortensis*. (You will often hear oregano called pot marjoram or wild marjoram.) Recently, several other plants collectively called Mexican oregano have become popular, although none of them is a true oregano. [*See chapter on Mexican herbs.*] Still, I find their flavors exciting and indeed piquant – excellent substitutes when other flavorful oreganos cannot be found. These oreganos especially complement the spicy foods that are enjoyed in the Southwest. Furthering the confusion, varieties of thyme, monarda, coleus, and savory mimic the flavor and aroma of oregano.

The oreganos most commonly associated with cooking are *Origanum onites, Origanum vulgare,* and *Origanum heracleoticum. Origanum onites,* also known as pot marjoram, is an upright plant about 2 feet tall, bearing resemblance to sweet marjoram. It is, however, a stiffer and taller plant with more pointed leaves that are not as perfumy or sweet as those of marjoram; instead they have a slightly sharp but pleasant flavor. Pot marjoram forms a spreading clump, which should be divided every few years for best results. This Mediterranean native grows attractively in pots, blooming in shades of white to pale pink—and can be moved inside in case of bitter freeze. Otherwise, it may be treated as a tender perennial—and used frequently in cooking. Steamed and sautéed vegetables especially are enhanced by this more subtle oregano.

Origanum heracleoticum has long been called winter marjoram in England because it was ready to be gathered much sooner than sweet marjoram. Sometimes also labeled Greek oregano, this plant makes an excellent seasoning. The leaves of this species are slightly pointed, aromatic, and slightly hairy underneath, and the flowers are usually white. Especially when grown in rather arid conditions, this species has a volatile and peppery taste that enlivens many dishes. Many consider herbs in this species the most piquant and flavorful.

Origanum vulgare, whose leaves are dark green and hairy underneath, often has slightly purplish stems and flowers that tend toward shades of pink and purple with reddish bracts. It is a less compact plant that spreads rapidly by rhizomes. It may become quite leggy when grown in rich soil with plenty of water; on the other hand, dry conditions cause it to grow more prostrate with a spicier flavor. This is the oregano that grows wild in England, carpeting the craggy limestone cliffs, where it is often called wild marjoram. Although to me the least desirable for cooking, oreganos in this species make pretty garnishes

and attractive ornamental plants in the garden. One particular favorite, *Origanum vulgare* 'Aureum,' sometimes called creeping golden oregano (or marjoram), tolerates summer's heat and endures mild winters. This thick, low-growing herb spreads quickly to fill in cracks in the rock garden and limestone paths. I first purchased it at a nursery in a 3 inch pot, and now sleepy paths of golden oregano creep through my yard. Unfortunately, its flavor, like that of most *Origanum vulgare,* is sleepy as well, but it does make an attractive garnish.

Thoroughly confused? Most people are when trying to differentiate among the many oreganos, and opinions and descriptions are about as varied as the genus itself. Finding your favorite culinary oregano is simply a matter of taste and will take some experimentation. Send off for some small plants from some of the mail-order catalogs that offer a variety. I find that purchasing transplants gives a better choice than growing oregano from seed. That way, you know exactly what you are growing.

It's appropriate that oregano derives its name from the Greek words *oro* (mountain) and *ganos* (joy). Its fresh fragrance and colorful flowers indeed call forth the "joy of the mountains." Summer finds this native Mediterranean bursting with flowers ranging from mauves to pinks and delicate whites. But oregano seems to feel just as much at home throughout much of the Southwest. Rocky soils, arid conditions, and relatively mild winters provide perfect growing conditions for this delightful herb.

Once established in the garden, oreganos require little special attention. In fact, as with many herbs, too much care can be detrimental. Some of the spiciest and most flavorful oreganos thrive in poor and dry conditions, whereas overwatering, fertilization, and too rich a soil may produce large leaves with little taste and may promote root disease. A loose, well-draining soil and plenty of sunshine are imperative, and I find that dividing the plants by the roots every few years, removing

▼▼▼▼▼▼▼▼▼▼▼▼▼▼▼▼▼▼▼▼▼▼▼▼▼▼▼▼▼▼

dead and woody branches, insures a more flavorful herb. Frequently cutting back new growth and pinching off the flowers also promote good growth and flavor.

I generally harvest my oreganos twice a year – once in June before flowering, then later in the fall. The fall harvest should be less drastic to avoid freeze damage. Although oregano generally dies back in the winter, it will return again in the early spring. A good way to preserve the oregano harvest (it is a fast and prolific producer) is to make gallons of vinegar. [*See chapter on vinegars.*] Oregano is an herb that I usually use in the dried form, which has the most intense flavor. During dry weather, I hang it upside down in small bunches or dry stems on a screen. When using it fresh in a recipe, remember to use two or three time as much as dried.

Oregano and parsley make good partners when combined with garlic and olive oil as a sauce for fish. *Ceviche* and broiled or grilled shrimp also benefit from a generous sprinkling of crumbled oregano (rubbing the leaves between the palms releases the volatile oils). Mexicans fry small chunks of pork called *carnitas*, then dunk them into a savory green *tomatillo salsa* flavored with garlic and oregano; in fact, oregano is probably the most ubiquitous seasoning used in the flavorful Mexican *salsas*. And a pot of *frijoles* lack flavor without this peppy herb.

Pesto made with oregano instead of basil makes a tasty condiment for fish, shrimp, steaks, or chicken. Toss pasta with oregano pesto, crumbled Montrachet goat cheese, a few tablespoons of freshly chopped oregano, and toasted pine nuts, or use the pesto in a layered cheese *torta* for a scrumptious appetizer. A festive and colorful medley of vegetables looks great and tastes wonderful served right out of a cast iron skillet: sautéed garlic, zucchini, crook-neck squash, onions, and red bell pepper. Sprinkle it generously with freshly chopped oregano or oregano pesto. Other vegetables including spinach, corn, tomatoes, squash, and the renowned eggplant dish *ratatouille* are especially enhanced by oregano.

Hearty beef and lamb stews, corn and seafood chowders, and thick and savory tomato sauces also benefit; add oregano the last 15 minutes of cooking so that it will not become bitter. Oregano's lively taste complements roasts, taco fillings, and meat marinades. And the fresh leaves may be used in a robust Greek salad, a spicy Mexican chicken salad, or cold beef salad.

By experimenting, you will soon find that oregano has as many culinary possibilities as it does botanical varieties. Make sure to grow several different varieties, including the Mexican oreganos, to have at hand for spirited seasoning of food. (*See Mexican herbs chapter.*)

OREGANO PESTO

Oregano gives basil some competition in this flavor-packed pesto. Fabulous tossed with jalapeño pasta, toasted pine nuts, and crumbled goat cheese; melted over steamed or sautéed squash; used in a luscious layered cheese torta; or served on baguette slices sprinkled with freshly grated Parmesan.

4–6 cloves garlic

2 cups fresh oregano, loosely packed

1 cup fresh parsley

½ cup pine nuts, lightly toasted [*for instructions, see Cooking Tips chapter*]

½ cup imported Parmesan cheese, freshly grated

½ teaspoon lime zest (avoid white pith)

1 teaspoon fresh lime juice

1–2 serrano chiles, seeded and finely chopped

¾ cup best quality olive oil (or more)

Chop the garlic, oregano, parsley, toasted nuts, and cheese in a food processor or blender, or pound with a mortar and pestle. Add the lime zest and juice and the chopped chiles. Slowly add the oil, adding a little more if necessary to make a thick, green paste. Spoon into 2 half-pint jars and top with ¼ inch melted butter.

NOTE: Use a good culinary oregano. Often, the Mexican oreganos are too strong; however, I may use 1–2 tablespoons of Mexican oregano for some of the oregano. This pesto freezes well.

OREGANO PESTO TORTA WITH ROASTED CHILE STRIPS AND TOASTED PINE NUTS

*This Italian-inspired appetizer uses pesto made with oregano instead of basil. South-western ingredients, zesty roasted and peeled red chile strips (*rajas*), and toasted pine nuts are alternated between colorful layers of green pesto and provolone, looking spectacularly colorful when sliced. Serve with homemade garlic croutons or thin slices of baguette.*

½ pound cream cheese, softened

4 tablespoons butter, softened

¾ cup oregano pesto

½ pound provolone cheese, thinly sliced

4 poblano or Anaheim chiles (preferably vine-ripened to red), roasted, peeled, seeded, and cut into *rajas* [*for instructions, see Cooking Tips chapter*]

¼ cup lightly toasted pine nuts [*for instructions, see Cooking Tips chapter*]

Fresh oregano sprigs for garnish

Blend cream cheese and butter with a fork; mix in oregano pesto.

Line a small (3-cup) loaf pan or bowl with plastic wrap, leaving several inches of overhang on each side. Place a thin layer of provolone slices on the bottom and partially up the sides. Top with ⅓ of the pesto mixture. Arrange 4–6 chile *rajas* in attractive horizontal patterns, and sprinkle with about 1 tablespoon toasted pine nuts.

Repeat until all ingredients are used, pressing down well between layers. The last layer should be pesto, depending on presentation (inverted or not). Reserve some of the toasted pine nuts and *rajas* (roasted pepper strips) for decoration. Chill several days or overnight, and serve at room temperature on a platter wreathed with fresh oregano sprigs. Reserved *rajas* may be arranged on top, and pine nuts pressed into the torta. Serves 10–12.

NOTE: This keeps for several weeks refrigerated. For less picante palates, roasted and peeled red bell pepper strips and/ or sun-dried tomatoes (approximately 4 tomatoes per layer) may be substituted for chile rajas.

▼▼▼▼▼▼▼▼▼▼▼▼▼▼▼▼▼▼▼▼▼▼▼▼▼▼

POLLO PICADO

This festive shredded chicken dish is brimming with color and flavor. Serve it in avocado halves drizzled with lime juice or on fresh salad greens. Roll it up in corn tortillas and fry in hot oil to make crispy flautas, or simply serve in warm corn tortillas or on tortilla chips. Simple party fare may be made by allowing guests to layer small fried tortillas with refritos (refried beans) [see recipe in epazote chapter], shredded lettuce, and the shredded chicken, topped with salsa picante.

1 3½-pound whole fryer chicken, boiled or roasted, with meat shredded
   from the bones
½ medium red onion, chopped
2 green onions with tops, chopped
2 medium tomatoes, chopped
⅓ pound Monterey Jack cheese, cut into ½-inch cubes
2–4 jalapeños, chopped
¼ teaspoon crushed red pepper (optional)
¼ teaspoon whole coriander seeds
½ teaspoon whole peppercorns, preferably white
½ teaspoon whole *comino* seed (cumin)
Salt to taste
2 tablespoons freshly chopped oregano
2 tablespoons freshly chopped cilantro
2 medium avocados, cut into bite-size cubes, sprinkled with fresh lime
   juice and salt
Juice of 1 or 2 limes
Shredded lettuce
Fresh oregano sprigs
Optional garnishes: chopped tomato, red onion rings, cheese cubes, lime
   wedges, salsa picante, chile *rajas*

In a large bowl, mix the shredded chicken with the chopped onions, tomatoes, cheese cubes, and chiles.

Grind the spices in a spice grinder and sprinkle with salt over the chicken. Add the freshly chopped herbs and mix well. Before serving, add the avocado cubes and the fresh lime juice, and toss well. Serve mounded on a platter of shredded lettuce with fresh sprigs of oregano and your choice of garnishes. Yields about 4 cups.

NOTE: If fresh oregano is not available, fresh cilantro may be substituted.

Flautas, meaning little flutes, are tightly rolled corn tortillas with savory fillings. Quickly fried in hot oil, they make tasty finger food when dipped into spicy hot

▼▼▼▼▼▼▼▼▼▼▼▼▼▼ ▼▼▼▼▼▼▼▼▼▼▼▼▼▼

sauce or guacamole. Place 1½ tablespoons of the shredded chicken filling (and a chile raja if desired) in a corn tortilla that has been softened on a hot griddle; roll up tightly and secure with a toothpick if neces-sary. Fry in ½ inch of hot oil, turning fre-quently, until crisp and golden (about 25 seconds). Flautas may be kept warm in a 250-degree oven until all are fried. Makes about 24.

GREEK SALAD

This fabulous salad evokes Mediterranean sunshine and sea breeze. Part of the fun is artistically arranging the crisp greens, crumbled feta, colorful sliced vegetables, and fragrant oregano sprigs. Serve as a light meal with wine and crusty bread, or on the side with grilled lamb or chicken.

THE DRESSING

½ cup best quality olive oil (or more)

3 cloves garlic, minced

¼ teaspoon crushed dried red chile pepper

2 teaspoons freshly chopped rosemary leaves

½ teaspoon crumbled dried oregano

½ cup Mediterranean marinade *or* basil-garlic vinegar, or oregano-garlic vinegar, *or* red wine vineger [*see chapter on herb vinegars*]

2 tablespoons fresh lemon juice

2½ teaspoons tomato paste

Salt and ½ teaspoon freshly ground pepper

Mix the olive oil, garlic, crushed chile, rosemary, and oregano in a small bowl. In a slightly larger bowl, combine the vinegar, lemon juice, and tomato paste. Slowly whisk in the spiced olive oil, adding a small amount more oil if desired. Salt and pepper to taste. Yields about 1 cup.

THE SALAD

¾ pound fresh spinach, carefully rinsed

1 head red-tipped lettuce

4 roma or pear tomatoes, sliced

1–2 medium bell peppers, sliced (preferably red and yellow)

1 cucumber, tined with a fork and sliced

1 small red onion, thinly sliced

1 large handful fresh oregano sprigs

¼ pound (or more) feta cheese, crumbled

Garnish: 2 artichoke hearts per person, 1 tablespoon toasted pine nuts per person, 4 Greek olives per person

▼▼▼▼▼▼▼▼▼▼▼▼▼▼▼▼▼▼▼▼▼▼▼▼▼▼▼▼▼▼▼▼

Arrange crisp greens on chilled salad plates, mixing in several whole fresh oregano leaves. Place groupings of tomatoes, bell peppers, cucumber, and red onion. Crumble feta over each salad and garnish with artichoke hearts, pine nuts, and Greek olives. Drizzle dressing over each and pass more dressing at table. Serves 4–6.

NOTE: Sometimes I add arugula to this salad and cold slices of grilled lamb. Try substituting Mardi Gras Montrachet [see recipe in thyme chapter] in place of feta cheese; allow 2–3 per individual salad serving. For instructions on toasting pine nuts, see Cooking Tips chapter.

PARSLEY

Petroselinum crispum
Apiaceae (Umbelliferae) family

Curly-leaf parsley is rich in vitamins.

Common Names:

French or curly parsley; flat-leafed, Italian, or Genovese parsley

Characteristics:

curly parsley's leaves are tightly curled and fringed into bright green clumps on strong stems; Italian parsley has flat, dark green, glossy leaves resembling those of celery; forms flowering umbel on long stalk, producing many tiny seeds; biennial

Conditions:

a rich and moist, well-draining soil; full sun or afternoon shade (in the summer)

Size:

curly parsley attains about 10 inches in height; Italian parsley grows to 1½ feet tall and 1½ feet wide

Propagation:

best grown from seed in the fall or very early spring; several plants of each kind per garden suggested; may be grown as a border

Fertilizer:

occasional light feedings of fish emulsion or manure; compost mulch especially during the winter and summer

Pests:

"parsleyworm" may be treated with bacillus thuringiensis; spider mites and aphids may be treated with insecticidal soap

Companions:

noted to aid growth of tomatoes and roses

"**E**at your parsley; it's good for you," my mother pleaded. "It has lots of vitamins." But to me, it just looked like little baby trees and was fun to play with. Indeed, while growing up, I agreed with Ogden Nash's "Parsley is gharsley," especially after tiring of the limp sprigs that often adorned dishes at restaurants.

Fortunately, things have changed. Now I find parsley's clean, crisp taste most appealing and love to munch on it in the garden. And, my mother was right. Parsley is rich in minerals (especially iron), chlorophyll, and Vitamins A and C. Consequently, I add handfuls of it to blender drinks. For instance, I fill the blender with tomato juice and add a generous handful of fresh parsley leaves, some celery tops, a few mint sprigs, 2 tender sorrel or comfrey leaves, the juice of a lemon, and a sprinkling of cayenne. Serve in a tall glass with ice, a lemon wedge, and a sprig of parsley. This healthful and refreshing tonic makes a great way to start the day and provides a revitalizing afternoon drink!

And I always eat my garnish! When stored properly (in a glass of water in the refrigerator, loosely covered with a plastic bag or in a tightly sealed container), parsley sprigs make attractive garnishes, especially when mixed with sprigs of other fragrant herbs. And for those of you who, like me, are garlic lovers, chewing parsley leaves will indeed freshen the breath.

Unfortunately, parsley has a reputation for being difficult to grow. In fact, an old wive's tale says that parsley seeds go to the devil and back nine times before the plant comes up. Actually, it is quite slow to germinate and can take as many as 4 weeks; however, there are a few tricks to facilitating its growth. Some soak the seeds for 24 hours in warm water; but this causes them to stick together, making them difficult to sow (mixing the soaked seeds with sand or dry coffee grounds helps). The renowned gardening expert Thalassa Cruso solves this problem by sowing the seeds in a shallow trench and then pouring scalding water down the row. As parsley is a cool-weather crop, I find that it needs a "false winter" to germinate properly, especially in our mild climate. Freezing the seeds in ice cubes, then burying the ice cubes is how

John Dromgoole, writer for *Organic Gardening*, deals with this problem.

But the most important factor in growing parsley is the soil. It must be rich, moist, and well-draining, and the seeds must not be allowed to dry out. Consequently, in the Southwest, it is best to sow parsley in the fall–and be patient! Like other members of the Apiaceae family (carrots, dill, cilantro), parsley's taproot makes it difficult to transplant, once it is established. Should you purchase it as a nursery transplant, make sure it is a very small plant (not root-bound) and with no yellowing of the bottom leaves. Keep parsley well fertilized with manure or fish emulsion, and give it adequate water and plenty of sunshine, although it can tolerate some afternoon shade. In late spring and summer, beware of the "parsleyworm," the larval caterpillar of the swallowtail butterfly, which quickly devours plants in the Apiaceae family. Aphids and spider mites can also bother parsley.

Although there are actually many kinds of parsley, the most common is curly parsley (*Petroselinum crispum*), sometimes known as French parsley, with leaves that are tightly curled and fringed into small, bright green clumps of foliage. Some varieties include moss curled and triple curled. Shepherd's Garden Seeds in California recommends Danish Afro, which has highly curled and fringed leaves on strong stems. Sometimes curly leafed parsleys taste slightly salty, bitter, or metallic; Danish Afro does not.

Another type of parsley that has rapidly gained popularity is Italian or Genovese parsley, often called flat-leafed parsley as well (*Petroselinum crispum* var. *neopolitanum*). Most chefs agree that this is the best cooking parsley, with its sweet and earthy flavor. Italian parsley's dark green, glossy, flat leaves somewhat resemble celery leaves and may even be confused with cilantro (also known as Chinese parsley). Its seeds often germinate more rapidly than curly parsley's.

In any event, no garden should be without parsley. Not only may it be mixed in with other vegetables in the garden, but it also makes a decorative border or container plant. (Try growing it in a deep container with chives and basil.) Although parsley is a biennial (setting seed the second year), I treat it as an annual. During our hot summers, it often becomes rather puny and loses its flavor, so I like to begin with fresh seed in the fall.

But what about the culinary uses of this tasty herb? The French have long extolled its virtues by joining it with tarragon, chervil, and chives in their *fines herbes* mixture, which is used for seasoning egg and fish dishes, as well as in *bouquet garni*, a collection of various herbs (usually thyme, bay, and marjoram) tied up with string or in cheesecloth and used in cooking stews, poultry, and fish. For me, homemade chicken broth is incomplete without a handful of parsley; so is *court bouillon*, a savory wine-and-herb broth used to poach fish and chicken.

Since parsley is available year round (if not in the garden, then at the market), it serves a very important purpose. If no other fresh herb is at hand, parsley gives a dish that essential "fresh and alive" flavor and texture. Fresh parsley reawakens dried herbs such as basil, tarragon, oregano, thyme, and marjoram. Simply mix the dried herbs called for in a recipe with a generous amount of freshly chopped parsley. And when that undeniable dead-of-winter craving for pesto attacks, parsley, in a pinch, may be substituted for basil.

You cannot add too much freshly minced parsley to dips, spreads, and salad dressings made with sour cream, cream cheese, or mayonnaise. And generous amounts may be added as well to rice, barley, or pasta dishes, especially when garlic predominates. My favorite way of eating mashed potatoes is with lots of minced parsley and green onions, butter, and fresh lemon juice; peas, carrots, and green beans may be similarly enhanced.

Try adding a handful of parsley sprigs to your next salad, making it extra nutritious.

▼▼▼▼▼▼▼▼▼▼▼▼▼▼▼▼▼▼▼▼▼▼▼▼▼

The New American Vegetable Cookbook, written by the founders of Le Marché Seeds International, gives a wonderful recipe for a salad whose greens are solely parsley, drizzled with a tangy vinaigrette and garnished with a chopped hard-boiled egg. Don't forget adding parsley to potato or seafood salads, and of course, vivid flecks of green parsley flavor the refreshing summer salad, *tabbouleh.*

Years ago I discovered one of my favorite condiments at an Argentine restaurant in Mexico City featuring meats *a la parilla* (grilled) and exquisite flaky meat-and potato-filled *empanadas* (turnovers). *Chimichurri,* a dark green garlicky vinegar sauce loaded with parsley and other herbs, was drizzled by the spoonful over the grilled meats and turnovers. This sauce also enhances grilled chicken or fish. A somewhat similar sauce, *salmorejo,* smothered over grilled fish in the Canary Islands, is made by grinding dried oregano, garlic, lime juice, olive oil, and lots of fresh parsley into a thick green paste.

And though some like to fry fresh parsley sprigs in very hot oil to make a crispy and unusual garnish, I think it is delicious and lovely as is, just as it's a shame to dry or freeze this herb, because it is readily available in markets at all times.

HERB SPIRAL BREAD

Ann Clark, author of Ann Clark's Fabulous Fish, *is a well-known teacher of French cooking in Texas. Her herb spiral bread is bound to add an extra touch of* joie de vivre *to any meal it graces—if you don't eat it right out of the oven!*

2 packages dry yeast

½ teaspoon sugar

¼ cup warm water

2 cups liquid: all whole milk *or* 1 cup whole and 1 cup skim *or* 1 cup milk, whole or skim, and 1 cup water

3 tablespoons butter *or* margarine *or* vegetable oil

1 tablespoon salt

2 tablespoons sugar

3 cups white flour: all-purpose *or* unbleached *or* a mixture of both

3 more cups flour

2 well-buttered loaf pans (8½ by 4½ by 2⅝ inches)

¼–½ teaspoon vegetable oil

HERB MIXTURE

¾–1 cup minced green onions with tops

1½ tablespoons sweet unsalted butter

½ cup minced parsley

½ cup minced fresh herbs [*see NOTE below for suggestions*]

Salt and pepper to taste

In a large mixing bowl, dissolve yeast and ½ teaspoon sugar in warm water. Place in a warm part of kitchen and proof 5 minutes. Place 1 cup of the liquid in a saucepan with butter, salt, and sugar. Scald and let cool. Be sure it is cool/lukewarm. Pour cooled liquid over yeast and add second cup liquid. Mix, and add half the flour (3 cups) one cup at a time. When all flour is added, beat vigorously for 3–4 minutes; it is important that the batter be very smooth.

Add the remaining 3 cups flour one cup at a time, using a spoon or dough hook. Add only as much flour as needed to allow dough to come away from the sides of bowl —usually 5½ cups. Knead carefully by hand for 10 minutes, or 5 minutes in a mixer with dough hook. Place in an oiled bowl, cover with plastic wrap, and let rise in a warm place until doubled—1 to 1½ hours.

In a large skillet, sauté the herb mixture (green onions, parsley, fresh herbs) in the butter. Add salt and pepper to taste. Remove from heat.

When the dough has doubled in size, punch it down and let it rest for 10 minutes. Divide the dough in half, and flatten each half into a rectangle, 12 by 8 inches, firmly pressing out air bubbles. Spread each rectangle with half of the sautéed herb mixture and press into the flattened dough, leaving a 1-inch margin on all sides.

Roll rectangles tightly, sealing ends by pinching. Tuck the ends under and place rolls in pans. Let rise until dough doubles or is at least 1 inch above edges of pan. (Let rise in refrigerator if desired.)

Place rolled loaves in preheated 375-degree oven and bake for 35–45 minutes. Remove loaves from pans immediately and cool on wire rack. Makes two loaves.

NOTE: Experiment with fresh herbs and combinations of herbs, such as: rosemary, oregano, and basil; marjoram, thyme, and chives; sage; or dill.

GARDEN DIP

Lots of ingredients, yet easy to make! Serve from a hollowed-out cabbage with crudités or crackers. Also delicious with cold sliced beef, as an artichoke dip, or thinned with lemon juice for a salad dressing. Tasty as a baked potato topping or omelet filling as well.

1 cup minced parsley

3 tablespoons minced fresh thyme (part lemon thyme preferred)

1 teaspoon minced fresh rosemary leaves

1 tablespoon minced fresh tarragon *or* minced fresh Mexican marigold mint

1 tablespoon minced fresh chives

4 cloves garlic, minced

2 medium-size shallots, minced

½ white onion, minced

12 ounces cream cheese, softened

8 ounces sour cream

1 2-ounce can anchovies, drained

3 tablespoons capers, rinsed

1 tablespoon Dijon mustard

Juice of 1 lemon (5–6 tablespoons)

½ teaspoon lemon zest

1 teaspoon pepper, freshly ground

¼ teaspoon crushed red pepper

2 tablespoons Parmesan, freshly grated

2 tablespoons olive oil

In a food processor, mince the fresh herbs and set aside. With the motor running, mince the garlic and shallots. Turn off processor and add the onion; mince. Add the chopped herbs and the other ingredients except the olive oil, and blend briefly. With the motor running, dribble in the olive oil, being careful not to overprocess. Adjust seasonings, but remember that the flavor will get stronger as it sits.

VARIATIONS

1. Substitute basil for parsley; parsley for thyme; oregano *or* marjoram for tarragon.
2. Use ½ cup dill and ½ cup parsley; omit thyme and rosemary, and add 2 tablespoons shredded sorrel leaves and 1 tablespoon minced mint leaves.
3. Use savory in place of thyme.

NOTE: If you don't have a food processor, you can still make this recipe, mincing the herbs and vegetables by hand and mixing them in a medium-size bowl with the other ingredients.

▼▲▼▲▼▲▼▲▼▲▼▲▼▲▼▲▼▲▼▲▼▲▼

CHIMICHURRI

I first tasted this sauce at an Argentine restaurant in Mexico City, where it was served as a table sauce to drizzle over meats cooked a la parrilla *(over a grill), as well as over savory empanadas. Not for timid palates, Chimichurri is a garlicky green sauce in which vinegar, herbs, and pepper predominate. It also makes a wonderful marinade for chicken or fish, with more sauce drizzled over portions before serving.*

6–8 cloves garlic, minced

2 tightly packed cups parsley (preferably Italian)

½ cup tightly packed cilantro

3 teaspoons best quality dried oregano

2 teaspoons best quality dried thyme

2 teaspoons chopped fresh rosemary

2 bay leaves

1 teaspoon whole black peppercorns

½–1 teaspoon dried crushed red pepper

¾ cup oregano-chile-garlic vinegar, *or* Mediterranean vinegar, *or* red wine
   vinegar plus 1 tablespoon water [*see chapter on herb vinegars*]

¾ cup olive oil

½ teaspoon salt

In a food processor or blender, grind the garlic and the herbs. Grind the bay and the peppercorns in a spice grinder, and add to the herb mixture with the crushed red pepper and vinegar. Add the olive oil and gently mix to blend; do not overprocess. Sauce should be slightly thickened. Let stand several hours or refrigerate and serve at room temperature. Drizzle over grilled or roasted meats, fish, or chicken. Also good on tomatoes or sandwiches. Yields 2 cups.

NOTE: Recipe may be halved. Keeps well several weeks in regrigerator.

ROSEMARY

Rosmarinus officinalis and *R. off. prostratus*
Lamiaceae (Labiatae) family

Tricia Shire

Lavender blossoms grace this rosemary plant.

Common Names:
rosemary; *romero* (Mexico)

Characteristics:
upright and creeping varieties; both have leathery and highly aromatic
needle-like leaves; lovely blue, white, or pink flowers; perennial

Conditions:
full sun; well-draining alkaline soil; do not overwater

Size:
upright varieties may attain 6 feet in height; prostrate varieties
approximately 12 inches

Propagation:
seeds rather difficult to germinate; purchase as transplants; root cuttings in
sand or layer them; 1–3 plants per garden suggested (more if used ornamentally)

Fertilizer:

occasional sprayings of foliage with seaweed and occasional light feedings of fish emulsion; mulch well when in danger of frost

Pests:

some spider mite or small webworm damage during periods of high heat and humidity

Companions:

strong, resinous odor seems to deter insects from the garden; grows well next to sage, dill, and cabbage; flowers attract bees into the garden, delicately flavoring their honey

In 1972, my younger brother, Stuart, and I drove an old blue Volkswagen from Amsterdam through Spain and ferried over to La Palma, a small island in the Canary Islands. I spent six weeks living in a Spanish-speaking fishing village, a pleasant respite from the sun-seeking Skandinavian crowds in Torremolinos. There I ate my evening meal at Manolo's, a tiny, open-air restaurant on the beach, and never grew tired of the cook's simple yet tasty fare. On cool winter evenings, a hearty stew of beef chunks, potatoes, and onions simmered in a kettle of red wine flavored with garlic and fresh rosemary. Sometimes I ate a meal of new potatoes roasted with a crusty layer of salt and rosemary, then dipped into a thick and garlicky red-pepper sauce.

On Christmas Eve, Manolo's family invited me to town for the *posada*. Accompanied by guitar, we went door to door singing carols, often welcomed by warming mugs of spicy, hot rum punch. Afterwards, we celebrated with the traditional spit-roasted *cabrito* (kid). Earlier in the day, Manolo had rubbed it with garlic, olive oil, and rosemary; later he slowly turned the spit to assure succulent slices of the Christ-mas treat. And to this day, I fondly remember that crisp, starlit sky, warm friends, and the pine tree fragrance of rosemary perfuming the night.

Sometimes on morning walks near the beach, I would brush against a rosemary plant, releasing its fresh, clean smell. This made me recall an old Spanish legend that rosemary-scented breezes often greeted weary sailors when they were still 20 miles away from shore; hence its name, *Rosmarinus*, meaning "dew of the sea." Women on the island taught me to make a hair rinse by steeping a large handful of rosemary in boiling water. Leaving it in after shampooing scents the hair with rosemary's seashore freshness and especially makes dark brown or black hair shine. Rosemary makes a fragrant addition to potpourris and gives its fresh scent to linens, deterring moths at the same time. For years, Europeans have burned rosemary as incense; occasionally, I burn sprigs on the gas burner of my kitchen stove to freshen the air.

But it is this strong, somewhat antiseptic characteristic that makes some wary of cooking with rosemary, and many are accustomed to using it only in its dried form, no matter how long it has been on the shelf! This is a shame, because the fresh herb imparts so much flavor. Otherwise bland potato dishes (mashed, baked, roasted, or in a salad with a tangy vinaigrette) come to life when sprinkled with rosemary leaves. Marinades for lamb, goat, veal, chicken, and game benefit from this herb, and also remember to rub the meat with the leaves. There is nothing as lovely as a wreath of fresh rosemary sprigs surrounding a holiday roast! Rosemary steeped in olive oil, garlic, and vinegar produces a delicious base for marinades and robust salad dressings. And don't forget to add a handful of rosemary sprigs to the hot coals directly before placing meat on the grill, to smoke in its delightful aroma.

Rosemary also lends itself to hearty fish stews, tomato-based pasta sauces, pizzas, and open-faced lamb, beef, or chicken sandwiches. It is also a savory addition to breads and rolls, cheese spreads, and butters. This flavorful herb makes a remarkable jelly for roasted meats and warm bread and may be used as a glaze for sautéed carrots, peas, or meats.

Surprisingly enough, rosemary can be used judiciously in drinks as well. A cup of soothing rosemary tea in the morning may refresh the mind and memory, and a cup before bed will help induce sleep. Try bruising a handful of the fresh leaves and chilling them overnight in apple or pineapple juice or fresh lemonade, then serve with lemon wedges and a sprig of the fresh herb. I enjoy doing this with a slightly sweet white wine or brandy to serve as a cordial to garden guests.

Fortunately, rosemary is an herb that thrives in gardens of the Southwest, favoring an alkaline soil similar to its native Mediterranean. But take caution not to overwater it! In fact, my healthiest plants grow in areas where they are sometimes neglected. In times of high heat and humidity, wet roots can cause fungal disease and untimely demise of rosemary, especially if grown in soggy soil. During droughts, frequent sprayings of water or a diluted seaweed mix (avoiding the roots) are also beneficial.

Rosemary loves the sun and good air circulation and seems to enjoy growing against a wall for protection against chilly winter winds. While its delightfully resinous odor is appealing to most people, it seems to deter insects from other plants. Occasionally, during times of heat stress, rosemary may suffer from some spider mite damage, and I have sometimes discovered tiny web worms nesting in the branches. Neither pest seems to do much damage; the first may be treated with a light spraying of insecticidal soap, and the latter with bacillus thurengiensis.

There are two kinds of rosemary: upright and prostrate (or creeping), and each has several varieties. With ideal conditions, the upright rosemary may attain 6 feet or more with a gnarled and twisted trunk, and it is winter hardy in our area. One such specimen grew against an adobe wall in the patio of my childhood home in El Paso. I have a vivid memory of it one winter, covered with delicate blue blossoms although its branches were laden with snow. 'Tuscan Blue,' a fast-growing broad-leafed variety, is popular. The tall and more slender variety R. off. 'Albus' seems especially winter hardy; surprisingly, its blooms are white instead of blue.

The upright varieties are bushy with stiff branches and lend themselves to shaping as hedges. The narrow and leathery leaves are greenish-gray and slightly silver underneath, resembling miniature pine needles. Rosemary's lovely blue flowers generally adorn the plant from spring to late fall and keep the bees busy. Their rosemary-flavored honey is considered a delicacy.

Valued more for ornamental purposes than culinary, prostrate rosemary makes an attractive plant in the garden, attaining approximately 12 inches in height. It especially lends itself to cascading over walls or barrels and growing in rock gardens or along borders. The leaves are generally shinier, smaller, and more dense in appearance than the upright varieties. Gardening friends in California may grow thick mats of this evergreen plant. Unfortunately, however, it is less winter hardy than its upright counterpart. If successive freezes don't kill it, it may be so severely damaged that it is simply more aesthetic to replace it. This plant is a heavy bloomer and makes an attractive hanging basket, in which it can be safely wintered indoors. Look for varieties such as 'Santa Barbara' or 'Lockwood de Forest' and a delicate pink-flowering variety called 'Majorca Pink.'

Rosemary is difficult to grow from seeds and takes a long time to germinate, so I recommend buying plants to transplant. Once established in the garden, rosemary can be propagated by cuttings in sand or by layering.

It is apparent why this often forgotten culinary herb is one of my favorites. Ironically, rosemary is the herb of remembrance. And so I try to remember to give a sprig to friends departing my garden, in hopes that they will remember to use it!

GARLICKY ROSEMARY SHRIMP NEW ORLEANS STYLE

My friend Danny Paquette shared this recipe—a version of the spicy shrimp served in New Orleans restaurants. Eat the shrimp with your fingers, sopping up the garlicky wine and rosemary sauce with crusty bread. Spinach fettuccine tossed with freshly grated Parmesan complements the bright pink shrimp.

1 pound medium unpeeled shrimp, rinsed and patted dry

¼ cup best quality olive oil

1 large head (or more) garlic, separated into cloves

3 bay leaves

1 generous teaspoon (or more) dried oregano

2 generous tablespoons chopped fresh rosemary, stems removed

½ teaspoon crushed dried red chile pepper (or more)

Salt and freshly ground pepper to taste

½ cup dry white wine

1 tablespoon Lovely Lemon vinegar or white wine vinegar [*see chapter on herb vinegars*]

Juice of 1 lemon

Freshly grated nutmeg

Heat olive oil in a 12-inch cast-iron skillet. Add the garlic cloves and sauté for 2 minutes over medium heat; do not brown! Add the shrimp and bay leaves, and continue to sauté, shaking the pan frequently. Follow with the herbs and crushed chile pepper, salt, and pepper, and toss well. Add the wine, vinegar, and lemon juice, and simmer until shrimp is pink and tender and garlic is slightly soft (approximately 5 minutes). Do not overcook! Before serving, adjust seasonings and sprinkle generously with freshly grated nutmeg.

Serve in bowls garnished with lemon slices. Peel shrimp at table. Wonderful as is, or serve over spinach fettuccine tossed with butter and freshly grated Parmesan, with cracked pepper on the side. Also tastes good the next day at room temperature. Serves 4.

NOTE: Traditionally, the shrimp is cooked until the shells are crunchy, and the shrimp is eaten, shells and all. The garlic cloves are also cooked in their skin, and eaten by squeezing the tender garlic clove from its skin into the mouth!

POMMES PEABODY

I know why these rosemary roasted potatoes are a favorite dish of my sister's family. Serve with roasts or grilled meats or for a special brunch.

2 medium-size Idaho potatoes, scrubbed, peeled, and cut into ¼-inch slices
2 tablespoons best quality olive oil
2–3 tablespoons minced shallots or green onions
1 tablespoon fresh lemon juice
1 generous sprinkling fresh rosemary sprigs
¼ teaspoon freshly grated nutmeg (optional)
¼ teaspoon crushed dried red chile pepper (or more)
Salt and freshly ground pepper to taste
1 tablespoon melted butter

Preheat oven to 400 degrees. Lightly coat a 10–12-inch cast-iron skillet with olive oil. Place the potatoes in a single layer overlapping slightly and lining the sides of the pan. Sprinkle with shallots and lemon juice. Tuck small sprigs of rosemary between the potato slices; drizzle with the remaining olive oil. Sprinkle with the grated nutmeg, crushed red chile, salt, and pepper. Cook for 50–55 minutes until lightly crisp and golden. Drizzle with melted butter and cook another 5 minutes. Serves 4 as a side dish.

NOTE: I often combine rosemary sprigs with fresh sage, thyme, and savory sprigs. If desired, generously sprinkle Parmesan on top of the butter before the last 5 minutes of cooking.

TEXAS GOAT CHEESE TART

This trendy tart comes from the Mozzarella Company in Dallas, purveyors of prize-winning Texas cheeses that often are flavored with herbs. It makes fine brunch fare accompanied by salad, and miniature tarts are a tremendous hit served as hors d'oeuvres.

12 ounces Texas goat cheese
½ cup fresh herbs, loosely packed (any combination of basil, parsley,
    marjoram, tarragon, rosemary, thyme, etc.)
1 small clove garlic, mashed (or more)
2 ounces unsalted butter
4 ounces fresh ricotta
3 ounces crème fraîche
2 tablespoons flour
2 eggs
Salt and freshly ground black pepper
1 9-inch pie crust, prebaked

Bring all ingredients to room temperature. Preheat oven to 375 degrees. In bowl of food processor, mince herbs and garlic. Add cheeses, butter, crème fraîche, eggs, salt, and pepper, and process until mixture is smooth. Pour into prebaked pie crust. Bake until puffed and golden, about 30 minutes. Serve warm or at room temperature. Serves 8 as first course, 6 for luncheon.

NOTE: My favorite combination of herbs for this recipe is ¼ generous cup parsley, 2 tablespoons fresh rosemary, and 2 tablespoons fresh basil. Often, I also add more garlic, 3 ounces of sun-dried tomatoes, and a generous sprinkling of toasted pine nuts.

▼▼▼▼▼▼▼▼▼▼▼▼▼▼▼▼▼▼▼▼▼▼▼▼

▲▲▲▲▲▲▲▲▲▲▲▲▲▲▲

BUTTERFLIED LEG OF LAMB LACED WITH GARDEN HERBS

▼▼▼▼▼▼▼▼▼▼▼▼▼▼▼

This lamb stuffed with slivers of garlic and chopped rosemary bathes in a robust marinade before grilling. Fragrant sprigs of rosemary, oregano, mint, and colorful red onion slices accompany the garlic, making a presentation that looks as good as it tastes and smells. Julia Child's suggestion to cut slashes lengthwise ⅔ the way through the meat gives it a more even thickness for grilling. Then it may be held together with 2 long skewers run crosswise through the meat, or grilled inside an oiled, two-sided wire basket.

1 5-pound leg of lamb, boned and butterflied with excess fat and skin trimmed

3 tablespoons olive oil

4–6 cloves garlic, slightly mashed

1 tablespoon chopped fresh rosemary

⅓ cup Mediterranean marinade vinegar, *or* oregano-chile-garlic vinegar, *or* red wine vinegar [*see chapter on herb vinegars*]

2 tablespoons sweet red vermouth

Freshly ground pepper

¼ cup fresh mint, loosely chopped, plus several 5-inch sprigs

¼ cup fresh oregano, loosely chopped, plus several 5-inch sprigs

Several sprigs fresh rosemary

½ medium-size red onion, cut in half, then sliced into ½-inch-thick slices

¼ teaspoon crushed dried red chile pepper (or more)

1 teaspoon paprika

Salt and pepper to taste

Place meat skin-side down in a shallow glass dish to marinate, and make approximately 5 lengthwise slits 2–3 inches apart in the thickest part. Rub both sides with the oil, 2–3 cloves of the mashed garlic, and the chopped rosemary. Drizzle the vinegar and sweet vermouth over the lamb, coating it well. Sprinkle with pepper, and marinate for 2 hours or overnight, turning occasionally. (If refrigerated, allow to come to room temperature before grilling.) Prior to grilling, fill the slits in the lamb with the chopped herbs, rest of garlic, and several sprigs of herbs. Place the onion slices round-edge up into each slit. Sprinkle with the crushed red chile pepper, paprika, salt, and pepper. Reserve marinade. Lamb may be grilled in a lightly oiled, 2-sided wire basket, or skewered (run one skewer end to end, securing the onions, and a second skewer through the other side so that the skewers cross at the tips). Use a drip pan. Before adding the lamb (5–6 inches from hot coals), add several rosemary sprigs to the coals; place lamb on grill and immediately cover (drafts open). Grill for 8–10 minutes per side (about 25 minutes total), turning 4 times and basting meat with the remaining marinade, using a thick rosemary sprig as a brush. Do not over-cook. Lamb should be crusty outside but pink inside. Let stand 10 minutes before serving. Serves 6–8.

NOTE: Lamb may be broiled in oven 6 inches from flame on oiled rack (about 10 minutes per side). Leftovers may be used in salads and sandwiches.

BABY ROUTH'S ROSEMARY MUFFINS WITH GOAT CHEESE

Rosemary, golden raisins, and a creamy goat cheese center make these muffins taste so special. Carla Wood, sous chef and butcher at Baby Routh in Dallas serves them with wild game, lamb, or pork dishes or with a festive luncheon salad.

¾ cup milk

¾ cup golden raisins

1 tablespoon chopped fresh rosemary leaves

¼ cup (2 ounces) unsalted butter

1½ cups all purpose flour

½ cup sugar

2 teaspoons baking powder

¼ teaspoon salt

1 large egg

8 tablespoons goat cheese

Simmer milk, raisins, and rosemary in a small saucepan for 2 minutes. Remove from heat; add butter and stir until melted. Let cool.

Mix dry ingredients in a large bowl. Beat egg into cooked milk mixture. Add to dry ingredients and mix lightly just until dry ingredients are moistened. Spoon ⅓ of the batter into 12 greased muffin cups. Place 2 teaspoons of goat cheese in center of batter in each cup. Cover cheese with remaining batter, divided among each of the muffins. Bake approximately 20 minutes in a preheated 350° oven, or until brown and springy in the center.

Serve muffins hot or cool. If desired, a ¾-inch cube of cream cheese may be substituted for goat cheese. Without cheese, muffins are still delicious!

SAGE

Salvia officinalis
Lamiaceae (Labiatae) family

A trio of sages. (*Clockwise*) Silver garden sage, variegated green/golden sage, tri-color sage.

Common Names:

sage, garden sage; *salvia* (Mexico); other varieties often named after color or other characteristics

Characteristics:

grayish green, variegated, purple, or tricolor rough and pebbly elongated leaves; highly aromatic; shrub-like with woody stems; double-lipped violet flowers form on square stems; perennial

Conditions:

full sun; loose and sandy alkaline soil; do not overwater

Size:

approximately 2–3 feet tall and 2 feet wide

Propagation:

seeds rather difficult to germinate; purchase as transplants; root cuttings in sand or layer them; larger, woody plants may be divided by roots in early spring; 1 of each variety per garden suggested (more if used ornamentally)

Fertilizer:

light application of fish emulsion in early spring

Pests:

set traps to deter pill bugs; use bacillus thuringiensis to kill worms; spray with insecticidal soap to kill mealy bugs

Companions:

grows well next to rosemary, lavender, and thyme; reputed to deter cabbageworms

It seems that once a year in many households, the jar of sage is removed from the pantry shelf (where it has sat for years!), and the pitifully pale and yellowed leaves are crumbled into the Thanksgiving stuffing. Then it is tucked away again behind the oregano and basil, where it sadly awaits another year, another turkey. Yet this infrequently used herb has exciting culinary offerings! Unlike the dried herb, which can taste somewhat bitter and medicinal, fresh sage is highly aromatic, reminiscent of rosemary and pine smoothly balanced with mint. It has long been a favorite cooking herb in Mediterranean countries, where it grows on hillsides bathed in sunshine and salty air.

But sage is also at home in gardens in the Southwest, favoring alkaline, sandy soil where the roots will not stay wet. Like rosemary and thyme, sage easily succumbs to fungal root disease when overwatered or planted in heavy soil. This disease generally strikes in late summer during times of high heat and humidity, and it is tragic to see a well-established plant slowly wither away from root rot. Placing several small limestone rocks along the base of the plant seems to keep water off the roots. I have also found that sage grows very well in large clay pots, which assure good drainage.

It seems that especially in early spring, pill bugs and small worms like to feast on tender sage leaves. Make sure to clean debris away from the bottom of the plant to discourage them. And if you find mealy bugs sucking the sap from a sage plant, it probably indicates that the plant is not happy with its environment, and these pests often appear when the plant is grown in a greenhouse. Try giving it less water or more sunshine and spraying it with insecticidal soap.

But don't let these potential problems dissuade you. Sage is an attractive plant in the garden and bears fragrant leaves year round if the winter is mild. During more severe winters, the leaves may drop and the branches get woody, but kept well mulched, sage will recuperate in the spring sunshine. Remember to keep woody branches continually trimmed to encourage new growth. Added attractions of this plant are the lovely violet-colored flowers that bloom on the thick, square stems in early summer to the delight of the bees.

You may choose from several varieties of sage to add color and texture to the garden. The common garden sage (*Salvia officinalis*) is the most easily recognized, with its gray-green leaves of a pebbly reptilian texture. This plant often attains 3 feet in height and looks pretty growing against a rock wall. There is also a fast-growing variety with large leaves called Holt's mammoth (*Salvia off.* var. *Holt's mammoth*) which fares especially well in heat and humidity, and a more compact dwarf variety, which grows well in a pot.

Sage leaves are handsome garnishes for platters of game or fowl and may be added to bouquets of white and lavender flowers to adorn the table or tucked into napkin rings. The leaves, dipped in flour and egg whites and fried, also make unusually tasty fritters, especially the large leaves of Clary sage. This particular sage is a biennial that sprouts a 4-foot-tall pink flower stalk. Its leaves are large and fuzzy and are favored by worms and pill bugs, making it difficult to grow. It is truly amazing to see what those voracious critters can do in one night!

One of my favorites, golden sage (*Salvia off. 'Aurea'*), has bright gold-and-green mottled leaves, which make an appealing contrast or border in the garden as well as a lovely garnish for food. An equally charming cousin with variegated leaves of green, white, and purplish red (*Salvia off. 'Tricolor'*) may be used in the same manner. Like other variegated plants, these are the weaker of the species and more susceptible to freeze and drought; thus they fare well in pots so that they can be moved easily. (Both grow approximately 18 inches tall.)

Red or purple sage (*Salvia off. 'Purpurascens'*) grows more compactly. It makes a lovely ornamental border and a delicious tea. Place a small handful of garden sage (red or gray) in a teapot and cover with boiling water. Allow to steep for 5 or 10 minutes, then sit down and relax. (Sage advice.) In fact, throughout history, sage has been extolled for its rejuvenative powers and for imparting wisdom and healing; salvia comes from the Latin word *salvar*, meaning "to heal."

A final favorite in the sage family is pineapple sage (*Salvia elegans*). There are many other Salvias used for ornamental purposes, and the leaves of pineapple sage resemble them. The leaves are only slightly rough, and they are pointed rather than pebbly and elongated like the other garden sages. The emerging bright green leaves smell distinctly like old-fashioned pineapple candies.

Pineapple sage is easily damaged by frost and will lose all of its leaves and possibly perish during extreme winters, so plant it against a protective wall and keep it well mulched. One extrememly cold winter, I was certain that I had lost my pineapple sage plant. While digging in the garden in early spring, however, I bruised one of its roots and quickly caught a whiff of its delicious tropical aroma. Then I knew that it would soon poke its head out of the ground.

Pineapple sage grows taller and bushier than the previously mentioned sages, eventually attaining 4 feet in height. It also requires more water than most sages. Its brilliant red flower spikes bloom in late summer and fall and sometimes in the spring as well, attracting bees and hummingbirds to the garden. Leaves and flowers both are beautiful in bouquets and as garnishes for flans, sorbets, delicately iced cakes, and other elegant desserts. They also are lovely as a garnish for fruit punches and sangría. Pineapple sage can flavor cream cheese and be added to fruit salads and pork or chicken dishes. And, fortunately, it roots quickly in water, so it can be easily shared with friends.

As for the culinary virtues of sage—what a gift! Italians use it generously as a savory complement to rich pasta and pota-

▼▼▼▼▼▼▼▼▼▼▼▼▼▼▼▼▼▼▼▼▼▼▼▼▼

to dishes. They wrap veal medallions and a thin slice of salty prosciutto (ham) around sage leaves, roll it up, and sauté it in butter and wine to create their renowned *saltimbocca*. Sage has long been used to flavor sausages, *pâtés*, goose, and rich pork dishes and is noted to aid in the digestion of such fatty foods. Throwing a large handful of sage onto the hot coals of the barbeque deliciously flavors game and fowl. French chefs stuff the cavities of hens and small game birds with fresh sage leaves and baste them with sage butter, while English cooks use it in roasting wild game and in stews and marinades.

Sage also gives a spirited kick to mild cheeses. Sage Derby is an English cheese streaked green with fresh sage – delicious with turkey or ham sandwiches and in casseroles! Montrachet goat cheese or cream cheese can be flavored with sage and other fresh herbs, as can festive holiday cheeseballs. Breads, especially those made with cheese, also benefit. Try making a bread pudding with layers of apples, onions, Swiss cheese, and sage, and add sage to baked apples or applesauce.

Heavy bean or split-pea soups also are enhanced by the addition of freshly chopped sage, as are potatoes. Whole tomatoes or onions baked with a peppery sage-and-cornbread stuffing are my favorites. And oh yes! We mustn't forget the Thanksgiving stuffing!

Although you may want to use fresh sage judiciously at first, once your palate becomes accustomed to its savory freshness, you will no longer leave it on the pantry shelf.

FESTIVE SAGE CHEESEBALL

This pecan-studded cheeseball flavored with fresh sage and dusted with grated nutmeg tastes delicious spread on crisp apple or pear slices. Served on a platter lined with grape leaves, it makes an exquisite holiday presentation.

8 ounces extra sharp Cheddar or English Sage Derby cheese
10 ounces sharp yellow Cheddar cheese
2 tablespoons freshly chopped sage
½ cup chopped pecans
½ teaspoon freshly grated nutmeg
½ cup sweet full-bodied port
30 pecan halves (approximately)

Grate the two cheeses and place in a bowl or food processor. Add the chopped sage, nuts, freshly grated nutmeg, and port; mix with fork, electric mixer, or food processor until well blended. Turn out on plastic wrap, and loosely form into a ball. Chill overnight or for several days.

When ready to serve, form into desired shape, stud with pecan halves, and dust with freshly grated nutmeg. Serve gar- nished with fresh sage leaves with slices of red starkrimson and Anjou pears, gold-speckled Asian or Bosc pears, red and green apples, or Carr's sweet crackers.

NOTE: Walnuts make an elegant substitute for pecans. Also may be made in a crock instead of studded with nuts. This recipe keeps well for over a month in the refrigerator.

▼▼▼▼▼▼▼▼▼▼▼▼▼▼▼▼▼▼▼▼▼▼▼▼▼▼▼

APPLE STUFFED PORK CHOPS IN CIDER-SAGE-MUSTARD MARINADE

Apples and onions sautéed with fresh sage and spices make a fabulous stuffing for pork chops. Using sage-flavored cider vinegar really makes a difference in the mustard-flavored marinade.

2 tablespoons butter

½ white onion, chopped

1 tablespoon minced shallots

¼ teaspoon whole juniper berries

¼ teaspoon whole cloves

½ teaspoon whole white peppercorns

¼ teaspoon ground cinnamon

1 medium winesap apple, chopped

1 tablespoon cider-sage vinegar *or* apple cider vinegar [*for recipe, see chapter on herb vinegars*]

1 teaspoon brown sugar

2 tablespoons freshly chopped sage *plus* 2–4 fresh sage leaves

2 center-cut pork chops, 1½ inches thick

2 tablespoons Dijon mustard

½ onion, sliced in ¼-inch slices

5 tablespoons cider-sage vinegar or apple cider vinegar

2 teaspoons brown sugar

Melt the butter; sauté the shallots and chopped onions. Meanwhile, grind whole juniper berries, whole cloves, and whole white peppercorns with cinnamon in a spice grinder. When shallots and onions are slightly softened, add the chopped apple and ground spices, and continue to sauté. Add 1 tablespoon vinegar and 1 teaspoon brown sugar, mixing well. Continue to sauté until apples are slightly softened. Remove from heat.

Cut a pocket through the middle of each pork chop and insert 1–2 sage leaves in each. Stuff each pocket with ½ of the onion/apple mixture. Place the sliced onions in a small, shallow pan. Rub each chop on both sides with mustard and place in the pan. Mix the remaining vinegar and sugar, and pour over the chops. Marinate overnight, turning and basting occasionally.

Cook chops for 18–20 minutes under a broiler, 6–8 inches from flame, turning and basting every 5 minutes with remaining marinade, and adding the onion slices from the marinade the last 5 minutes. Serve each chop with some of the onions and remaining pan drippings. Serves 2.

NOTE: If you prefer, you can ask your butcher to cut pockets in the pork chops for you.

TRICOLOR PEPPER PASTA WITH GARDEN SAGE

A feast for the eyes! Colorful, ripe, and sweet red, golden, and green bell peppers tossed with pasta, freshly chopped sage, grated Parmesan, and lots of garlic make a simple yet elegant meal.

¾ cup sage oil, strained (recipe follows)

2 cups each red, golden, and green bell peppers cut into ½–¾-inch pieces

½ teaspoon crushed dried red chile pepper

1 large red onion, roughly chopped

4–6 large cloves garlic, minced

½ teaspoon white pepper, freshly ground

½ teaspoon paprika

½ cup sweet vermouth *or* Spanish Oloroso sherry

3–4 tablespoons chopped sage (or more if desired)

3 tablespoons minced parsley

Salt and freshly ground white pepper to taste

Freshly grated Parmesan cheese

Fresh sage sprigs

1 pound fresh pasta cooked *al dente* [*for instructions on cooking fresh pasta, see Cooking Tips chapter*]

SAGE OIL

¾ cup extra virgin olive oil

6 cloves garlic

8 large sage leaves or more

Bruise garlic and sage with the back of a wooden spoon in the oil. Allow to sit, covered, several hours or overnight, bruising occasionally with the spoon.

Heat sage oil in a deep skillet; add the bell peppers and coat well with oil. Add the crushed red pepper and mix well. Add the chopped onions and minced garlic, and sauté about 5 minutes. Sprinkle with white pepper and paprika, then add the vermouth or sherry and cook until tender-crisp. Do not overcook! Add the freshly chopped sage the last minute of cooking. Turn off heat and add parsley. Salt and pepper to taste.

Fill individual warmed bowls with cooked pasta and cover generously with pepper mixture, tossing well with about 2 tablespoons freshly grated Parmesan; add a sage sprig to each bowl for garnish. Pass small bowls of Parmesan and crushed red pepper at the table. Serves 6.

NOTE: Make sure that peppers are cooked in time for the pasta. Cheerful butterfly-shaped farfalle, or corkscrew-shaped fusilli are my favorite pastas for this dish. Immediately toss with the peppers. Leftovers may be eaten as a pasta salad. Simply drizzle lightly with a garlic vinaigrette and add some more freshly chopped sage and parsley.

SKILLET SAGE AND PEPPERED CORNBREAD

Dunk this dense, country-style cornbread in beans, hearty stews, or gravy. The smoky flavor of bacon and fiery peppers is complemented by the fresh flavor of sage.

6 slices bacon
1¼ cups corn meal
¾ cup white flour
½ teaspoon salt
3 teaspoons baking powder
½ teaspoon crushed dried red chile pepper
¼ teaspoon ground white pepper
1 teaspoon paprika
1¼ cups buttermilk
1 egg
2 tablespoons molasses or honey
3 generous tablespoons freshly chopped sage
2 tablespoons green onions, chopped
2 tablespoons freshly grated Parmesan cheese

Preheat oven to 425 degrees. In a 9–10-inch cast-iron skillet, fry bacon until crisp; reserve fat. Crumble bacon.

In a medium size bowl, mix the cornmeal, flour, salt, baking powder, peppers, and paprika; blend with a fork.

In a small bowl, mix buttermilk, egg, and molasses or honey, then mix with dry ingredients. Add the chopped sage, onions, Parmesan, and crumbled bacon.

In skillet, heat ¼ cup of the reserved bacon fat to near smoking, and pour into the cornmeal mixture. Immediately return to the hot, greased skillet and bake in oven 20–25 minutes until golden brown on top. Do not overcook!

NOTE: Try making this recipe in a cast-iron cornpone mold. (Vegetarians can substitute ¼ cup oil for bacon fat.) Use leftovers to make cornbread stuffing—delicious in baked onions, tomatoes, or pork chops.

SALAD BURNET

Poterium sanguisorba
Rosaceae family

Salad burnet potted in a whimsical animal planter.

Common Names:
salad burnet, burnet

Characteristics:
grows in a rosette clump with bending stems and small, rounded, serrated leaves with a cucumber-like taste; flower heads form in the summer of the second year with crimson styles and pale yellow-green stigmas; biennial

Conditions:
fairly dry, chalky, limestone soil preferred and full sunshine (can tolerate some afternoon shade)

Size:
from 12 to 15 inches tall and about 1½ foot wide

Propagation:

readily reseeds itself; seeds should be planted in the fall and/or very early spring; clump may be divided in the spring or fall; 1–2 plants per garden suggested or several plants for ornamental border

Fertilizer:

none required; some mulch in summer beneficial

Pests:

some pill bug damage possible

Companions:

grow with other low-growing and aromatic herbs such as thyme and mint

Salad burnet, an herb with a subtle, cucumber-like taste, is often overlooked. In fact, most people do not realize that this attractive and easy-to-grow plant offers exciting culinary possibilities. As its name suggests, salad burnet makes a sprightly salad green, and its delicately serrated leaves (resembling those of the related wild roses) also make lovely garnishes.

I must admit, however, that it tastes especially wonderful in a gin and tonic on a hot summer's day. (Keep the bottle of gin ice cold in the freezer.) Gently bruising the leaves of the herb releases its unique flavor–the unmistakable cucumber taste, which quickly permeates the icy gin with a smoothness that is truly elegant and indeed cooling! (Try a cucumber slice for garnish.)

Other cold drinks–iced tea, lemonade, tomato juice, and even simple mineral water–are similarly enhanced by salad burnet. In fact, noted herbalist Mrs. Grieve says in *A Modern Herbal* that its generic name, *Poterium*, comes from the Greek word *poterion*, meaning "drinking cup," as the fresh-tasting leaves were used for their cooling effect in wines and ales.

Try bruising a few sprigs and adding them to a chilled glass of white wine. Or follow British example and steep some of the leaves in an iced glass of Pimms (an aromatic herbal aperitif), then serve with a crisp cucumber slice.

The wispy stems of this plant have small, serrated leaves that grow opposite one another and resemble small fluttering wings. These gracefully bending stems lend themselves to adorning platters, and small sprigs are quite eye-catching when used to garnish soups or open-faced sandwiches. For a special treat, freeze sprigs in ice cube trays and use the decorative ice cubes in cool drinks.

Salad burnet grows in a compact rosette clump with the new leaves bursting forth from the center and the older leaves hanging towards the ground. Because of this growth pattern, one of my favorite English herbalists, Dorothy Hall, calls it the "fountain plant." A biennial, it sends up long stems in late spring/early summer of its second year with rather inconspicuous flowers. These resemble the knotted shape of a green raspberry but are coarse with tiny crimson styles and pale yellow-green stamens that may be noted under close observation.

Once established in the garden, salad burnet readily reseeds and can even become invasive. It's a good idea to keep most of the flower heads pinched (this also prevents the leaves from tasting bitter) and to allow only a few plants to go to seed. Because salad burnet is a gregarious plant and likes to grow among its fellow plants, it should be planted in groups–along paths or as a border. I remember a spectacular sight at a country home where whimsical clumps of salad burnet formed a bumpy green carpet–the lower leaves hugging the ground and the newer leaves spouting forward. A single plant, however, does look pretty cascading from a pot.

The seeds of salad burnet are easily propagated, especially when sown in the fall, although seeds also may be planted in very early spring. The best method is to scatter them, keeping them well watered and transplanting the seedlings to 12 inches apart after they are established. Dividing the clump in early spring or in the fall is another method of propagation.

Salad burnet does have some special requirements. A soil that is too rich–especially when combined with high heat and humidity–can cause the roots to rot. This plant's native environment is the limestone downs of Southern Europe, where in the the chalky soil it generally attains only 4–5 inches. (In richer soil, it grows to about 1 foot tall and up to 2 feet when in flower.)

The pleasure of growing this plant is that it remains in the garden year round; consquently, it should always be used in its fresh form (or steeped in vinegar). In the summer, it requires more water and the leaves and stem have a tendency to be rather tough and bitter. This is also true of the plant when it gets too old, so remember to replace old plants with new ones every few years. Always use the tender sprigs in food and drinks. The bottom leaves may be trimmed off to prevent pill bugs and worms from foraging, although these leaves often compost themselves into the ground.

Salad burnet, called *pimpinella* by Italians, is their beloved salad herb; they say "a salad without *pimpinella* is like love without a girl." Fortunately, these leaves may be used in a winter salad when many other herbs are unavailable. My grandmother's favorite summer sandwich was brown bread spread lightly with mayonnaise and thin slices of cucumber sprinkled with black pepper. A generous handful of salad burnet sprigs makes it even better! Salad burnet also enhances cottage cheese with chives or a cream cheese-mayonnaise-chive combination to use as a spread for canapés.

A cool and refreshing sauce for cold poached fish or grilled salmon may be made by mixing finely chopped cucumbers, shallots, and salad burnet with crème fraîche. Or try chilled cucumber soup enticingly garnished with salad burnet sprigs. Tomato juice, Bloody Marys, and gazpacho are similarly enhanced. And an absolutely lovely but simple presentation may be made by garnishing a platter of sliced cucumbers and/or other fresh raw vegetables (drizzled with lemon juice–or better yet, salad burnet vinegar) with salad burnet sprigs and nasturtiums, borage flowers, chive blossoms, or cilantro flowers.

To make decorative cucumber slices, tine an unpeeled and unwaxed cucumber with a fork; rub with a lemon half, squeezing plenty of juice on the cucumber, then slice thinly and garnish each slice with a salad burnet sprig. And of course, don't forget this herb in cold drinks (its cooling properties come from its ability to promote perspiration) and in fruit cups. I especially like it with slices of cantaloupe or honeydew melon sprinkled with fresh lime juice.

From its native windy limestone bluffs to the Tudor knot gardens to the tidy kitchen gardens of the American colonists, this cheerful herb (perky in the winter when other herbs are dormant) has brought joy. Even the early Greeks imbibing wine steeped with salad burnet leaves said it rejoiced the heart. So, cheers!

▼▼▼▼▼▼▼▼▼▼▼▼▼▼▼▼▼▼▼▼▼▼▼▼▼▼▼▼▼▼▼

SALAD BURNET SANDWICHES

Beautifully garnished open-faced sandwiches make a lovely luncheon in the garden and tempting appetizers as well. These taste good on dark rye or pumpernickel party bread.

THE HERB CHEESE SPREAD
▼▼▼▼▼▼▼▼▼▼▼▼▼▼

8 ounces cream cheese, softened

2 green onions with tops *or* 1 small shallot, minced

3 tablespoons chopped fresh salad burnet

3 tablespoons chopped fresh dill

1–2 tablespoons mayonnaise *or* sour cream

½ teaspoon dried mustard

1½ teaspoons curry powder

2 teaspoons chopped fresh chives

1 pinch salt

Blend cream cheese with onions, herbs, and mayonnaise or sour cream. Add the mustard and curry, and blend in the chives. Flavors increase as it sits. Keeps several days refrigerated. Yields approximately 1¼ cups.

THE SANDWICHES

Cut bread into festive shapes with cookie cutters. Spread generously with the cheese spread. Place a thin slice of tined cucumber on each sandwich and garnish with a sprig of salad burnet and/or dill. Serve on a wicker tray lined with nasturtium flowers. Remember: the petals and leaves are edible, too!

NOTE: If desired, substitute dill, mint, or parsley for the salad burnet.

GRILLED SALMON WITH SALAD BURNET/SHALLOT CRÈME FRAÎCHE

The delicately scalloped leaves of salad burnet lend their subtle cucumber flavor to this creamy sauce. Delicious served with grilled or poached fish (hot or cold), tossed with cucumber slices, used as a topping for baked potatoes, or used in place of mayonnaise.

1 cup crème fraîche

2 tablespoons salad burnet vinegar, *or* Lovely Lemon vinegar, *or* bouquet garni vinegar, *or* fresh lemon juice [*see chapter on herb vinegars*]

1½–2 tablespoons minced shallots

1 teaspoon dried mustard

¼ teaspoon freshly ground white pepper

3 tablespoons chopped salad burnet leaves

2 teaspoons chopped chives

Salt to taste

Several hours before serving, mix all the ingredients. (Keeps several days in the refrigerator.) Serve at room temperature. When serving with fish, place a generous dollop on each portion and garnish with a sprig of salad burnet. Makes about 1 cup.

VARIATIONS

1. Replace salad burnet with fresh dill. Add 1 teaspoon capers or horseradish (optional).
2. Replace salad burnet with fresh mint and use mint vinegar. Add ½ teaspoon lemon zest (optional).
3. Replace salad burnet with fresh chiffonade of sorrel leaves.

TO COOK SALMON

Sprinkle 6-ounce salmon steaks with salt, pepper, and a pat of butter. Broil 6 inches from flame (preheated) 4–6 minutes, depending on thickness. Do not overcook!

GIN AND TONIC WITH SALAD BURNET SPRIGS

It's amazing how the seemingly subtle flavor of salad burnet can perk up cold drinks. A single stem in a glass of ice water gives it a refreshing flavor. But in gin, it's pure heaven! For a special touch, freeze sprigs of salad burnet in ice cube trays, and place a few cubes in each glass.

1½–2 ounces gin per glass (keep in freezer)
Tonic water
Juice of ½ small lime
1 dash or more bitters (optional)
1–2 sprigs salad burnet
1 cucumber slice (optional)

Fill tall glass with several ice cubes. Add gin and tonic, juice of the lime, and bitters if desired. Garnish with a fresh sprig of salad burnet and a cucumber slice. Stir and sip.

NOTE: For a festive presentation, place a bottle of gin in a slightly larger container (plastic jug with the neck cut off or a large milk carton will work well). Arrange long sprigs of salad burnet and colorful flowers (purple pansies look good) around bottle, then cover with cold water that has been allowed to sit for several hours. Make sure that some leaves and flowers are near the base by pushing them down with a long-handled spoon. Freeze indefinitely. When frozen, remove container and place ice-covered gin bottle on an attractive shallow dish on serving table.

Angostura and Peychaud's bitters are mixtures of aromatic oils with essences of herbs and other plants in an alcohol base used to give a bitter flavor to drinks. Pink gin, popular in England, is gin and Angostura bitters swirled around in a glass until the mixture becomes pink.

SAVORY
Satureia species
Lamiaceae (Labiatae) family

Winter savory trailing from a terracotta planter.

Common Names:
winter savory; summer savory

Characteristics:
winter savory grows compactly with woody branches, small dark green aromatic leaves, and small star-shaped white flowers, perennial; summer savory is a taller plant with more succulent leaves and delicate pinkish flowers, annual

Conditions:
loose, well-draining soil and plenty of sunshine for winter savory; summer savory benefits from a slightly richer and moister soil

Size:
winter savory attains 8–12 inches in height and spreads; summer savory reaches about 2 feet high

Propagation:

winter savory best propagated from root divisions, cuttings, or layering; summer savory sown from seeds in early spring; several of each variety per garden suggested

Fertilizer:

light applications of fish emulsion and compost mulch for summer savory

Pests:

summer savory sometimes bothered by spider mites

Companions:

plant near beans or onions for mutual benefit

Savory's complex flavors merrily dance, tingling tastebuds with a combination of a feisty piquancy and a subtle sweet spiciness. To me, savory captures the essence of other herbs, notably thyme, oregano, and marjoram, and consequently blends well with them in recipes.

French cooks frequently incorporate *sarriette*, or savory, into their *bouquet garni* or throw sprigs of it on the coals before grilling. Mediterranean cooks adore this herb, and Germans call it *bohnenkraut*, the bean herb, because of its natural affinity to beans. Its perky flavor enhances the otherwise bland legumes: navy beans, limas, garbanzos, split peas, and lentils. Although savory was one of the herbs brought to America by the Pilgrims, it is an herb too often forgotten here today.

What a shame, because this herb comes in two different forms—summer savory (*Satureia hortensis*) and winter savory (*Satureia montana*)—making it accessible in the garden year round. On a cold winter's day, winter savory sprigs may be freshly picked to add to a simmering stew; likewise, summer savory sprigs enhance a crisp summer salad.

Winter savory's small dark green, narrow leaves grow from woody stems. This compact and low growing (8–12 inches) plant is ideal for rock gardens, container growing, or borders. Look for other varieties of ornamental value in herb catalogs. Its shiny leaves have a strong and piquant aroma, and in the summer, tiny white starlike flowers shine on the branches. Best propagated from root divisions, layerings, or cuttings, winter savory thrives when given proper conditions. These include plenty of sunshine and a loose, though not necessarily rich, well-draining soil. Shade produces a woody and leggy plant. To promote more growth, trim dead and woody branches in early spring and again after flowering. Do not cut the plant too far back in autumn or it will be more susceptible to a hard freeze. Like thyme, savory plants should be divided by the roots every few years, discarding the woody mother plant.

On the other hand, summer savory is a more wispy plant—attaining about 2 feet—with a more delicate flavor. The appearance of this plant is much softer than that of winter savory, with somewhat larger and rounder leaves that grow sparsely along the soft stem. The stem often becomes purplish in summer and may become weak or top-heavy, a condition which is discouraged by frequent pinching. Growing plants close together or among beans and onions also gives them support.

Summer savory is an annual that readily reseeds. Plant seeds in early spring – they germinate within a week – and make successive sowings for a continuous crop. Thin to about 8–10 inches apart. Full sun is a must, and summer savory benefits from a slightly richer soil and more water than does winter savory. Its delicate pinkish flowers entice bees into the garden.

Although I prefer to use savory in its fresh form, it may be successfully dried. Harvest right before the plant flowers, and hang bunches upside down or on a screen rack to dry. Winter savory takes a long time to dry because of its resinous leaves. Both savories may be frozen; however, since one or the other is available in the garden year round, why bother? I prefer to preserve the harvest by making savory herb butter or savory vinegar, which tastes delicious on bean salads and as a marinade for beef or chicken.

Summer savory's fresh taste benefits steamed vegetables – green beans, squash, and artichokes particularly. I simply place a bouquet of the fresh herb on top of the vegetables as they steam. Winter savory lends itself to cooking with stronger vegetables – cabbage, brussel sprouts, and turnips – and lessens their strong odor as they cook. Soups, stews, and casseroles are especially enhanced by this peppery herb, sometimes called the "pepper herb." And it certainly adds flavor for those whose salt intake is restricted.

Savory is a beloved herb among Greek cooks, who use is in their renowned spicy beef stew, *stifátho*, while French chefs use it to flavor their traditional *cassoulet*, a hearty casserole made with beans, vegetables, and assorted meats and served from an earthenware pot. In Venice, Italians serve *risi e bisi*, a traditional dish of rice and peas simmered with savory. Sausages and stuffings are complemented by this aromatic herb, as are any dishes that use thyme or oregano. Savory asserts itself politely; its flavor dances among more subtle company, as did its botanical namesake, *Satureia*, the satyr.

▼▼▼▼▼▼▼▼▼▼▼▼▼▼▼▼▼▼▼▼▼▼▼▼▼

SAVORY GREEN BEAN SALAD

This colorful and crunchy salad is one of my favorites. Green beans may be arranged in spoke fashion with artichoke hearts, red onion rings, and crumbled feta cheese in the center, or the salad may be simply tossed. Either winter or summer savory may be used, but remember that winter savory is stronger tasting.

1½ pounds fresh green beans, cut in half with ends trimmed

¼ cup bouquet garni vinegar, *or* Lovely Lemon vinegar, *or* white wine vinegar [*see chapter on herb vinegars*]

3 tablespoons fresh lemon juice

1 teaspoon dried mustard

½ teaspoon brown sugar

1 tablespoon minced red onion

1 tablespoon finely chopped fresh savory

¼ teaspoon freshly ground white pepper

Salt to taste

½ cup best quality olive oil

2 6-ounce jars marinated artichoke hearts, drained

½ medium-size red onion, sliced into thin rings, *plus* 2 tablespoons minced red onion

2 tablespoons chopped fresh parsley

2 tablespoons chopped fresh savory

Optional garnishes: cherry tomato halves, crumbled mild feta cheese, toasted pine nuts or walnuts [*for instructions on toasting nuts, see Cooking Tips chapter*]

Steam green beans with a few sprigs of savory until crisp-tender (do not overcook!); immediately plunge into ice water. Drain and pat dry.

Mix vinegar, lemon juice, mustard, sugar, 1 tablespoon minced onion, 1 tablespoon chopped savory, salt, and pepper; slowly drizzle in the olive oil. Gently toss the green beans in the vinaigrette, adding the other ingredients. Sprinkle with freshly grated white pepper and salt if desired. Serves 6.

NOTE: Green beans may be cooked several hours in advance and chilled; vinaigrette may be mixed ahead and chilled also. Dress the salad just before serving.

SAVORY CHEESE BISCUITS

In the English tradition, these resemble cookies, rather than American biscuits, and are tasty with hot tea, sherry, or wine. Richard Cilley of Austin shared his recipe, and I added some fun variations.

MASTER RECIPE

½ pound salted butter (2 sticks), room temperature

1 pound double Gloucester or sharp Cheddar, grated and room temperature

4 cloves garlic, minced

1 tablespoon chopped fresh chives

3 tablespoons chopped fresh savory

1 teaspoon cayenne *or* dried crushed red chile pepper (or less)

2½ cups white flour

2 cups walnut or pecan pieces (optional)

Blend the butter and cheese together. (A food processor or hand mixer works well for this.) Add the garlic, chives, savory, pepper, and nuts, mixing thoroughly. Slowly add the flour until you have a stiff dough.

Divide the dough into portions, and roll it out, one portion at a time, to ¼-inch thickness on a lightly floured board. Cut into rounds, or use decorative cookie cutters; with a fork, make a criss-cross pattern on each. Place on baking sheet in a preheated 375-degree oven for approximately 10–12 minutes until slightly golden. Cool; store in airtight tin in refrigerator for several weeks, or freeze. Makes approximately 5 dozen biscuits.

VARIATIONS

Omit the nuts and savory in the master recipe. Divide dough into 4 equal parts, and add one of the following to each part.

1. 1 tablepoon fresh basil, minced
   1 teaspoon dried oregano
   1 tablespoon Parmesan cheese
   ⅛ teaspoon crushed red pepper
   2 teaspoons chopped fresh chives
   ¼ cup pine nuts (optional)

2. 4 tablespoons chopped fresh savory
   ¼ teaspoon cayenne
   ½ cup walnut or pecan pieces

3. 3 tablespoons chopped fresh sage
   ¼–½ teaspoon crushed red pepper
   ½ cup walnut pieces

4. 1 teaspoon caraway seed
   1 teaspoon dill seed
   2 teaspoons chopped fresh chives
   3 tablespoons chopped fresh dill

NOTE: These biscuits are best when served warm. Simply reheat in a low oven for a few minutes before serving.

STIFÁTHO (GREEK BEEF STEW)

Richard Cilley, a scholarly Austin chef, attended one of my first herb classes and over the yars has provided me with much insight and inspiration. I have adapted his recipe by adding fresh herbs and spices. Their aroma simmering in wine is entrancing on a winter's night. Crumbled feta and walnut pieces garnish this hearty beef stew.

½ cup best quality olive oil *plus* 3 tablespoons

3 pounds lean rump roast, cut into ¾-inch cubes

1½ pounds small boiling onions with papery skin removed

4–6 cloves garlic, chopped

2 cups dry red wine

1 6-ounce can tomato paste

4 tablespoons Mediterranean marinade vinegar *or* oregano chile garlic
    vinegar *or* red wine vinegar [*see chapter on herb vinegars*]

1 teaspoon brown sugar

½ teaspoon whole allspice, freshly ground

½ teaspoon pepper, freshly ground

1 teaspoon whole coriander seeds, freshly ground

1–2 3-inch sticks cinnamon

2 tablespoons chopped fresh savory

1 2-inch sprig rosemary

1 teaspoon dried oregano

2 bay leaves

Salt to taste

½ cup walnut pieces (optional)

8 ounces feta cheese cut into ½-inch cubes (optional)

Heat ½ cup olive oil in a 10-inch skillet. Brown the meat in batches and set aside. Discard remaining oil and wipe skillet clean.

Add 3 tablespoons olive oil to pan and heat; sauté onions until gently browned on the outside (shake the pan frequently). Remove onions with a slotted spoon. Set aside. Briefly sauté the garlic in the remaining oil; do not brown!

In a large stewpot over medium heat, dissolve the tomato paste in the wine and vinegar; add the sugar and garlic. Grind the spices in a spice grinder and add to the pot, along with the cinnamon sticks. Add the meat, savory, rosemary, oregano, and bay; bring to a boil. Reduce heat and simmer, covered, for 30 minutes. Add salt and onions and simmer another 30 minutes until meat is tender. Add the walnuts and feta the last 5 minutes of cooking. Add 2 teaspoons freshly chopped savory and allow stew to sit covered a few minutes before serving. Serves 6–8.

NOTE: Stifátho is delicious as is or served over noodles or rice with a green salad. If using summer savory, add it toward the end of cooking. Mexican oregano (Poliomintha longiflora) or fresh thyme may be substituted for savory.

SORREL

Rumex species
Polygonaceae family

Sorrel and leeks (*in basket*) grow well together in the garden.

Common Names:

common or garden sorrel; French sorrel; wild sorrel

Characteristics:

rosette-like clump with bright green leaves that are broad and oval or arrow shaped with distinct tart and lemony flavor; flower stalk with tight clusters of greenish flowers in summer; perennial

Conditions:

rich, moist, well-draining soil (preferably acidic) and some afternoon shade; even moisture is beneficial

Size:

1½–3 feet tall and 2 feet wide

Propagation:

sow seeds in fall or very early spring; readily reseeds if flower stalks not cut; roots may be divided in early spring or fall; purchase as transplants; 2 plants per garden suggested (more if used ornamentally)

Fertilizer:

compost mulch, especially in summer; regular light applications of manure and fish emulsion helpful

Pests:

caterpillars, snails, and slugs chew holes in the leaves—use bacillus thuringiensis on caterpillars and set traps for the slugs and snails

Companions:

grow near leeks and other alliums

I remember as a child munching on the leaves of "sour dock," or the seed pods of the clover-leafed oxalis. Although concaved cheeks and grimaces followed, the mouth-puckering tang gave me great pleasure. Sorrel is an herb that recaptures that same delight. Its tart flavor has been highly prized in European cookery for centuries, perking up soups and sauces, potato salads, and baked fish with its lemony freshness. Suzanne McLucas, author of *A Provençal Kitchen in America*, says that sorrel is a favorite of Provençal cooks, who call it *eigreto*, deriving from the French word *aigre*, meaning sour, and add the young and tender leaves to salads and soups.

Fortunately, however, sorrel has finally gained acclaim in America, where innovative chefs have paired it with grilled swordfish in salads and mixed it with shallots and wine to make a savory sauce for poached salmon. John Sedlar, the talented chef of Saint Estèphe in Manhattan Beach, California, uses a sorrel sauce as one of his "Indian paints" to decorate Southwestern

motifs on some of his dishes. For instance, in his recipe for "Salmon Painted Desert" in his recently published *Modern Southwestern Cuisine*, a pattern of the desert mesas is painted with a sorrel sauce and served with steamed salmon. But for me, sorrel is the quintessential soup herb, enlivening hearty fish chowders, creamy purées, and green borscht.

I first learned about sorrel when a friend's mother arrived from Minnesota with a jar of her daughter's favorite Ukranian green borscht. It was absolutely delicious! And I was fascinated by the refreshing tartness, mistaking it for lemon. It was several years before I discovered a small sorrel plant at a nursery. I must admit, the first year of growing it was quite frustrating, and I was beginning to think that sorrel could only grow in Minnesota. But as I catered to its needs, it quickly became an herb that I could not do without.

Summertime is a difficult season for this cool-weather plant. It droops during the sweltering days and longs for water, but a

▼▼▼▼▼▼▼▼▼▼▼▼▼▼▼▼▼▼▼▼▼▼▼▼▼▼▼▼

drip irrigation system will greatly diminish this problem. At this time of year, I cut the plant back (it often dies back on its own), apply a compost mulch, and try to keep it moist. Another devastating problem for sorrel, especially in the spring, is that caterpillars, worms, slugs, and snails adore it, marring its leaves with unsightly holes. These creatures feed at night and hide under leaves during the day, when they may be picked off and discarded. Frequent sprayings of bacillus thuringiensis will exterminate them. But sorrel comes into its own as soon as cooler weather approaches. With renewed vigor, its bright green leaves gently unfold. And during this time, insect attack is minimal and more easily controlled. Sorrel is one of the first herbs to reappear the following season–often in January. Although a freeze may cause a setback, a few warm days will see it poke its head out once again.

It dismayed me to harvest most of my first plant when the recipe for sorrel soup required 10 cups of the leaves, but within a few days, the plant had miraculously sprouted new leaves; in fact, the more it is picked, the faster sorrel grows. Like spinach, however, sorrel shrivels and reduces drastically when cooked, so it's a good thing it rejuvenates so quickly! When harvesting sorrel, simply cut off the individual leaves as needed, preferably from the center of the plant.

There are many varieties of sorrel, ranging from the smaller leafed and more sour tasting wild docks to the less acidic and broader leafed cultivated ones. French sorrel (*Rumex scutatus*) with its fleshy, heart-shaped leaves is the favored species for cooking and is more tolerant of dry conditions. Blonde de Lyon, with its thick, large leaves that fare well in warm weather, and Belleville de Chambourcy, another large-leafed French variety, are now available in many seed catalogs. Seeds germinate rapidly; sow directly in rich, well-draining (preferably acidic) soil in rows 1–1½ feet apart, and thin to 8–10 inches apart. I generally plant seeds in mid September

and again in February or simply purchase a few plants at the nursery. Keeping the seedlings well watered and partially shaded in warm weather is imperative. Also, sorrel may be propagated by division of the clump in very early spring or in fall.

Sorrel is a most attractive plant that has purpose as an ornamental or border plant as well as in the kitchen. It grows in large rosette-like clumps with bright green, glossy leaves that may be broad and oval or have pronounced arrowhead or shield-shaped leaves. The more common or "wild" garden sorrel, *Rumex acetosa*, has leaves that are arrow-shaped at the base and has somewhat reddish stems. You will find discrepancy in seed catalogs and herb books as to which in *Rumex scutatus* and which is *R. acetosa;* fortunately, both impart the welcome lemony tang. In the summertime, sorrel plants send up a flower stalk with tight clusters of green flowers that ripen to a rusty brown and may be used in flower arrangements. Make sure to keep this stalk cut off at the base to keep the plant from going to seed and to keep the leaves tasting succulent.

This perennial produces well for about 3 or 4 years but should then be dug up and replaced, for it tends to rob the soil of nutrients. Rich in Vitamins A and C, potassium, and calcium, sorrel supplies the body wth essential vitamins and minerals, and its inherent potash salt supplies flavor for those on salt-restricted diets; however, as is true of all plants that produce oxalic acid, sorrel should be consumed with moderation. Like spinach and other highly oxalic vegetables, sorrel should always be cooked in an enamel or stainless steel pot, and a stainless steel knife should be used when chopping it to prevent darkening of the blade. A French friend told me that she rubs sorrel leaves on copper pots to brighten them and makes a strong infusion of the leaves to remove stains from linens.

Although the young, tender leaves taste best in salads, the larger leaves may be used in soups and sauces. One note of caution: the thick midrib vein must be removed before cooking, as it gives a hairy consistency. (Fold large leaves in half and cut fleshy part away from the midrib.)

A chiffonade of sorrel makes a tasty addition to soups or salads and may be used in sauces. I particularly like to steam spinach and sorrel together and serve them with butter and finely chopped scallions. Bright green flecks of chopped sorrel look appealing and give a lively spark to potato or tuna salads. For centuries in England, a thick green sorrel sauce has accompanied lamb, veal, and fish; a more delicate version made with butter and cream similarly enhances poached fish and baked chicken. And homemade mayonnaise flavored with freshly chopped sorrel and green onions perfectly complements seafood or chicken salads.

So try a handful of sorrel leaves torn into bite-sized pieces in your next spinach salad, or a sorrel chiffonade in garden-fresh pea soup. Grinding a few tender leaves in the blender with some cucumber slices and tomato juice makes a great pick-me-up cocktail. Indeed, sorrel is a versatile herb brimming with flavor! This pretty plant will unfurl its bright green leaves in the garden almost year round, an especially welcome sight in the dreary winter.

FRENCH SORREL SOUP

The lively lemony tang of this sprightly soup promises spring on a cold winter evening. It's delicious served hot or cold, preferably in a bowl that will contrast with its rich herbal green color.

5 cups fresh sorrel, tightly packed

½ stick butter

1 medium shallot, chopped

1 medium leek, white part only, chopped

1 medium onion, chopped

2 medium white potatoes, peeled and chopped

4 cups rich chicken stock [*for recipe, see Cooking Tips chapter*]

1 tablespoon fresh thyme (preferably lemon thyme), finely chopped

Salt to taste

½ teaspoon white pepper, freshly ground

¼ teaspoon crushed dried red chile pepper (optional)

2 tablespoons chopped fresh marjoram

2 tablespoons chopped fresh parsley

2 tablespoons chopped fresh dill (optional)

⅓ cup green peas, frozen

Freshly grated nutmeg to taste

Lemon slices for garnish

Optional garnishes: sorrel butter [*see chapter on herb butters*], fresh dill
    sprigs, sour cream, chives, chiffonade of sorrel, 2 boiled shrimp per bowl

Fold sorrel leaves in half and trim away the thick midrib. Slice the leaves into chiffonade to make 5 cups tightly packed. Set aside. In a stock pot, slowly sauté the onions, shallot, and leek in the butter until slightly translucent. In batches, add the sorrel chiffonade and toss until wilted. (It will lose its bright green color and reduce greatly.) Add the potatoes, stock, thyme, salt, pepper, amd crushed chile. Bring to a boil; reduce heat and simmer 20 minutes. Add the fresh herbs and peas, adjust seasonings, and simmer 10 more minutes. Purée in batches in a blender. Return to simmer, and sprinkle with freshly grated nutmeg and white pepper. Serve with a sorrel butter curl and a lemon slice, and garnish with sorrel chiffonade; or serve chilled with a dollop of sour cream and some of the optional garnishes. Tastes best made a day in advance. Serves 4–6.

NOTE: See Cooking Tips chapter for instructions on making a chiffonade of herbs.

▼▼▼▼▼▼▼▼▼▼▼▼▼▼▼▼▼▼▼▼▼▼▼▼▼▼▼

▲▲▲▲▲▲▲▲▲▲▲▲▲

SPICY SHRIMP AND SORREL SALAD

▼▼▼▼▼▼▼▼▼▼▼▼▼▼▼

I like serving this beautiful salad as a main dish in the springtime. The lemony tartness of sorrel complements the spicy shrimp and avocado. In Southeast Asian tradition, encourage guests to wrap shrimp and vegetables inside a lettuce leaf with a piece of sorrel and a garlic chive, then drizzle with extra dressing. Serve with ice cold beer.

THE SHRIMP
▼▼▼▼▼

2 tablespoons fresh lime juice

2 large cloves garlic, minced

1 teaspoon fresh ginger, minced

Salt and pepper to taste

¼ teaspoon crushed dried red chile pepper

2 tablespoons safflower oil

2 teaspoons Oriental sesame oil

1 pound medium shrimp, shelled and deveined

Mix ingredients (except shrimp) in a glass dish. Add shrimp, gently tossing to coat well. Marinate at least 30 minutes, tossing occasionally. Set aside, chill.

SPICY LIME DRESSING
▼▼▼▼▼▼▼▼▼▼

½ cup Chinese Five vinegar *or* rice wine vinegar [*see chapter on herb vinegars*]

4 tablespoons fresh lime juice

1 teaspoon freshly grated ginger

2–4 cloves garlic, minced

1–2 red serrano chiles, thinly sliced

1½ teaspoons (or more) honey

1 tablespoon best quality fish sauce (optional)

¼ teaspoon crushed dried red chile pepper (optional)

Combine all ingredients and set aside. Keeps several days and may be made in advance. Remaining dressing may be used as a marinade for shrimp or drizzled over seafood salads.

▼▼▼▼▼▼▼▼▼▼▼▼▼▼▼▼▼▼▼▼▼▼▼▼▼▼

THE SALAD
▼▼▼▼▼

3 small, tender sorrel leaves per serving

4 large bibb or Boston lettuce leaves per serving

1 medium red onion, sliced into thin rings

1 small cucumber, unpeeled, tined, and sliced

2 limes, sliced

3 small carrots, grated

2 avocados, cut into wedges and drizzled with fresh lime juice

1 small handful mung bean sprouts per serving

1 tablespoon toasted sesame seeds per serving [*for toasting instructions, see Cooking Tips chapter*]

1 tablespoon chiffonade of sorrel per serving [*for chiffonade instructions, see Cooking Tips chapter*]

3–4 fresh mint springs per serving

3 (or more) long garlic chives per serving

Bring shrimp to room temperature and preheat broiler. Arrange the sorrel and lettuce leaves attractively on 4 large chilled salad plates. Evenly distribute the red onion rings, cucumber and lime slices; arrange the grated carrots, avocado wedges, and mung bean sprouts in clusters.

Place the shrimp in a small, foil-lined broiler pan and place under the broiler for about a minute per side, basting as you turn, until shrimp are slightly curled. Do not overcook! Mound shrimp in the center of each salad, sprinkle with toasted sesame seeds and chiffonade of sorrel. Garnish with mint sprigs and garlic chives. Drizzle each salad with the dressing and pass remaining dressing at the table. Serves 4.

NOTE: Chinese Five vinegar adds a great deal of flavor to this dressing, so if you're using rice wine vinegar instead, you may want to increase the chile, garlic, and ginger. Sometimes I pass a bowl of cooked vermicelli noodles, room temperature; a few teaspoons may be wrapped in the lettuce with shrimp and vegetables for a more substantial dish. If desired, substitute grilled fish or chicken for the shrimp. If sorrel is unavailable, substitute Napa or Savoy cabbage for color, and increase mint. Cilantro may be used as well.

▼◆▼◆▼◆▼◆▼◆▼◆▼◆▼◆▼◆▼◆▼◆▼◆▼◆▼◆▼◆▼◆▼◆▼

SORREL-WRAPPED SALMON WITH LEMONY BEURRE BLANC

Ron Estill has cooked in some of Austin's finest restaurants. During an improvisational evening in my kitchen, we produced this elegant yet easy dish—rosy salmon wrapped in sorrel leaves in a golden, lemony beurre blanc sauce with flecks of green sorrel. Don't worry if this sauce seems quite tart when you taste it during cooking; with the salmon, it's perfect.

2 12-ounce salmon steaks, split through the bone lengthwise to form
    4 fillets

4 teaspoons oil

Salt and pepper

4 sorrel leaves, midribs removed and halved lengthwise

8 long chives

BEURRE BLANC
▼◆▼◆▼◆▼◆▼◆

½ cup fresh lemon juice

3 tablespoons minced shallots

2 tablespoons Lovely Lemon vinegar *or* white wine vinegar [*see chapter
    on herb vinegars*]

1 stick butter

Salt and pepper

¼ cup chiffonade of sorrel [*for instructions on herb chiffonade, see Cook-
    ing Tips chapter*]

Thin lemon slices for garnish

Preheat broiler. Place the lemon juice, shallots, and vinegar in a small saucepan; cook over medium-high heat until liquid is reduced by slightly more than half. Over very low heat, swirl in the butter, a tablespoon at a time, to obtain a creamy consistency. Salt and pepper to taste and keep warm in a thermos or *bain marie* until serving.

In a broiler pan, drizzle the oil over the salmon fillets, making sure to coat both sides as well as the pan. Sprinkle both sides with salt and pepper. Place 4 inches from heat and broil 6 minutes, or until salmon is firm and skin is crispy on the edges.

Quickly wrap 2 halves of each sorrel leaf around the center of each fillet with 2 chives sticking out, and place on plates (or cut fillets into appetizer size servings). Add the chiffonade to the sauce and spoon sauce on the plate to the side of salmon. Garnish with lemon wedges. Serves 4.

NOTE: Work quickly when preparing this dish, as sorrel loses its bright green color when exposed to heat. I usually broil the salmon while the sauce is reducing; however, the sauce may be made several hours earlier (without the sorrel chiffonade) and kept warm in a thermos. This sauce also tastes good with broccoli, asparagus, and any grilled fish. If a less tart sauce is desired, substitute ¼ cup white wine and ¼ cup lemon juice for the ½ cup lemon juice in the recipe.

THYME

Thymus species
Lamiaceae (Labiatae) family

Three thymes contrasted in a clay pot. (*Clockwise*) Silver thyme, green lemon thyme, golden variegated lemon thyme.

Common Names:
French thyme; English thyme; and assorted varieties

Characteristics:
upright and prostrate varieties; small (⅛ to ¼ inch long) slightly pointed leaves–ranging from glossy dark green to wooly silver or variegated green and gold–are highly aromatic; woody stems; tiny star-like flowers bloom throughout the summer in shades from crimson to pink or white; perennial

Conditions:
well-draining soil imperative with plenty of sunshine

Size:
ranges from 2 inches to 1 foot high; prostrate varieties may spread vigorously

Propagation:

seed, cuttings, or root division in early spring; several varieties per garden suggested

Fertilizer:

none required; smaller leaves yield most flavor

Pests:

quite susceptible to root rot and fungal disease when grown in soil that is too moist and heavy

Companions:

grows well with lavender and sage; attracts bees into the garden; acts as a moth repellent among linens; repels cabbageworms

Picture Provençe in the summertime: a thick, lilac-colored carpet of blooming thyme is interspersed with wispy silver stems of purple lavender, and the air is heavily perfumed and alive with the intoxicating buzzing of bees. Or envision the English countryside, where thick clumps of matted thyme form lawns, releasing a fragrant, heady aroma when trod upon.

Thyme, the legendary romantic herb of fairies and young maidens, is a most enjoyable herb to grow. Innumerable varieties (and over 100 species) abound much to the delight and confusion of gardeners and botanists. Thyme may have bright green, glossy leaves; wooly silver leaves; lavender-gray leaves; or sunny golden leaves flecked with green. There are upright, shrubby varieties, creeping and sprawling ones, and tiny clumps that nestle between rocks or stones in pathways. Throughout the summer, small starry flowers blossom in shades from deep crimson to rose and pristine white. And varieties with tantalizing aromas mimic the smells of caraway, lemon, orange, nutmeg, pine,

coconut, camphor, and oregano. Fairman and Kate Jayne list 40 different thymes in their beautifully calligraphed catalog, *The Sandy Mush Nursery Handbook.*

But to simplify matters, I recommend members of *Thymus vulgaris,* growing less than 1 foot tall as the best culinary thymes. French thyme, with its narrow, ⅛-inch gray-green leaves, seems to fare the best during our hot and humid summers and has a good, strong flavor. Its shrubby nature produces gnarled and woody trunks as the plant gets old. English thyme's leaves are broader, greener, more oval, and about ¼ inch long. It makes a lively seasoning as well.

When slightly crushed, the leaves of *Thymus x citriodora,* or lemon thyme, surrender a redolence of fresh lemons. The taste is heavenly as well when added to cottage cheese or steaming vegetables (especially artichokes), stuffed under chicken breasts, and used in sauces for fish or poultry. It also makes a soothing and delightful tea. Lemon thyme may be found in upright varieties with glossy, green leaves or with green and gold variegation. Prostrate or creeping varieties exist as well. These may be green, variegated green and gold, or silver. Lemon thyme may be more susceptible to frost (especially the variegated ones) than other thymes. Fairman Jayne says that all variegated herbs are generally weaker and more prone to freeze damage and disease than their solid-color relatives.

Wild thyme, *Thymus serpyllum*, has a creeping, prostrate, mat-like nature and tolerates cool weather. It is attractive to grow, and its flavor is mild. One of my favorite creeping thymes is caraway thyme (*Thymus herba-barona*), a 4-inch-high matting plant with dark green, shiny leaves and bright pink flowers. For centuries, it has been rubbed on beef to impart its sweet caraway flavor. I like to add its leaves to *pâtés* and cheese spreads. Unfortunately, it is a slow grower. Do experiment with growing some of these spreading thymes for their ornamental value (tuck them among rocks in the rock garden) and their exquisite flowers.

But I must warn you. Thyme, like its companions lavender and sage, can be somewhat difficult to grow, especially during hot and humid summers. It is highly susceptible to root rot and fungus, especially when grown in a soil that is too moist and rich. Planting thyme on a sloping hill or terraced rock garden assures good drainage. Thyme likes rather loose, dry soil, as long as it is well draining (and preferably alkaline); in fact, some of the most flavorful thyme is grown under arid, adverse conditions.

Another problem in growing thyme is that gardeners often overlook planting the roots deep enough. As Adelma Simmons, owner of the renowned herb farm Caprilands in Connecticut, says, "Because thyme *seems* to be flat, it is often planted in a very shallow way, is easily uprooted, and the roots burned by the sun before they can take hold." I often place flat limestone rocks at the base of the plant to hold the roots in place.

I learned my lesson the hard way. One spring, I zealously planted several varieties of creeping thyme among the cracks in my flagstone walk. They did fine at first, but the burning August sun was just too much for their shallow roots. That is often the case in growing the prostrate thymes in the Southwest – they miss the sea breeze of the Mediterranean, which moistens the leaves but does not soak the roots. The adverse combination of spring showers and 90-degree days often steams the plants and causes their demise. I must stress the importance of a well-draining soil (try adding sand), and I must admit that the fragrant and colorful blooming thymes have yet to carpet my yard in summertime!

Although *Thymus vulgaris* may be planted from seed, especially when planted as a border, the seeds are slow to germinate. To assure the desired taste, I recommend growing thymes from nursery transplants. Once established, they may be propagated by cuttings, root division, or layering. "As a general rule, the bushy, upright growers propagate best from cuttings, while the creepers divide easily," says Fairman Jayne.

"Also remember," reminds Diane Barnes of It's About Thyme in Austin, Texas, "to keep the woody branches cut back to encourage new growth and to discourage woodiness." Because woodiness is the nature of this plant, start with new plants every 3–4 years for best results. Remember that thyme likes plenty of sunshine and really requires no fertilizer, except perhaps a light application of fish emulsion to get it started.

Thyme is best harvested right before it flowers and may be hung in bunches to dry. Do not harvest too heavily in the fall, or it will be more susceptible to freeze damage. Thyme retains its pungence when dried; in fact, many prefer to use it in that state. Thyme sprigs may be steeped in olive oil with lots of garlic cloves for use in salad dressings and marinades as well as for sautéeing. It also may be used to make a savory herbal vinegar, and wild thyme honey has long been considered a delicacy.

It's hard to imagine that an herb that has been used as a fumigant and as an antiseptic—whose volatile oil, thymol, is an active ingredient in mouthwash and cough drops—could be of such culinary importance. But, indeed, its clear, sharp, and warming pungence is a welcomed seasoning in many cuisines. *Provençal* cooks crumble it over succulent baked garlic drizzled with olive oil, and over crisp salad greens topped with chèvre. Unlike many herbs that should be added toward the end of cooking, thyme has a flavor that may be slowly simmered in hearty beef or wild game stews, soups, and sauces. From peasant fare to *haute cuisine*, thyme lends its spicy flavor. Add the sprigs to *bouquet garni* or throw them on the grill to envelop the meat in thyme's smoky redolence.

Thyme has always been a key element in Creole and Cajun seasonings, as it balances the fiery pepper and spices, just as it does in piquant Mexican sauces. *Tomillo*, as thyme is called in Spanish, is the favored herb for pork and *tomatillo* dishes, hearty *guisados*, and soups throughout Mexico. I tasted an unforgettably delicious soup of Spanish origin in a small, family-operated cafe in Mexico City where, I am glad to say, the cheerful cook shared her recipe with me. Cloves from three heads of garlic were sautéed in oil, then simmered in a tomato-based broth, rendering them sweet and mild. A generous sprinkling of thyme further enhanced the flavor.

A simple dinner may be made by stuffing the cavity of a chicken (or the skin of chicken breasts) with minced garlic and lots of fresh thyme. Dot with garlic butter and a dash of dry white wine, then bake or grill. Similarly, you can insert slivers of garlic and crumbled thyme in small slits in lamb or beef. Rich pâtés also benefit from thyme's fresh flavor.

Baked onions, zucchini and tomatoes sautéed in olive oil and garlic, steamed squash, and casseroles are brightened with thyme, and of course, vinaigrettes and marinades become livelier as well. Or roll Montrachet goat cheese into bite-sized balls, roll in finely chopped thyme (lemon thyme is delicious, too), and pop in your mouth!

Although thyme requires some tender loving care, remember that too much pampering can be detrimental. Overfertilization yields lush but flavorless leaves; overwatering and too moist a soil cause root disease. Remember thyme's homeland: the dry and rocky hillsides of the Mediterranean!

SOPA DE AJO

Three heads—not cloves, heads—of garlic! Don't panic: as they cook, they become sweet and irresistibly flavorful, producing a rich and mellow soup garnished with croutons, grated Gruyère, and fresh sprigs of thyme.

¼ cup best quality olive oil

3 heads garlic with loose skin removed but unpeeled

8 cups rich, homemade chicken stock [*for recipe, see Cooking Tips chapter*]

1½–2 cups puréed tomatoes, skins and seeds removed (best-quality canned tomato purée may be used in a pinch)

1 bay leaf

1 handful fresh thyme sprigs (or 2 teaspoons dried)

2 tablespoons chopped fresh marjoram (or 1 teaspoon dried)

Salt to taste

½ teaspoon freshly ground white pepper

½ cup Manzanilla or other dry sherry

Garnishes: garlic croutons, fresh thyme sprigs, and freshly grated Parmesan or Gruyère cheese

Heat olive oil in a large pan. Add the separated garlic cloves and sauté, mashing them with the back of a wooden spoon; sauté until slightly browned.

Place garlic in a large stock pot and add chicken stock, puréed tomatoes, and bay leaf. Bring to a boil; reduce heat and simmer 30 minutes; add fresh thyme and marjoram and simmer another 20 minutes. Strain soup and simmer while adding salt and pepper and adjusting seasonings; add sherry last, and serve in heated, oven-proof bowls.

Top each bowl with a garlic crouton and large sprig of fresh thyme. Freshly grated Parmesan and/or Gruyère cheese may be passed around the table. Serves 8.

NOTE: In Spain and Mexico, the hot soup is often ladeled over a raw egg (which poaches it). This soup should be rich and slightly thick with a deliciously mellow flavor.

▼▼▼▼▼▼▼▼▼▼▼▼▼▼▼▼▼▼▼▼▼▼▼▼

MARDI GRAS MONTRACHET

Bite-size balls of Montrachet cheese rolled in fresh thyme, golden marigold petals, and lilac-colored chive blossoms make a confetti of colors. Serve as appetizers with a glass of wine and thin slices of crusty baguette, or as garnish for soups and salads.

1 11-ounce log of Montrachet (preferably garlic-herb flavored), cut into ½-inch slices, then each slice rolled into 2 bite-size balls

½ teaspoon chopped fresh herbs per ball, such as: thyme (try several varieties, such as French, lemon, and golden variegated lemon); marigold petals; chive blossom petals; chives; marjoram; savory; basil (try several varieties, such as dark opal, lemon, and the smaller-leafed varieties); sage; dill; fennel; salad burnet (press 3 leaves into cheese)

Roll the cheese balls in your choice of several herbs or press tiny sprigs of herbs or small flowers such as Johnny jump-ups into them. May be made early in the day, and keeps well for several days in the refrigerator, although some herbs (rosemary, basil) will darken. Serve on a tray or board lined with grape leaves and bunches of red and green grapes. Yields about 30 bite-size cheeseballs.

NOTE: I often press down slightly on the round balls to form Montrachet Medallions. These look attractive in salads and may be marinated beforehand in olive oil, minced garlic, and cracked pepper. Once they are drained, the remaining olive oil may be used to make a vinaigrette.

THYME ROASTED CHICKEN WITH BABY LEEKS

This is the perfect dish to make after thinning leeks (as well as shallots, chives, green onions, or other alliums) from the garden. Fragrant sprigs of thyme stuffed inside the cavity and under the skin of the bird further the flavor. Not only is this dish simple to make, but it also looks lovely served on a platter wreathed with fresh herbs and flowers. Serve hot or cold slices accompanied by bread and zesty herb butter.

1 whole chicken, 3½–4 pounds

1 lemon

2 tablespoons butter, softened

½ apple, quartered

1 large handful tender baby leeks with tops or other alliums such as scallions, unpeeled garlic cloves, etc.

1 loosely packed cup fresh thyme sprigs (Lemon thyme is wonderful in this.)

1 teaspoon paprika

Freshly ground pepper

Salt to taste (optional)

Preheat oven to 450 degrees. Cut 3 slices, ¼ inch each, from the lemon. Ream the remaining lemon and rub about 1 tablespoon of the juice inside the cavity of the chicken and another tablespoon on the outside. Rub the butter inside and out as well.

Stuff the cavity with the lemon slices, apple slices, leeks, and some of the thyme sprigs, reserving some to stuff under the skin of the chicken on the outside. Rub chicken with the paprika and a generous sprinkling of freshly ground pepper.

Place on a foil-lined roasting pan in the middle rack of the oven, and cook for 15 minutes at 450 degrees. Baste, and reduce heat to 350 degrees; bake for about 45 minutes, basting every 15 minutes, until tender and golden. Allow to rest 10 minutes before serving, sprinkling with salt and pepper if desired.

VARIATIONS

1. Replace thyme with fresh rosemary sprigs (decreasing the amount), and use an orange instead of lemon.
2. Use savory, marjoram, or sage instead of thyme.
3. Replace thyme with a combination of lemon verbena, lemon balm, and lemon thyme.
4. Experiment until you find your own favorite combination.

NOTE: Sometimes, I place slivers of garlic cloves under the skin of the chicken with the fresh herbs.

GRILLED SPRING CHICKEN WITH A SPICY RED ONION–POBLANO CHILE RELISH AND SMOKED RED AND YELLOW BELL PEPPER SAUCE

The noted acclaim of Dean Fearing, executive chef at The Mansion on Turtle Creek in Dallas and the Southwest advisor for the Culinary Institute of America, comes from his imaginative combination of indigenous ingredients and his innovative style. This recipe, first celebrated at the Texas Hill Country Wine and Food Festival, makes a light and refreshing summertime meal for friends.

6 (1 pound) spring chickens, split in half, tip of wing removed *or* 2 three-
 pound chickens
⅛ cup olive oil
⅛ cup peanut oil
salt and freshly ground pepper, to taste
2 limes
2 lemons
juice from 2 limes and 2 lemons

Preheat grill.

Combine both oils for basting.

Season all chicken (inside and out) with salt and pepper.

Brush oil over all chicken and grill to your own specification, baste with remaining oil.

After chickens are grilled, brush with the juice from lime and lemon.

Cover the bottoms of each hot plate with half smoked red and roasted yellow bell pepper sauces. Add chickens to the middle of plates and garnish with relish.

SMOKED RED AND ROASTED YELLOW BELL PEPPER SAUCE

4 red bell peppers, smoked for 20 minutes, and 4 yellow bell peppers,
 charred, peeled, and deseeded
2 tablespoons peanut oil
1 onion, small, diced
1 small bunch thyme
3 cups chicken stock
3 cups heavy cream
2 cloves garlic, peeled
salt and lemon juice, to taste

Bring a medium to large sauce pot to medium heat and add oil.

Add onion and sauté until transparent.

Add thyme and chicken stock. Reduce by half (12 minutes).

Add cream and boil hard for 3 minutes. Remove from fire and divide liquid mixture in half. Remove thyme sprigs.

In a small blender add the red bell peppers, the liquid mixture, and 1 clove garlic.

Blend until smooth and adjust seasoning.

Repeat the same blender method for the yellow bell pepper sauce.

SPICY RED ONION–POBLANO CHILE RELISH

3 tablespoons olive oil
2 medium red onions, medium diced
3 medium poblano peppers, charred, peeled, deseeded, and medium diced
1 large clove garlic, minced
1 tablespoon mint, finely chopped
1 tablespoon scallions, finely chopped
2 tablespoons balsamic vinegar
1 tablespoon white wine
juice from 1 lime
salt to taste

Bring a large sauté pan to medium heat and add oil.

Add onions to pan and sauté until soft, but not mushy, about 5 minutes.

Place onions in a medium bowl and add all the other ingredients.

Toss and let relish marinate for 20 minutes. Serve at room temperature.

Pottery by Finn Alban

Herb butters garnished with fresh sprigs of Mexican marigold mint, scented geranium leaves and chive blossoms.

HERB BUTTERS

It's amazing what a splendid flavor herb butters (also called compound butters) can give, adding a gourmet touch to simple dishes. Because they may be frozen for several months, they provide a good way to preserve the herb harvest, lending their summery freshness throughout the winter. A varied assortment of fresh herbs and spices, citrus zest, and liqueurs may be used to make them. Not only do these butters taste delicious on breads, but they also enhance soups, sauces, pasta and rice dishes, vegetables, and any grilled foods. Need something simple to take to a pot luck? Arrange a tray with assorted bread slices and a big crock of herb butter. If you have time, spread assorted herb butters on baguette slices and garnish each with complementary fresh herb sprigs.

Herb butters also add a festive touch to the table. Try making them in wooden butter molds or plastic candy molds in decorative shapes. I sometimes make them in miniature heart-shaped ice cube trays. They are easiest to remove from the molds when frozen first, then allowed to come to room temperature before serving. Serve on bread plates with fresh herb sprigs for garnish. Or place the butter on a scented geranium leaf.

These tasty butters when softened may be stored easily: spread them across a length of waxed paper or plastic wrap, then roll it back and forth to make a smooth tube approximately 1¾ inches thick. Twist the ends and store in the refrigerator, or label and freeze in freezer-proof bags. This butter may then be easily sliced. Try serving a combination of colorful butters with grilled fish, chicken, or corn on the cob.

Packed in attractive jars or crocks, herb butters make special gifts. Fill a basket with assorted breads and one or two crocks of herb butter, or give an assortment of savory butters. Lids may be covered with festive fabric or paper and tied with ribbons or raffia.

Herb butters are easy to make. Simply grind or chop the herbs, garlic, and whatever other ingredients are called for and blend in the softened butter (often wine or lemon juice are added as well). Remember, if you are using a food processor and you have rinsed the fresh herbs, they must be perfectly dry to chop well; do not overprocess. If you are making herb butters by hand, simply cream the butter and the herbs with the back of a wooden spoon. The following recipes include serving suggestions.

▼▼▼▼▼▼▼▼▼▼▼▼▼▼▼▼▼▼▼▼▼▼▼▼▼

SWEET HERB BUTTERS

3 tablespoons sweet-scented herbs (mints, lemon balm, or lemon verbena)

1 teaspoon orange zest (optional)

2 tablespoons fruit preserves (strawberry, raspberry, or orange marmalade are especially good), or honey

1 tablespoon brandy or sweet liqueur such as Grand Marnier, Framboise, or Chambord

1 tablespoon or more chopped pecans or almonds (optional)

¼ pound unsalted butter (one stick)

Delicious with croissants and homemade breads or muffins. Spread on party bread cut into decorative shapes with cookie cutters, and garnish with fresh fruit slices and a fresh sprig of herb.

HERB BUTTER TIPS

Use sweet, fresh, unsalted butter. Salted butter has a longer shelf life, so it may not be as fresh, and some brands of salted butter are so salty that they overpower the flavor of the herbs. I add my own salt and freshly grated pepper to taste.

Experiment with various flavorings such as finely minced onions, shallots, garlic, chives, green onions, and garlic chives. They are interchangeable according to the flavor (and strength) desired.

Citrus zest gives a burst of fresh flavor to herb butters. Make sure that you remove none of the white pith while zesting, or the butter may become bitter.

If you grind the herbs in a food processor and you have rinsed them previously, make sure that they are patted dry or they will become mushy when chopped. Garlic should be dropped in with the motor running. Do not overprocess.

Remember that the flavor of herb butters gets more intense as they sit. If you are going to use a butter soon after preparing it, you may make it stronger, increasing the garlic and herbs.

Because flavors and strengths of various ingredients vary, rely on your own taste-buds and sense of smell to judge. Above all, be creative! Experiment with different herbs and flavorings.

Store herb butters in the refrigerator for 1–2 weeks, or in the freezer for 2–3 months. Butter made with nuts have a shorter shelf life as the nuts tend to mold, especially when frozen.

ANCHO-OREGANO-PECAN-BUTTER

3 cloves of garlic

1 ancho chile, briefly toasted and ground in spice grinder (approximately 4 teaspoons)

2 tablespoons chopped fresh oregano

1 tablespoon gold tequila

3 generous tablespoons chopped pecans

Salt and pepper to taste

¼ pound unsalted butter (1 stick)

My brother keeps me well supplied with chiles and pecans from his farm in New Mexico, so I keep this pumpkin-colored butter on hand to add to squash, corn, soups, sauces, and pasta, and to melt over grilled fish, chicken, or steaks.

BASIL-GARLIC-PARMESAN-BUTTER

4–6 cloves garlic, minced

½ cup freshly chopped basil

3–4 tablespoons lightly toasted pine nuts or more (optional)

1 tablespoon white wine

2 tablespoons freshly grated Parmesan cheese

Salt to taste

Crushed dried red chile to taste

½ pound unsalted butter, softened (2 sticks)

Delicious with corn, whether roasted, steamed, or in corn soup; with green beans, squash, spinach, or baked tomatoes; with rice, pasta, or on sliced baguette (sprinkled with Parmesan); and on grilled chicken or fish.

SPICY CILANTRO BUTTER

3–4 cloves garlic, minced

4 generous tablespoons chopped fresh cilantro

1 or 2 jalapeños *or* 1 serrano chile (preferably red), seeded and finely chopped

1 teaspoon lime zest

2–3 teaspoons fresh lime juice

Salt to taste

Crushed dried red chile to taste

¼ pound unsalted butter (1 stick), softened

Wonderful with grilled or broiled fish, shrimp, or steak; pasta; rice (add curry powder, pecans, and green onions); and squash, corn, or eggplant. Roll corn on the cob in this butter, then sprinkle with fresh lime juice and freshly grated Parmesan.

DILLY BUTTER

1 green onion with tops *or* 1 medium shallot, minced

4 generous tablespoons chopped fresh dill

½ teaspoon lemon zest (optional)

¼ teaspoon dried mustard

2 teaspoons fresh lemon juice or white wine

2 teaspoons chopped fresh chives (optional)

Salt and freshly ground white pepper to taste

1 hard-boiled egg, yolk and white ground separately with a Mouli grinder or ricer, (optional)

¼ pound unsalted butter (1 stick), softened

When using the hard-boiled egg, mix the yolk with the butter and other ingredients. Gently blend in the whites at the end. Add a generous pat of this butter to grilled fish or chicken; steamed cauliflower or broccoli; baked, roasted, or sautéed potatoes. Swirl into carrot, beet, potato, or sorrel soups, and spread it on cucumber sandwiches made with dark bread.

FABULOUS FENNEL BUTTER WITH PERNOD

1 green onion with top, finely chopped (optional)

4 generous tablespoons finely chopped fennel leaves

1 teaspoon orange zest (optional)

Salt and freshly ground white pepper to taste

1 tablespoon Pernod or dry vermouth

¼ pound unsalted butter (1 stick), softened

Fabulous with fish, especially when grilled wrapped in fennel leaves; delicious with cauliflower, broccoli, or potatoes; add to Portuguese white bean and sausage soup and fish chowders. Good on black bread.

ELEGANT LEMON BALM BUTTER

⅓ cup lightly toasted almonds, crushed

½ tightly packed cup chopped lemon balm (some lemon thyme, lemon verbena or lemon basil may be used)

1 teaspoon lemon zest

1 tablespoon lemon juice (or more)

Salt and freshly ground white pepper to taste

½ pound unsalted butter (2 sticks), softened

Tastes truly elegant with any steamed or sautéed vegetable, especially asparagus and new potatoes; with fish or chicken; and with croissants. This recipe may be halved.

▼▼▼▼▼▼▼▼▼▼▼▼▼▼▼▼▼▼▼▼▼▼▼▼▼▼▼

LUSCIOUS LEMON BASIL BUTTER

Follow instructions for basil-garlic-Parmesan butter halfing the recipe. If desired, use 1 or 2 green onions instead of the garlic; substitute lemon basil (some lemon verbena or lemon thyme may be used also) for the basil in the recipe; also use 1 tablespoon fresh lemon juice instead of wine and omit chile. Heavenly in rice and pasta dishes, over any steamed vegetable (especially artichokes), in soups, and over fish or chicken.

MEXICAN MARIGOLD MINT BUTTER

1–2 green onions with tops, or 1 medium shallot, finely chopped

2–3 tablespoons finely chopped Mexican marigold mint leaves (some of the golden petals may be used as well)

½ teaspoon orange zest (optional)

2–3 teaspoons fresh orange juice *or* white wine *or* dry vermouth

1–2 tablespoons chopped pecans or more (optional)

Salt and white pepper to taste

¼–½ teaspoon dried mustard (optional)

¼ pound (1 stick) unsalted butter, softened

This tasty butter complements fish and fowl, grilled or baked, and is especially good with quail. Try it with steamed sweet potatoes or carrots; use it in stuffings and sauces. Garlic may be substituted for green onions.

FRESH MINT BUTTER

4 tablespoons chopped fresh mint
1 teaspoon or more honey
3 teaspoons or more fresh orange juice
1 teaspoon orange zest
Salt and freshly ground white pepper to taste
¼ pound unsalted butter, (softened)

This butter tastes wonderful on steamed peas or carrots. Often, I add chopped shallot, garlic, or green onion, omit the honey, and substitute fresh lemon juice and zest for the orange. I usually add some crushed dried red chile and use it with fish (especially salmon), lamb, or new potatoes.

TEQUILA OREGANO BUTTER

4 or more cloves garlic, minced
½ generous cup chopped fresh oregano
2 tablespoons chopped parsley
½ teaspoon crushed dried red chile pepper
2 teaspoons chopped fresh chives
1 tablespoon or more gold tequila
Salt and pepper to taste
½ pound unsalted butter (2 sticks), softened

This butter is one of my favorites. Serve with zucchini and corn dishes; rice, pasta, or bread; and especially on grilled fish, chicken, or steak.

REGAL ROSEMARY BUTTER

2–3 cloves garlic, minced

3 teaspoons fresh rosemary leaves, removed from stem

½ teaspoon orange or lemon zest

1 tablespoon white wine *or* orange juice *or* lemon juice

¼ teaspoon or more crushed dried red chile pepper (optional)

Salt and pepper to taste

¼ pound unsalted butter (1 stick), softened

Try a dab of this melted on steak, lamb chops, or veal. Also excellent with fish, chicken, and potatoes.

SAVORY SAGE BUTTER

1 tablespoon finely chopped onion

4 tablespoons freshly chopped sage

2 tablespoons finely chopped peeled apple

2 teaspoons lemon juice *or* white wine

Salt and pepper to taste

¼ pound (1 stick) unsalted butter, softened

This butter tastes wonderful rubbed on chicken and other fowl before baking, as well as on grilled fish or chicken. Use in stuffings and sauces and on potatoes.

GREEN SORREL BUTTER

2 tablespoons minced shallots
1 loose cup watercress leaves
1 loose cup chiffonade of sorrel [*for chiffonade, see Cooking Tips chapter*]
½ teaspoon dried mustard
1 tablespoon fresh lemon juice *or* white wine
2 tablespoons chopped fresh chives
Salt and pepper to taste
½ pound unsalted butter (2 sticks), softened
Salt and pepper to taste

Try this melted over fish or chicken; fabulous with asparagus, artichokes, and other steamed vegetables. Also swirl into soups, especially sorrel soup and fish chowders. Recipe may be halved.

Jewel-like bottles of vinegar on a windowsill.

HERB VINEGARS

Bottles of vinegars preserve the herb harvest in jewel-like colors of ruby, amber, and garnet, a delightful sight in glistening bottles on the sills of sunny kitchen windows. These vinegars, made throughout the summer and fall, make unusual and impressive holiday gifts. I generally make my vinegars in large gallon glass jars, then strain them into smaller decorative bottles and I add a fresh bouquet of herbs to each bottle. For further festive touches, I tie dried red chile peppers and herb branches in raffia strands or ribbons around the neck of the bottles, seal them with corks dipped in colorful wax, and paste on handlettered labels.

But aside from their value as gifts, these delicious vinegars add new and exciting dimensions to cooking. Most often associated with pickling, salad dressings, and marinades, vinegar can enliven other foods as well. Instead of fresh lemon or lime juice, I frequently drizzle aromatic herbal vinegar over foods—a flavorful substitute that especially brings out the best of raw and cooked vegetables. Fish and steaks also benefit, and herb vinegars may be used instead of wine to flavor a dish or deglaze a pan to make a tasty sauce.

Herb vinegars give an almost magical uplift to soups, sauces, and stews. Try a generous dash of spicy oregano-chile-garlic vinegar with spaghetti sauce, dill vinegar with beet soup, tarragon or marigold mint vinegar in béarnaise sauce. Even beverages may be enhanced: a dash of basil vinegar in tomato juice or Bloody Marys; lemon vinegar in pineapple juice; mint vinegar in apple juice. Somehow, vinegar just seems to give the right balancing touch. Accidental oversalting can sometimes be remedied with a generous dash of vinegar and a pinch of sugar.

When preserving herbs in vinegar, always invest in the best quality vinegars that you can find: red wine, white wine, champagne, rice, or apple cider vinegars. Distilled white vinegar is simply too harsh. These vinegars may be purchased in gallons at restaurant supply and specialty food stores. Eventually, you may choose to make your own vinegar by saving the dregs of good bottles of wine and purchasing a vinegar culture.

Always use an enamel or stainless steel pan when heating vinegar, as aluminum will react adversely with it; neither should you use metal lids or canning tops, funnels, spoons, or strainers. Sterilize jars and bottles by the traditional canning method or by pouring boiling water into them and letting them stand for 10 minutes; sterilize corks by boiling them and then drying them in a low oven.

Although many books advise placing fresh herbs in vinegar and allowing them to steep in the sunlight for a few weeks, I do not recommend this method for residents of the Sunbelt. While visiting Adelma Simmons' Caprilands Herb Farm in Connecticut, I noticed many gallons of herb vinegar lining the pathways of her gardens, bathing in the gentle sunshine. Unfortunately, our sun is just too hot and direct, causing vinegar to fade and lose its intense flavor, so I make herbal vinegars by another method. I twist or wring bunches of fresh herbs to release their

▼▼▼▼▼▼▼▼▼▼▼▼▼▼▼▼▼▼▼▼▼▼▼▼▼

volatile oils, and cover them with vinegar that has been heated (but never boiled). Then I allow them to steep for a few weeks, stirring occasionally. Next, I strain these vinegars (paper coffee filters give the most clarity, but a double layer of cheesecloth will suffice in a pinch) into sterilized bottles with a fresh bouquet of herbs in each one. Dried red chile peppers, small chunks of peeled ginger, or peeled garlic may be impaled on bamboo skewers; ¼-inch spirals of lemon or orange peel and/or flower petals may provide additional embellishment and flavor. For optimum flavor, these vinegars should be stored in a cool, dark place and used within 6–8 months.

To prevent clouding, make sure that the herbs are free of moisture before you pour the heated vinegar over them. I spray the desired herbs in the garden with the hose in the early morning to remove any dirt, then let them dry naturally. Next, I cut them and take them into the house, where I carefully remove any damaged leaves. I will use the leaves and stems of tender herbs such as basil, dill, oregano, marjoram, lemon balm, mint, and salad burnet, although I often remove the stems from woodier herbs such as rosemary, winter savory, and marigold mint.

I suppose that one could infuse dried herbs in warm vinegar; however, unless you are certain of the quality and age of the herbs, why bother? On the other hand, dried seeds and spices such as coriander, peppercorns, cloves, bay, chiles, fennel, allspice, and dill may be steeped in vinegar to create winter vinegar (about 2 tablespoons per quart). Similarly, these dried ingredients may augment herbal vinegar; add a few teaspoons of slightly cracked black pepper to *bouquet garni* vinegar, or a few teaspoons of dill seed to dill vinegar. When using seeds and spices, they should be lightly crushed or bruised with a mortar and pestle.

The most difficult thing to do when making herb vinegars is deciding which herbs to use. There are many combinations that give exciting results. A single herb may be used or a combination of several. There is no hard-and-fast rule, and experimentation is part of the fun. The following vinegars are my favorites.

▼▼▼▼▼▼▼▼▼▼▼▼▼▼▼▼▼▼▼▼▼▼▼

GENERAL DIRECTIONS FOR MAKING HERB VINEGARS

▼▼▼▼▼▼▼▼▼▼▼▼▼▼▼▼▼▼

1. Gently rinse herbs; shake out excess moisture and allow to dry naturally, or pat dry carefully. Remove any damaged or discolored leaves and woody stems. Twist or wring the herbs to release their volatile oils, and fill a clean glass gallon jar ⅔ full of the herbs. Add other flavorings as desired (peeled garlic, dried red chiles, citrus peel, flower petals, ginger, spices). Ginger and garlic should be peeled and gently mashed with the back of a wooden spoon; spices should be slightly crushed with a mortar and pestle.

2. Heat a good quality vinegar until warm to the touch, but do not allow it to boil. Pour the vinegar over the herbs, stirring well and gently bruising the herbs with the back of a wooden spoon. Cover with plastic wrap or a non-metal lid, and store in a cool place for a few weeks, stirring occasionally.

3. Strain into sterilized decorative bottles, using a non-metal funnel and best quality paper coffee filters or double layers of cheesecloth, taking care not to disturb sediment on the bottom of the large jar. Place a fresh, unbruised herb branch (and/or chiles, garlic, citrus peel, and such) into each bottle for garnish. Cork or cap bottles, and store in a cool, dark place away from direct sunlight. Use within 6–8 months.

4. As in fine wine, sediment naturally occurs in vinegar and will not impair flavor. Red wine vinegar and cider vinegar are apt to develop sediment, as are herb vinegars augmented with spices. Peeled garlic cloves will darken or discolor when left in the bottle. As you use the vinegar, remember to remove or submerge decorative herb sprigs that are no longer covered.

NOTE: A small electrical appliance that peels lemons and oranges in a continual spiral comes in handy.

DARK OPAL BASIL VINEGAR

Fill jar ⅔ full of fresh dark opal basil; the dark purple leaves will turn the vinegar a jewel-like crimson color. Cover with white wine vinegar or champagne vinegar. This elegant vinegar makes a delicious salad dressing, or simply drizzle it over avocado halves. It makes a beautiful pale pink poppyseed dressing. Use it in a marinade for chicken, pork, or veal, as well as in soups and to deglaze pans.

BASIL CHILE GARLIC VINEGAR

Fill jar ⅔ full of fresh basil (experiment with various varieties of basil), the peeled cloves of 2 or 3 heads of garlic, and about 6–15 dried red chiles. Cover with heated red wine vinegar. This vinegar is fabulous sprinkled over slices of garden-fresh tomatoes and may be used to make a zesty salad dressing or beef or chicken marinade with the addition of olive oil. Add a dash to a glass of tomato juice or a Bloody Mary, and simply sprinkle a little over vegetables, steaks, or grilled chicken. Delicious in beef stew, spaghetti sauce, and tomato soup.

GINGERED THAI VINEGAR

Fill jar ⅔ full of fresh reddish purple Thai basil, ½ pound peeled and sliced ginger, and 1–2 tablespoons Szechuan pepper. Cover with rice wine vinegar, and it will turn a lovely crimson color. When straining, reserve the ginger slices and enough of the vinegar to cover them, and keep to use in marinades, dressings, and stir-frys (they store indefinitely refrigerated). Remember to skewer a few ginger slices and add to each bottle along with a Thai basil sprig, once you have strained the vinegar. This vinegar enlivens Oriental foods and wok stir-frys and is also a good marinade for chicken and pork. With sesame oil and garlic, it makes a delicious dressing for chicken salad.

CHIVE VINEGAR

Fill a jar ½ full of chives; a combination of other herbs may be added as well. Remember to use the chive blossoms, which will impart a delicate pinkish color. Cover with white wine vinegar, and use in salad dressings and marinades and sprinkled over vegetables.

DILLY VINEGAR

Fill jar ⅔ full of fresh dill; stems and stalks may be used as well as flower heads and unripened seeds. A few teaspoons of dried dill seeds may be added. (Occasionally, I add the spiraled peel of one or two lemons, along with the peeled cloves of a head of garlic or several chopped shallots.) Cover with heated white wine vinegar or champagne vinegar. After you've strained the vinegar, you'll see that a golden dill flower head looks lovely in each bottle. Delicious to use in a salad dressing or marinade, especially with fish and shellfish. Also enhances potato salad, cole slaw, or cucumber salad. May be drizzled over vegetables, especially broccoli, cabbage, beets, carrots, and cucumbers; enhances soups made with these vegetables as well.

LOVELY LEMON VINEGAR

Fill jar ⅔ full with a combination of: lemon balm, lemon basil, lemon thyme, lemon verbena, root stalks of lemon grass (sliced and slightly crushed). Add spiraled peels of 2 or 3 lemons. Cover with white wine vinegar or champagne vinegar. Once you have strained it, remember to add a fresh spiral of lemon peel to each bottle and a bouquet of the lemony herbs. Use this fresh and citrusy vinegar over cooked and raw vegetables, in zesty salad dressings, and in marinades for chicken or fish. It also imparts a lovely flavor to sauces and soups.

GARDEN MINT VINEGAR

Fill jar ⅔ full of fresh mint. Experiment with a combination of mints. (I find Egyptian mint especially flavorful.) Spiraled peels of one of two lemons and garlic may be added, but the mint aroma is delightful as is. Cover with white wine vinegar or apple cider vinegar. Mint vinegar tastes delicious sprinkled over raw vegetables or used in a salad dressing, and try it in fruit salads. Make a mint sauce with it or a marinade for lamb or venison.

TEXAS TARRAGON (MEXICAN MARIGOLD MINT) VINEGAR

Fill jar ½ full of fresh Mexican marigold mint. (I generally remove the leaves from the stems so the vinegar won't taste too strong or become dark.) Cover with heated white wine or apple cider vinegar. After straining, I often add small bouquets of marigold mint's colorful golden flowers to each bottle. This vinegar's strong, anise-like aroma greatly enhances vegetables and soups. I like to use it in pickling beets and in making a zesty vinaigrette with Dijon mustard and honey. It makes a wonderful marinade when oil and garlic are added for wild game, chicken, and pork. Delicious with seafood salads and in homemade mayonnaise.

OREGANO-CHILE-GARLIC-VINEGAR

Fill jar ⅔ full of fresh oregano; make sure you use a flavorful oregano or a combination of several types (don't forget the Mexican oreganos). Add 2 or 3 heads of peeled garlic and 6–15 dried red chiles. Cover with red wine vinegar. Once strained, impale a few cloves of garlic and red chiles on a bamboo skewer, and place them with a few sprigs of oregano in each bottle. This peppery vinegar makes a delicious and robust salad dressing or marinade for fajitas, steaks, and chicken when olive oil is added. Add some to your favorite tomato sauce, hot sauce, barbecue sauce, and spaghetti sauce. Try it in stews and soups as well.

ROSE GERANIUM VINEGAR

Fill a jar ½ full of rose geranium or lemon geranium leaves, discarding any woody stems. Cover with white wine vinegar or champagne vinegar, and a few teaspoons pure rose water if desired. This makes a flowery and delicate vinegar to use in salad dressings, rice salads, and fruit salads. It also is soothing when poured in the bath.

TEXAS CIDER SAGE VINEGAR

Fill a jar ½ full of sage leaves and only the tender stems (discard woody ones). Add 5 or 6 small cinnamon sticks, 1 teaspoon of whole allspice, and ½ teaspoon of whole cloves. Cover with apple cider vinegar. After straining, garnish each bottle with a cinnamon stick and a sprig of sage. This deliciously spicy vinegar (mixed with oil) makes a wonderful marinade for quail, dove, and other game—especially when honey and mustard are added. Use it in a glaze for ham or pork chops and in a fruit salad with apples and pears.

SALAD BURNET VINEGAR

Fill jar ⅔ full of fresh salad burnet; add some chives or shallots if desired. Cover with white wine vinegar. Salad burnet imparts a delicate cucumber taste and the palest rose color. After straining the vinegar, salad burnet's attractive serrated foliage looks especially pretty in each bottle. This vinegar is simply delicious sprinkled over raw vegetables or used in a salad dressing and is lovely drizzled over fish or chicken. Use it over cucumbers and in cucumber soup.

BOUQUET GARNI VINEGAR

Fill jar ⅔ full of a combination of fresh herbs—making certain that they are complementary; for example, marjoram, salad burnet, and lemon balm; thyme, rosemary, oregano, and basil; or tarragon, lemon thyme, and chive blossoms. Find your own favorites. An exquisite addition is several handfuls of marigold petals, which will create a delicate peach color. Cover with white wine vinegar or champagne vinegar. After straining, fill each bottle with a small bouquet of mixed herbs and marigold petals. This attractive vinegar may be used in salad dressings and in marinades for chicken, fish, pork, or veal. And just sprinkle it over cooked or raw vegetables.

CHINESE 5 VINEGAR

In a gallon jar: peel and slice ½ pound ginger; peel the cloves of 2–3 heads of garlic. Slightly mash 6 lemon-grass stalks (or more) and slice them into 1-inch pieces. Add about 12–15 dried red chiles. Cover with rice wine vinegar. After straining, add a small lemon-grass stalk, 2 red chiles, and 2 garlic cloves impaled on a bamboo skewer. This richly amber-colored and spicy vinegar makes an unforgettable marinade, salad dressing, or dipping sauce.

FOUR FLOWERS VINEGAR

Fill a jar ½ full of a variety of flowers, such as nasturtiums, chive blossoms, marigold petals, and borage flowers. Or simply add flowers to one of your favorite herb vinegars. Cover with white wine vinegar. After straining, add a bouquet of flowers to each bottle. This delicate vinegar makes a delicious salad dressing and may be sprinkled on vegetables.

MEDITERRANEAN MARINADE

Fill jar ⅔ full with a combination of oregano, basil, and rosemary (remove rosemary leaves from their stems). Add 2 or 3 heads of peeled garlic cloves and a handful of dried red chile peppers. Cover with red wine vinegar. After you have it strained, add a small bouquet of the three herbs to each bottle with a red chile pepper. This makes a delicious marinade for lamb or beef and a zesty salad dressing as well. Use it in stews, soups, and sauces.

Oriental herbs. (*Clockwise, above soup*) makrood leaves, chopped lemon grass, rau ram, ginger, chiles, garlic chives, mint and Thai basil in basket.

ORIENTAL HERBS

The influx of Southeast Asian immigrants to the Southwest – especially Thais, Vietnamese, and Malaysians – has caused their cuisines rapidly to gain popularity here. And the subsequent increase of Oriental food markets makes the unique ingredients used in preparing their cuisine more readily available. The provocative and spicy food native to Southeast Asia easily beckons American palates already accustomed to the spirited food of the Southwest. Indeed, Southeast Asian and Mexican food share some of the same crucial seasonings: fiery chiles, refreshing cilantro and mint, and lots of garlic.

But there are other herbs used in Oriental food that also can grow in American gardens. Most of these plants especially thrive in the hot and humid areas of South and Central Texas, the Gulf Coast, Florida and the mild temperatures of Southern California. Many lend themselves to greenhouse or patio container growing, as they require winter protection.

BASILS
Ocimum species
Lamiaceae (Labiatae) family

After spending a few weeks in France, I was desperate for hot peppers and garlic. Wandering into a Thai restaurant on the Left Bank, I literally gulped spoonfuls of the fiery *nam prik*, a slightly sweet and sour table sauce made with fish sauce, fresh lime juice, chopped chile peppers, and garlic. Immediately, the owner took me under her wing and invited me to eat with the family.

My favorite dish was a spicy, rich, and smooth chicken curry flavored with a purple-tinged herb that resembled basil. *Bai grapao*, sometimes called *bai krapow* or Thai basil (also called holy basil or Tulsi basil in India and sacred to the Hindus), has highly aromatic, slightly downy leaves with reddish-purple markings and small, tight clusters of similarly colored seed stalks. The more sun this 3-foot-high shrubby plant gets in the garden, the redder its color. Thai cooks use this sweetly perfumed herb with fish, chicken, and beef curries. I find that it makes a delicious ruby-colored herb vinegar when flavored with ginger slices. I also add it to stir-frys and chicken salad, and I flavor a spicy Szechuan sauce with it that tastes delicious with grilled chicken or fish.

Sometimes a basil with sprawling branches and pale green hairy leaves and stems (attaining about 2 feet in height) is also called holy basil. Its lavender flowers bloom all summer and it is a rampant self-seeder. The sweet leaves remind me of overripe apples and often have a rank and pungent odor. They are traditionally used in stir-frys and curries. This plant readily reseeds and becomes a volunteer in the garden the following season.

Thai and Vietnamese use basil, cilantro, mint, and mung bean sprouts as edible garnish, often setting a platter piled high with these refreshing herbs on the table. They are then added to rice and noodle dishes and envelop various spicy fillings to serve as wrappers. The famed *nam prik* sauce (and the similar *nuoc cham* in Vietnamese cuisine) is often drizzled over the herbs, then eaten as a salad.

One of my favorite Vietnamese appetizers, *chá giò*, is made by rolling minced pork, water chestnuts, crabmeat, and vegetables inside thumb-sized rice paper wrappers. They are fried until slightly crisp and golden, then wrapped in lettuce leaves with sprigs of cilantro, basil, and mint, then dunked into *nuoc cham*. The fresh herbs provide a refreshing foil to the hot chiles, adding texture and color as well.

Other varieties of basil favored by Thais include cinnamon and anise-scented basils [*see chapter on basil*]. Marilyn Hampstead, founder of Fox Hill Farm in Michigan, says that Thais also use *Thrysiflora* basil, one that she features in her extensive catalog. This basil has a unique pyramid shape with silky green leaves and a very sweet perfumed flavor.

For more information, see chapter on basil.

CHINESE CHIVES
Allium tuberosum
Liliaceae family

Look for bundles of these chives for sale in Oriental markets. They make a peppy addition to stir-frys, but overcooking diminishes their flavor. Chinese chives, often called garlic chives or *gow choy*, have a mild, garlicky flavor. Their lovely star-like white blossoms may be used as garnish and tossed in salads or stir-frys.

For more information, see chapter on chives.

CHINESE PARSLEY
Coriandrum sativum
Apiaceae (Umbelliferae) family

Like mint and basil, coriander (better known as cilantro in the Southwest) has a cooling and balancing effect on the chiles, ginger, and garlic used in Chinese and Southeast Asian foods. It usually accompanies mint, basil, and mung beans on garnish platters at Thai and Vietnamese meals. It also garnishes soups, stir-frys, and rice or noodle dishes. Chinese, Thais, and Vietnamese all have a variation of a whole crispy fried fish in a sweet hot chile sauce liberally sprinkled with fresh cilantro. Thai cooks use the flavorful roots in marinades and curries, and coriander seeds are ground into the renowned Thai curry pastes. A nutritious plant, coriander is rich in vitamins A and C, iron, and calcium.

For more information, see chapter on cilantro.

LEMON GRASS
Cymbopogon citratus
Poaceae (Gramineae) family

Once, a visitor to my garden asked, "Why do you have Johnson grass growing in your garden?" Indeed, this tall clump of reed-like leaves resembles the invasive weed. It has grayish-green spear-shaped leaves that are 2–3 feet long, and rough to the touch, but it is the slightly enlarged, bulbous and juicy base that is highly esteemed, especially in Thai and Vietnamese cuisines.

Oriental markets usually stock bunches of the fibrous stalks, and if you are fortunate enough to find one with its roots still intact, it may be planted in a rich, well-draining soil. Otherwise, it may be ordered from herb catalogs or divided from an existing clump. It can tolerate full sun, but its roots like to remain moist; some afternoon shade during the summer is preferred. During fairly mild winters, the plant can stay outside with a good mulch, but I generally transplant it into pots in the greenhouse.

During one growing season, the plant may spread at the base to a clump of 8–10 inches. As you dig it up, it may be separated into numerous new plants. I share some of these with friends who own Oriental restaurants, use some in cooking, and repot the rest. In the spring, I plant them outside again. The clumps give good ornamental contrast, especially when grown near a fountain or pond or as a background plant.

New shoots of lemon grass respond well to light feedings of fish emulsion. Aphids can be a problem but may be dislodged with a strong spray of the hose or with sprayings of insecticidal soap.

A sweet and citrusy tea is made from the leaves and bulbous base by pouring boiling water over them and allowing them to steep. To release the flavor of the bulbous base, mash it slightly with the back of a knife, then slice it thinly (only use the lower white portion of the stalk). It gives a fabulous lemon flavor and aroma to marinades and vinaigrettes, although its traditional use is with beef, shrimp, chicken, and hot red pepper stir-frys and curries, as well as a flavoring for soups. When heated, its lemony aroma permeates the air. Lemon grass is a crucial ingredient in Thai curry paste, a smooth, moist paste made by grinding lemon grass, red hot chiles, shrimp paste, coriander seeds, garlic, and other spices with a mortar and pestle. It also makes a lively condiment when steeped in rice wine vinegar with lots of garlic and dried red chiles. Lemon grass stalks may be frozen or stored in the refrigerator in a paper bag.

MAKRUT or MAKROOD
Citrus hystrix
Rutaceae family

Sol Meltzer, author of *Herb Gardening in Texas*, first shared this highly aromatic citrus tree with me. I soon learned that to displaced Thais, this plant is "green gold," as it is often sold here for more than $50. No wonder. When gently rubbed, the richly pefumed leaves release the most luscious citrus scent. Apparently, this plant is so expensive because it is difficult to propagate. But Sol Meltzer solved the problem by rooting cuttings in #3 rooting powder in a light potting medium and misting them frequently. Now, not only is he known as "the herb man" in Houston but also as "the magic man" to his grateful Thai friends.

If you are fortunate enough to find a small plant at a nursery or Oriental market, plant it in rich, well-draining soil. The many branches of makrood host smooth, glossy leaves formed in the shape of an 8 – actually like two leaves growing back to back. And its numerous stiff 1¼-inch thorns can cause much distress: handle with caution! Sol recommends adding phosphorus (bone meal), trimming off the thorns to encourage growth, and keeping the plant staked if necessary. In Thailand, both the leaves and the grated rind of the plant's small, bumpy fruit are treasured, but my plants have never produced fruit.

This plant must be wintered in the greenhouse, although I transplant it outdoors to a sunny spot with afternoon shade after all danger of frost has passed. Also, remember to give it adequate water and regular light feedings of fish emulsion. At this writing, my 2-year-old plants are about 3½ feet tall and may ultimately attain 8–10 feet. When harvesting leaves, snip off each one individually instead of cutting lengths of the branch. Often, fresh leaves are sold packaged in plastic bags in the refrigerated sections of Oriental markets.

Known as *bai makrut* or *bai makrood* in Thailand and kaffir lime to Westerners, the dried rind may also be found in powdered or grated form in Oriental markets and is used in curries, and curry pastes, and soups. Steaming bowls of hot and sour shrimp soup, redolent of lemon grass and *bai makrood*, is a beloved Thai soup, and variations abound. The rich broth is flavored with garlic, fresh lime juice, fiery peppers, fish sauce, and fresh shrimp, garnished with chopped cilantro and green onions. I like to float a *makrood* leaf in each bowl. This intriguing soup is as welcomed on a hot summer's night as on a cold winter's eve.

MINT
Mentha species
Lamiaceae (Labiatae) family

Like cilantro and basil, mint has cooling effects that help balance the incendiary

▼▼▼▼▼▼▼▼▼▼▼▼▼▼▼▼▼▼▼▼▼▼▼▼▼

chiles used in Southeast Asian cuisines. Oriental markets often have many varieties of fresh mint available throughout the warmer weather months.

Thais enjoy a refreshing summer salad of squid or fresh shrimp marinated in fresh lime juice and fish sauce flavored with ginger, lemon grass, hot red chiles, and lots of freshly chopped mint. With cilantro, basil, and mung bean sprouts, mint provides edible garnish for noodle and rice dishes, stir-frys, soups, and salads.

For more information, see chapter on mint.

PERILLA
Perilla frutescens
Lamiaceae (Labiatae) family

There are at least six species of this coleus-like plant, often known as the beefsteak plant. All of them offer important ornamental value in the garden by providing an appealing contrast. Perilla's serrated leaves may be variegated or almost purplish-black, bronze, or green, depending on the variety. The dark purple form, *Perilla 'Atropurpurea,'* sometimes called *Ocimum crispum*, is also known as ornamental basil. Its large, crinkly leaves resemble a popular new basil cultivar, 'Purple Ruffles.'

Perilla can reach 3 feet in height with rather large crinkly leaves and thick square stems. Its pinkish flowers bloom throughout the summer. Plant perilla in rich, well-draining soil in a sunny area (some afternoon shade is tolerated). Although an annual and quite susceptible to the first frost, it reseeds itself, producing many volunteers in the spring.

Perilla has culinary value as well, especially in cuisines of Japan (where it is known as *shiso*), Korea, and Vietnam. The spicy-scented leaves are used to flavor pickles, cucumbers, tofu dishes, and tempura. The Vietnamese often use perilla in eggplant dishes, and its crinkly green leaves often accompany *sushi* dishes, as do its tiny, spicy sprouts. The purple-leafed variety is used to color pickled ginger, and its seeds are eaten as well. I enjoy wrapping the leaves around shrimp, fish, chicken, or beef, then dipping them in spicy sauces.

PEPPERS
Capsicum species
Solanaceae family

The incendiary chiles widely used in the cuisines of tropical countries promote perspiration, consequently cooling the body temperature. There are innumerable varieties with different degrees of piquancy, but generally speaking, the smaller the chile, the hotter. Chiles that grow pointing upwards are reputed to be the hottest. I grow one small, bushy shrub with ½-inch green peppers pointing towards the sun; they are commonly called Thai peppers (a variety of *Capsicum annuum*). They ripen to a colorful reddish-orange and are indeed fiery! Other varieties may be larger and longer, some more *picante* than others. Chiles are freshly chopped or used in their dried forms in stir-frys, curry pastes, and marinades. Fresh chiles are also often artistically carved into flowers for garnish.

Chile peppers thrive in the Southwest, as they require plenty of sunshine. Plant them in a rich, well-draining soil with adequate water and occasional light feedings of manure or fish emulsion. They may be picked green or allowed to ripen on the vine. The available types of peppers that may be substituted for Thai peppers are the serrano and the tiny, fiery chile piquín or chiltepín. Le Marché Seeds International offers Thai peppers in their catalog. Small (2–3 inches), thin (¼ inch), dried red peppers called *japónes* (Japanese chiles) are used whole in stir-frys and soups, in hot oil, and in chile and curry pastes.

Many of my Thai friends plant peppers in pots so that they may be brought inside during the winters – Thai peppers fare surprisingly well indoors by a window. Look for Thai peppers at Oriental markets –

they can be successfully frozen for use in soups and stir-frys.

RAU RAM
Polygonum odoratum
Polygonaceae family

I hesitate mentioning this plant because I have been unable to find nursery sources (except Richters and Companion Plants, where it is known as Vietnamese coriander), but it is often available in Oriental markets, especially during the warm months. Rau ram is a rapidly spreading plant, as long as it is given enough water and partial shade. Its requirements are similar to those of mint, and it roots readily in water. The lower stems tend to get rather woody with yellowing of the leaves, especially if not given adequate water. Keeping the plant cut back encourages better growth.

Rau ram has ¾-1-inch green lanceolate leaves with a unique aroma reminiscent of cilantro. Its scent seems stronger than its taste, and its flavor is milder than cilantro's, with a hint of lemon and a peppery aftertaste. Mary Dunford, founder of Nature's Herbs in San Antonio, says that many who have an aversion to cilantro can tolerate rau ram, and its fresh flavor enhances soups and salads. Vietnamese traditionally eat it – get ready – with embryonic duck eggs. They also serve it with an appetizing salad of shredded chicken, cabbage, and onions drizzled with a slightly sweetened vinegar sauce. Although, like cilantro, this herb may be an acquired taste, it adds as interesting flavor to foods that normally use cilantro and makes a unique garnish. And it often accompanies basil, mint, cilantro, and mung bean sprouts on salad platters at Vietnamese restaurants.

Vietnamese plant specialist Kim Kuebel says to keep this tender perennial in a greenhouse during the winter. It rarely blooms in our country.

▼▼▼▼▼▼▼▼▼▼▼▼▼▼▼▼▼▼▼▼▼▼▼▼▼▼▼▼

▲▲▲▲▲▲▲▲▲▲▲▲

SPICY HOT AND SOUR SHRIMP SALAD (PLÁ-GOONG)

▼▼▼▼▼▼▼▼▼▼▼▼

Foo Swasdee, a Thai friend, shared her recipe for this simple salad which tastes particularly refreshing in the summertime, garnished with fresh mint and cilantro. The delicate citrus flavor of lemon grass soothes the fiery chiles and pungent garlic.

½ pound fresh shrimp, boiled and deveined (*see Spicy Oriental Shrimp Boil*)

½–1 tablespoon nampla (*bottled Thai fish sauce*)

2–3 tablespoons fresh lime juice

¼ teaspoon (or more) crushed dried red chile pepper

3–4 Thai peppers, minced, *or* 2–4 serranos, sliced

½ teaspoon sugar

2 tablespoons chopped red onion

1 generous tablespoon finely chopped lemon grass (use only the white part of the stalk)

1 tablespoon chopped green onion

Lettuce leaves

Fresh mint leaves

Fresh cilantro

Place cooked shrimp in a bowl. Add fish sauce, lime juice, peppers, and sugar; mix well. Toss in the red onion, lemon grass, and green onion. Line a small platter with lettuce leaves, fresh mint, and cilantro. Place the shrimp in the center and top with fresh mint leaves. Drizzle with remaining marinade. Serves 2.

SPICY ORIENTAL SHRIMP BOIL

▼▼▼▼▼▼▼▼

1. Fill a medium pot with water and add 2 slightly crushed lemon grass stalks, 2–3 makrood leaves, several garlic cloves, ¼ onion, 1 stalk celery, 1 carrot, 1–2 dried red chiles, ½ teaspoon seeds, 3 lemon slices, ½ teaspoon peppercorns, and salt to taste.

2. Bring to boil for 5–8 minutes; add shrimp and return to boil. Immediately turn off heat and remove shrimp in 2–3 minutes. Do not overcook!

THAI HOT AND SOUR SOUP (TOM YUM GOONG)

This flavorful soup is my adaptation of several Thai recipes. Tart and tangy lime juice, lemon grass, and makrood leaves complement hot chile peppers and shrimp in a delicious broth, accented with colorful condiments.

6 cups chicken broth [*for recipe, see Cooking Tips chapter*]

2–3 stalks lemon grass, slightly mashed and cut into 1-inch lengths

4–6 fresh makrood leaves

4–6 Thai peppers (or more), mashed, *or* 2–4 serrano peppers (or more), finely chopped

2–3 tablespoons nampla (bottled Thai fish sauce)

1 cup straw mushrooms (canned), optional

¾ pound fresh shrimp, peeled and deveined

4 tablespoons freshly squeezed lime juice

Garnish: chopped fresh cilantro, chopped green onions, slivered serrano peppers, lime slices

Bring broth to boil; add lemon grass, makrood, and chiles. Reduce heat and simmer, covered, 15 minutes. Add the fish sauce and bring to a boil; add the straw mushrooms and shrimp; cook 2–3 minutes. Turn off the heat, and add fresh lime juice. Adjust seasonings, adding more lime-juice, chiles, or fish sauce if needed. Serve immediately, garnished with chopped cilantro, green onion, and slivered serranos. Pass steamed rice. Serves 4–6.

NOTE: For exceptional flavor, reserve the peeled shrimp shells and sauté in 2 teaspoons light oil. Bring to boil with the broth, but strain before serving. Although canned straw mushrooms are traditionally used in this recipe, I prefer fresh mushrooms which may be added at the same time as the shrimp. For a Southwestern flavor, garnish with avocado chunks. Straw mushrooms and nampla are available at Oriental markets, as is lemon grass. Shrimp may be replaced with chicken (Tom Yam Gai) or fish (Tom Yam Fla).

SHRIMP WITH HERBS AND VERMICELLI IN RICE PAPER WRAPPERS WITH HOISIN AND PEANUT SAUCE

This popular appetizer is served at Austin's Sea Dragon restaurant, where the specialties are Vietnamese food and friendly service. It makes a great light summer meal and lends itself to fillings of your own choice: spicy shredded chicken or beef, grilled fish, or grated vegetables.

1 package rice paper (each round rice paper sheet is about the size of a flour tortilla)

1 package rice vermicelli noodles

½ pound freshly boiled shrimp, peeled and deveined; [*see Spicy Oriental Shrimp Boil*]

1 head Boston or bibb lettuce

1 generous handful mung bean sprouts

40 mint leaves (approximately)

8 cilantro sprigs (or more)

8 garlic chives (or more)

Cook noodles in boiling water for 10 minutes. Drain in a colander, rinse with cool water, and set aside to cool. Fill a pan (slightly larger than the rice paper) with warm water. Dip rice papers, one at a time, in the warm water (to soften), then drain, arranging them in a single layer on a clean dish towel. Slice the boiled shrimp in half lengthwise.

For each serving, take 1 lettuce leaf, about 10 bean sprouts, 5 mint leaves, and 1 or 2 cilantro sprigs, and roll up tightly to make a small bundle. Place 4–6 sliced shrimp halves, cut-side up, about ½ inch from top edge of a softened rice paper sheet. Place approximately 2 heaping tablespoons vermicelli on top of the shrimp, then top with one lettuce bundle. Roll the paper neatly, folding in the side edges as you go (like a burrito); when it is rolled half way, place a long garlic chive horizontally, so that it pokes out; continue to roll into a neat little bundle, but do not wrap too tightly, as it will cause the delicate rice paper to tear. Serve seam-side down on a plate with a bowl of hoisin sauce. Serves 4 (2 rolls per person).

HOISIN SAUCE WITH PEANUTS

½ cup hoisin sauce
2 tablespoons lime juice, Chinese Five vinegar, *or* rice wine vinegar [*see chapter on herb vinegars*]
¼ cup cold water
2 tablespoons roasted peanuts, crushed

Mix the hoisin, lime juice or vinegar, and water to form a slightly thickened sauce. Just before serving, garnish with the roasted peanuts.

NOTE: Traditionally, a bowl of hoisin sauce is passed at the table as a dipping sauce. I also like to pass a bowl of Spicy Lime Dressing (see recipe accompanying Spicy Shrimp and Sorrel Salad). Rice paper, rice vermicelli noodles, and hoisin (a thick, dark, fermented bean sauce) are available at Oriental markets. At the Sea Dragon, 2–3 slices of cooked pork accompany the shrimp; I substitute more shrimp for the pork. Be creative, and invent your own fillings!

Mexican Herbs. (*Left to right*) epazote, Poliomintha longiflora (mexican oregano), Mexican Marigold mint. (*Back row, left to right*) aloe vera, Lippia graveolens (mexican oregano).

MEXICAN HERBS

CHILE PEPPERS

Capsicum species

Chiles, like garlic and onions, are crucial ingredients in many of my recipes. In fact, they deserve more attention than space allows in this book. Fortunately, my special friend Jean Andrews has written a fascinating book, *Peppers: The Domesticated Capsicums* with information on everything from growing to cooking, as well as her original color illustrations of the various peppers. I also recommend Diana Kennedy's books *Recipes from the Regional Cooks of Mexico* and *The Cuisines of Mexico* for further information on Mexican chiles.

I grew up in El Paso, Texas, and my younger brother, Stuart Hutson, now raises chiles in the renowned nearby chile-growing Mesilla Valley of Las Cruces, New Mexico. The fresh green chile peppers grown there can be quite *picoso*, often more piquant than their California counterparts called Anaheim peppers. The hot and arid climate in that part of the country allows the chiles to be strung outside in *ristras* to dry. The dried *chiles colorados* (red chiles) are then ready for grinding into thick enchilada sauce. This is made by soaking the dried chiles in hot water to soften, them grinding them with garlic, spices, and some of the reserved soaking liquid. This sauce is far superior to the chile powder gravy thickened with flour or cornstarch, that too often passes for enchilada sauce in Mexican restaurants in the United States!

FRESH CHILES

The fresh chile peppers referred to in the recipes in this book include the small, glossy, bright green serrano chile, which is most *picante;* the larger jalapeño, whose flavor ranges from mild to hot; the pointed, glossy, light green chile verde, often known as the Anaheim, California, or New Mexico chile pepper, which varies from mild to quite *picoso;* and the thick, wrinkly, very dark green poblano, which also varies from mild to hot.

Chiles may be eaten when green or when ripened to red, at which point they are usually sweeter. I especially like to mix colorful chiles whenever possible– particularly the red Fresno jalapeño and the yellow-skinned *güero*. Serranos and jalapeños are generally used raw, while the Anaheim and poblanos need to have their tough outer skins removed. This is done by charring and blistering the peppers, then steaming them briefly until the skin peels off easily.

Poke the chiles with a fork to keep them from bursting, then place them directly on the flame of a gas burner, turning them until evenly blistered; or place them on a foil-lined baking sheet in a preheated broiler 4–6 inches from the flame. I prop an oven mitt in the oven door to keep it slightly ajar, so that I can carefully watch the chiles and turn them frequently. Another good way to char chiles is over the open flame of the barbecue grill.

After roasting, place the chiles in a plastic bag (or to be more aesthetic, a damp dish towel) and leave them to "steam" for about 15 minutes. Then you can easily peel them by removing the charred skin. Do not rinse under water or you will wash away the flavor! The chiles may be frozen in their charred skins, which are easily peeled when thawed.

To make chile *rajas* (strips), peel the roasted chiles. Remove the stem, scoop away the seeds and veins (to decrease the piquancy), and cut into 3-by-⅜-inch strips. These may be tossed with minced garlic and used in *salsas, quesadillas, chile con queso*, stews, soups, and marinated salads, and to top steaks or hamburgers.

If the chiles are to serve as shells for salads or savory fillings, remove the seeds and veins by making a small slit along top of each chile, leaving the stem intact. Marinate them in a garlicky vinaigrette, and later stuff with salad fillings such as guacamole, squash salad, tuna or salmon salad, chicken salad and so forth.

DRIED CHILES

For simplicity's sake, the dried chiles mentioned in my recipes are ones readily available in markets in the Southwest. These include: the chile colorado (New Mexican ristra chile), which is essentially the dried form of the Anaheim or New Mexican chile; the ancho, which is the dried poblano; the pasilla, which has a round tip and a rich, piquant flavor; the guajillo, a long and pointed chile that may be quite *picoso;* and the narrow pointed chile de árbol, which may be used interchangeably with the japón or the dried cayenne, ground in a spice grinder to make crushed red chile flakes. For an even more fiery taste, use the small round chiltepín or slightly oval chile piquín, often volunteers in Southwestern gardens.

Because the size, the freshness, the weight, and the piquancy of chiles vary so, their use is simply a matter of taste. Both dried and fresh chiles may be augmented in a dish by the addition of crushed red chile,

just as the poblano or chile verde may be augmented by the addition of chopped jalapeños or serranos. Do remember, however, to exercise caution when preparing chiles, as their volatile oils can cause distress and serious stinging to the hands hours later. Wearing gloves while handling chiles is one way to solve the problem. I find that rubbing my hands afterwards with fresh lime juice and salt or rubbing my hands with olive oil before handling prevents stinging.

Chile peppers grow well in the warm climate of the Southwest. For further information and seed sources, send for Shepherd's Garden Seeds Chile Pepper Collection; The Redwood City Seed Company's booklet *Peppers: Pickled, Sauces, and Salsas* and their *Catalog of Useful Plants;* and Le Marché Seeds International's extensive chile pepper collection.

CILANTRO
Coriandrum sativum
Apiaceae (Umbelliferae) family

Cilantro is one of the most popular herbs in Mexican cuisine, balancing the fiery chile peppers. There is no substitute, and it must always be used in its fresh form: its refreshing, bittersweet pungence is what gives it character. Cilantro is to Mexicans what parsley is to Americans; however, Americans often send parsley sprigs back to the kitchen untouched, whereas Mexicans eat cilantro sprigs with gusto. Cilantro floats in their soups and broths, is wrapped up in savory tacos, sprinkled over spicy guacamole, and eaten as a salad with shredded lettuce, chopped tomatoes, onions, and fresh lime juice. Emerald green flecks of cilantro flavor the tomato and chile *salsas* found on tables throughout Mexico and spooned over tacos, crisp fried tostada chips, and grilled meats.

Fortunately, cilantro is readily available in produce departments throughout the Southwest and thrives in the garden during the cooler months. Unfortunately, many people have a downright aversion to its taste, so it should be used with discretion when cooking for guests. But then there are we cilantro aficionados who welcome its refreshing and distinct flavor; to us, many dishes are not the same without it.

Cilantro's seeds, called *semillas de cilantro*, or coriander seeds, have a mellow, citrus-like flavor and are not interchangeable with the pungent, fresh leaves. Mexicans use them in broths, soups, and sauces, and often in festive, brightly colored candies.

For further information, see chapter on cilantro.

EPAZOTE
Chenopodium ambrosioides
Chenopodiaceae family

Although not often used in cooking in the northern border states of Mexico, epazote is used throughout Southern and Central Mexico. Because of its tenacious character and ability to withstand less than optimum growing conditions, epazote remains unmatched in traditional Mexican cuisines.

Epazote is popular as well as a medicinal herb; Mexican mothers steep it in milk and sugar to rid their children of intestinal parasites. And it is known to prevent the aftereffects of eating beans. These medicinal values (as well as its accessibility) account for epazote's value as a culinary herb. In her well-researched book *The Cuisines of Mexico*, Diana Kennedy says that the word *epazote* comes from the Nahuatl words *epatl* and *tzotl*, meaning an animal with a rank odor. Indeed, epazote has a potent aroma, smelling to me much like turpentine. But don't let this discourage you! Its pungence and refreshing camphor and minty overtones can lend a pleasing contrast to many foods.

For further information, see chapter on epazote.

ESTAFIATE
Artemisia ludoviciana
Asteraceae (Compositae) family

Estafiate, a willowy plant with downy silver foliage, is used primarily in Mexico and the Southwest to treat stomach ailments, but the leaves make unique and attractive garnishes, especially for wild game and pork dishes. Lining a platter of venison with a wreath of estafiate's silvery leaves makes a regal presentation. Add a mere ½ teaspoon of chopped leaves to rich sauces and gravies made by deglazing the pan with juices of the meat and the addition of wine or other spirits. The sharp and bitter flavor of estafiate contrasts well with sweeter sauces flavored with lingonberries or currants and served with wild game. But because it is quite bitter, use this herb in moderation, reserving it mostly for garnish.

Just as estafiate gives its attractive silvery contrast as a garnish, it does so in the garden as well. It looks pretty as a background plant among brighter colored herbs and flowers and makes an excellent material for dried wreaths. It also tolerates dry and arid conditions, often attaining 3 feet in height. The most common *Artemisia* found in the Southwest is the variety *mexicana;* however, nurseries are more apt to carry cultivars such as Silver King and Silver Queen, which make the most popular ornamental and border plants. If not kept contained, these artemisias can be quite invasive. The plant may be divided in early spring and transplanted into other areas of the garden or shared with friends. Full sun promotes less leggy and more upright plants.

HOJA SANTA
Piper auritum
Piperaceae family (often misclassified as Piper sanctum)

Hoja santa has brought me much joy, and many comments from passersby in my garden. The plant is semi-woody and has new shoots frequently emerging from its base, forming a clump of individual plants. Each plant is multi-branching and hosts large, velvety, heart-shaped leaves (often 8 by 10 inches or more), giving the clump an umbrella-like shape. When rubbed, the leaves release a musky scent reminiscent of sarsaparilla and licorice, which is probably why it is sometimes called the "rootbeer plant." Throughout the summer, strange-looking, slightly rough white appendages appear, actually cylindrical flower spikes about 4 inches long. Other curious characteristics of this plant are its oil glands, tiny, gelatinous balls that form on the underside of its leaves.

Although a native of tropical Mexico, hoja santa grows well in parts of the humid Southwest: the problem is finding "starts." Once established in the garden, the emerging new plants may be transplanted, and the clump has a tendency to spread like bamboo. In fact, it has done so along the river walk in San Antonio, where many of the plants attain 10 feet or more in height. Hoja santa also makes a unique and attractive container-grown plant. I have a clump growing in a large terra cotta pot adorning my patio, and it would look great in large pots around a swimming pool. The plant dies back with a freeze, but new shoots appear in the spring. During a hard freeze, container-grown plants will need more protection than those growing in the ground. Hoja santa tolerates full sun if frequently watered but appreciates some afternoon shade and a rich, well-draining soil.

Besides ornamental value, hoja santa has its share of culinary virtue. I first tasted it in Oaxaca in tamales wrapped up tightly in banana leaf packets. As I opened one, a sweet and musky flavor escaped in the rising steam, and I quickly devoured the moist masa filling laced with tender pieces of shredded pork and a rich, dark, slightly sweet *mole* sauce. In her book *The Cuisines of Mexico*, Diana Kennedy has a variation of this recipe, *Tamales Estilo Veracruzano*, made with a *chile ancho* sauce.

While in Oaxaca, I also ate chicken cooked in a pan layered with hoja santa leaves, then smothered in a spicy *mole* sauce. Cooks in Southern Mexico also tear up the leaves and use them to season sauces, tamale fillings, and dried shrimp and fish dishes.

I have enjoyed creating new ways to use this aromatic herb, especially using the large leaves as wrappers around savory fillings, imparting the unique fragrance of hoja santa. Sometimes I make a spicy, shredded pork filling in a *chile ancho* sauce or slightly sauté squash, corn, onions, and tomatoes, then wrap them up in a leaf and bake until warm. Or I marinate boneless chicken breasts in orange juice, white wine, oil, and crushed red pepper, then wrap them up in the leaves with orange slices, red bell pepper slices, and chopped green onions and bake until tender (basting occasionally). I usually add a fresh sprig of *yerbanís* (Mexican marigold mint), which pleasantly complements the flavor of hoja santa.

My favorite way to use hoja santa, though, is with fish. Fillets may be prepared like the chicken breasts above or smothered in a creole sauce redolent of cinnamon and sweet spices, savory herbs, and peppers, all of which partner well with the sarsaparilla flavor of the leaves.

In any event, this hard-to-find plant is well worth the search.

MEXICAN MARIGOLD MINT
Tagetes lucida
Asteraceae (Compositae) family

Yerbanís, as Mexican marigold mint is commonly known in its native Mexico, is used only occasionally as a culinary condiment for boiled green corn or *chayote* squash. Primarily, it is used as a medicinal tea to calm stomachs and nerves, cure colds, and to alleviate the ill-fated hangover, according to ethnobotanists Dr. Robert Bye and Dr. Edelmira Linares of the Universidad Nacional Autónoma de Mexico. This plant grows throughout Central and Southern Mexico, where it is sometimes known as *hierba de las nubes*, from a Nahuatl word meaning cloud plant, or as *pericón*. The Tarahumara Indians of Chihuahua and the Huichol Indians of Jalisco and Nayarit especially favor this herb and use it in religious rituals. According to Gilbert Voss, curator of Quail Botanical Gardens in California, Aztecs used it as an ingredient in a numbing powder blown into the faces of sacrificial victims to calm them before their hearts were plucked.

Also called marigold mint, mint marigold, or "Texas tarragon," yerbanís has gained popularity as a tarragon substitute, but I find its lively flavor a welcome addition to a variety of foods. Its strongly anise-scented leaves enliven salads, fish, and quail and turkey dishes. Mexican marigold mint also makes a delicious tea. Simply place a large handful in a small china teapot and cover with boiling water; allow to steep 6–7 minutes and serve with a fresh sprig of the herb. I also sometimes add the leaves to orange-flavored tea and find the flavors quite complementary.

Mexican marigold mint graces the garden with cheerful, bright golden marigold-like flowers in the fall. They are attractive in bouquets, as garnish, and in potpourris. If not kept in check, however, Mexican marigold mint can be invasive. A perennial, it is quick to poke its head up in early spring.

For further information, see chapter on Mexican marigold mint.

MEXICAN OREGANOS

One popular Mexican oregano, *Poliomintha longiflora* in the Lamiaceae family, is an attractive, shrub-like plant with small, glossy, and highly aromatic leaves that grow on woody branches. During cold winters, the plant may be deciduous, al-

though it often remains semi-evergreen with a woody trunk.

"I have seen Mexican oregano reach 6 feet in the San Antonio area, although 3 to 4 feet in the norm," Manuel Flores of Native Plant Design Nursery in San Antonio told me. Abundant tubular flowers bloom throughout the spring and summer in lovely shades ranging from pale pink to violet. "It tolerates arid conditions, withstands the freeze, and makes an attractive landscape plant," Flores added. *Poliomintha longiflora* needs a somewhat sandy, well-draining soil and plenty of sunshine, although it can tolerate some afternoon shade. This herb makes a spicy condiment when steeped in red wine vinegar with garlic and chiles, and sprigs of it may be added to the hot coals before grilling steaks. I often add some of the leaves to meat or chicken marinades, and it imparts a lively taste to beef stews and *frijoles* (beans). Its branches, especially when in flower, make attractive garnishes for meat platters as well.

Another Mexican oregano, *Lippia graveolens*, is really in the verbena family. It, too, is a shrubby bush (attaining 4–6 feet in height) with long, woody stems hosting slightly rough elliptical leaves with delicately scalloped edges. These highly aromatic leaves have a taste that is sweet and fruity yet quite *picante*. *L. graveolens* has clusters of tiny cream-colored flowers that bloom almost all year, especially after rains. This is the plant commonly sold in its dried form in markets in Mexico as *orégano*, and it is used to flavor thick and spicy *guisados* (stews) and pots of *frijoles*. But it also asserts itself in pizzas and tomato sauces, sautéed vegetables (especially squash, corn, and eggplant), stews, and marinades. Sometimes I place a large branch of the fresh herb on top of a roast, then wrap it in foil to cook. Hang bunches of *orégano* upside down to dry, then store it in jars and use sparingly as needed (it has a tendency toward bitterness).

Native to rocky slopes, arroyos, and the arid conditions of South and Central

Texas, Mexico, and Central America, *Lippia graveolens* also adapts to home gardens. It benefits from dry, sandy soil, sunshine, and adequate room for its willowy branches. A rich soil and partial shade make it rather leggy and increase leaf size but decrease piquancy. It is susceptible to freeze damage but will generally return from its woody trunk in Southwestern gardens. No insect damage occurs.

Three other Mexican oreganos are members of the *Monarda* genus. Ben and JoAn Martinez of Herb Valley outside of Dallas grow *Monarda fistulosa* var. *menthifolia*, whose aromatic, serrated leaves are favored by chefs in the area as an oregano flavoring and an attractive garnish. The Mozzarella Company in Dallas finds that its unique oregano-like flavor augments semi-soft ricotta cheese. The leaves have traditionally flavored *cabrito*, wild game, and meat. The Martinezes have seen fields of this plant with its showy orchid-colored pom-poms growing wild in the Midwest, where it is known as wild bergamot, blooming May–July. Although this 4-foot-tall plant is fairly adaptable, they recommend growing it with adequate sunshine to prevent powdery mildew. This monarda tolerates more arid conditions (limestone fields are ideal) than most monardas. Although it dies back with the freeze, this perennial will make a welcomed return.

Monarda austromontana's flavor also mimics that of oregano. The leaves of this rather low-growing and fast-spreading plant are elliptical and slightly rough; it is called Pima oregano in the *Native Seed/Search* catalog and has long been used by Indians of Northern Mexico and the Southwest. It fares best at high, arid elevations. The mint-like leaves are best used in the dried form; they are quite spicy with a slightly bitter aftertaste, according to Fairman Jayne of The Sandy Mush Herb Nursery in North Carolina. Still, it may be used in soups, stews, and beans as one would use oregano.

A plant that I recently acquired, *Monarda punctada*, also has an apparent oregano taste and smell. It is a 3-foot plant with purplish square stems and pointed, slightly serrated leaves. It produces lovely pale yellow and pink orchid-like pompom flowers. Use leaves fresh or dried.

For further information, see chapter on oregano.

YERBA BUENA
Mentha species
Lamiaceae (Labiatae) family

Literally translated, *yerba buena* means the "good herb," and it has been a favored herb of Mexicans for centuries. It is used as a simple, soothing medicinal tea to ease stomachaches, headaches, and childbirth, or brewed with cinnamon, clove, and nutmeg to cure *la cruda* (a hangover), according to L.S.M. Curtin in *Healing Herbs of the Upper Rio Grande*. This easily accessible herb also finds its way into food. Mexican cooks often add it to a pot of chicken soup toward the end of cooking; it really gives a surprisingly pleasant and refreshing flavor. They frequently add it to tomato-based soups as well. Yerba buena is chopped and added to *albóndigas*, little meatballs that are usually served in a savory tomato broth.

I have seen many varieties of mint called yerba buena in my travels to Mexico. It is generally a variety of spearmint (*Mentha spicata*), but a smaller, darker green variety than what we usually see growing in American gardens. In Mexico, cooks often use a wild spearmint found growing along streambeds.

One early morning while visiting the market in the Pacific resort town of Zihuatanejo, I encountered a traveling nursery. Strolling through the aisles, an Indian woman balanced on her head a bright yellow plastic tub planted with vigorous sprouts of yerba buena. (She had obviously dug up a large clump of the herb somewhere to sell in town.) As she made a sale, she would lower her cargo and carefully dig up a small clump with a big spoon and wrap it in newspaper for the buyer to take home.

For further information, see chapter on mint.

FRESH CHILES

Name(s)	Description	Size
Serrano	small and narrow, glossy, bright green; hot	1½ inches long, ½ inch diameter
Jalapeño	plump, dark green; mild to hot	2½ inches long
Chile verde, Anaheim, California, New Mexico	pointed, glossy, light green, long and smooth; mild to hot	6 inches long, 1½ inches diameter
Poblano	triangular, thick, wrinkly, greenish black; mild to hot	about 5 inches long, 3 inches diameter

DRIED CHILES

Name(s)	Description	Size
Chile colorado (dried Anaheim, ristra chile)	smooth, glossy reddish brown; mild to hot	5–6 inches long, 1½ inches diameter
Ancho (dried poblano)	wrinkled, deep reddish brown; mild	4–5 inches long, 2½–3 inches diameter
Pasilla	long, slender, reddish black; mild to hot	6 inches long, 1 inch diameter
Guajillo	long, pointed, brownish red; hot	5 inches long, 1¼ inches diameter
Chile de árbol	small, narrow, pointed, bright orange-red; hot	2½ inches long, ½ inch diameter

QUESITOS

This variation on the recipe for Mardi Gras Montrachet gives the tasty bite-size cheese balls a decidedly Mexican flair.

Chopped fresh Mexican marigold mint

Mexican marigold mint flower petals

Chopped fresh oregano (try a combination of Mexican oreganos)

Chopped fresh epazote

Chopped yerba buena (mint) leaves

Crushed red chile pepper (Ancho chile or mild chile colorado are the best
to use, as cayenne or japónes may be too *picoso*. Grind the chiles in a
spice grinder, but do not overgrind into a powder.)

NOTE: Chill hoja santa leaves first to prevent their wilting.

Follow the recipe for Mardi Gras Montrachet [*see recipe in thyme chapter*], allowing approximately ½ teaspoon of the following herbs per cheese ball. Serve on a wicker tray adorned with hoja santa leaves.

▼▼▼▼▼▼▼▼▼▼▼▼▼▼▼▼▼▼▼▼▼▼▼▼▼▼

▲▲▲▲▲▲▲▲▲
MEXICAN MAY WINE
▼▼▼▼▼▼▼▼

Serve this festive wine punch in a large clear glass punch bowl, decorating the base with long stems of Mexican marigold mint, colorful daisies, Johnny jump-ups, scented geranium leaves and the garden's loveliest flowers and herbs. Float them in the punch bowl, too. Whole strawberries, small peaches, and orange and lime slices further the festivity. I like using a blush-colored white zinfandel, but any fruity white wine will do.

4 bottles white zinfandel (chill 3 bottles)

1 cup Mexican marigold mint, stems removed, loosely packed

1 tablespoon coriander seeds

2 pints (or more) fresh strawberries

1–2 tablespoons sugar

1 orange, thinly sliced

1 lime, sliced

1 bottle champagne

Additional Mexican marigold mint and/or lemon verbena sprigs

Heat 1 bottle wine. Remove from heat and add the Mexican marigold mint leaves and the coriander seeds. Cover and let steep overnight.

Strain. Pour into a large (gallon) container with remaining chilled wine. Slightly mash 1 pint strawberries (reserving rest for garnish) with the sugar and add to the wine. Chill and serve within 2–3 days.

To serve: pour into the punch bowl, adding the strawberries (sliced or whole), orange and lime slices, additional sprigs of marigold mint and flowers, reserving some for a garland around the base of punch bowl. Add champagne just before serving. Pour into small cups, each with an herbal ice cube [*see Cooking Tips chapter*], a sliced strawberry, and a fresh sprig of marigold mint.

NOTE: Pineapple sage, lemon verbena, lemon balm, mint, and lemon thyme may be substituted or used in combination with Mexican marigold mint.

PESCADO CON HOJA SANTA

Red snapper or redfish fillets wrapped in sarsaparilla-flavored hoja santa leaves and accompanied by a spicy creole sauce make this dish unusually delicious. Serve with black beans and rice.

6 redfish or red snapper fillets (6–8 ounces each)

6 tablespoons butter, preferably Mexican marigold mint butter [*for recipe, see chapter on herb butters*]

1 tablespoon (approximately) Spicy Seasoning (recipe follows)

6 large hoja santa leaves

1 orange, thinly sliced

6 sprigs Mexican marigold mint

3 green onions with tops, chopped

SPICY SEASONING

½ teaspoon whole black peppercorns

1 teaspoon whole coriander seeds

½ teaspoon whole allspice berries

¼ teaspoon whole cloves

½ teaspoon cayenne

1 teaspoon paprika

¼ teaspoon cinnamon

1 teaspoon dried thyme

1 teaspoon dried oregano

Grind the whole spices in a spice grinder.
Mix in the dried herbs.

▼▼▼▼▼▼▼▼▼▼▼▼▼▼▼▼▼▼▼▼▼▼▼▼▼▼▼

CREOLE SAUCE
▼▼▼▼▼▼▼

3 tablespoons oil

1 medium-size onion, chopped

4–6 garlic cloves, minced

2 celery stalks, chopped

3 bay leaves

1 medium-size green bell pepper, chopped

2 serrano or jalapeño peppers, chopped

1 tablespoon Spicy Seasoning (recipe above)

1 teaspoon brown sugar

1 cup broth

4 large tomatoes, peeled, seeded, and chopped [*see Cooking Tips chapter*]

Salt and pepper

Heat the oil in a large skillet and sauté the onion, garlic, and celery for approximately 5 minutes. Add the bay leaves and peppers; continue to sauté until vegetables are slightly tender (about 3 minutes). Add the remaining Spicy Seasoning, sugar, and broth, and bring to boil; reduce heat and simmer 5 minutes. Add the tomatoes and simmer about 10 minutes. Sauce should be thick. Remove bay leaves. Salt and pepper to taste.

Preheat oven to 400 degrees. Brush both sides of fish fillets with melted butter and sprinkle with Spicy Seasoning. Place each fillet on a hoja santa leaf, cover with ⅓ cup of the Creole Sauce, 2 thin orange slices, a sprig of Mexican marigold mint, and some chopped green onions; roll up tightly in leaf, and place seam-side down in a lightly oiled baking dish. Bake 15 minutes for redfish, 12 minutes for red snapper. Heat any remaining sauce, and serve over fish. Serves 6.

NOTE: The Creole Sauce is wonderful on chicken, in omelets and egg dishes—and even in black beans.

FIESTA TEQUILA

My friends Mercedes Klein and Nick Jones shared this festive idea with me. What a delight at a party: a bottle of gold tequila frozen in a block of ice with brilliant golden Mexican marigold mint flowers, lime slices, and red and green serrano and jalapeño peppers!

1 bottle gold tequila
2–3 limes, sliced
1 large bunch Mexican marigold mint, preferably in flower
6 fresh red and green serrano peppers
6 fresh red and green jalapeños

Place bottle of tequila in a slightly larger plastic pitcher or milk carton. Add 2 inches water, and place slices of 1 lime and several peppers around the bottom of bottle. Press a few long stems of Mexican marigold mint and peppers close to the sides. Freeze until slightly frozen, then fill with water and add more lime slices, marigold mint stems, and peppers in an artistic fashion.

When the ice block is completely frozen, remove from carton or pitcher, and place on a Mexican pottery dish surrounded with lime slices, a small bowl of salt, and small shot glasses. The traditional way to drink tequila is to rub lime juice on the back of the hand, then sprinkle salt on it. In quick succession, bite into a lime wedge, lick the salt from your hand, then down the shot of tequila.

NOTE: Arranging the ingredients in the ice may take some patience; use chopsticks or a long-handled wooden spoon, and make sure that the peppers don't all float to the top. Bright yellow daisies and fern fronds may be substituted for Mexican marigold mint.

TEQUILA MARGARITA CHEESEBALL

This unique and truly Southwestern appetizer is a party favorite, served on a platter garnished with fresh cilantro and clusters of small dried or fresh red peppers. Spread on crusty garlic croutons or crisp tostada chips (for recipes, see Cooking Tips chapter), with Margaritas or ice cold beer. Don't even taste this cheeseball until it has aged a few days; just trust me.

½ pound sharp Cheddar

½ pound mild Cheddar

4–6 cloves garlic, minced

1 bunch green onions, chopped (including green tops)

8 ounces cream cheese, room temperature

Grated zest of one orange

1½ teaspoons curry powder

1½ teaspoons mustard powder

1 teaspoon ground coriander

½ rounded teaspoon cayenne

2 tablespoons gold tequila

2 tablespoons Grand Marnier liqueur

2–3 dried ancho chiles, stems and seeds removed, ground lightly in a spice grinder, *or* crushed dried Italian red pepper

A food processor blends this cheeseball nicely. Grate the Cheddar cheeses, then blend in the garlic and green onions. Add cream cheese, orange zest, curry powder, mustard powder, coriander, and cayenne. Mix well. With food processor running, slowly add tequila and Grand Marnier. Form mixture into a rough ball, wrap in plastic, and refrigerate. When slightly firm, form into the desired shape and roll it in finely chopped dried chile peppers or crushed Italian red pepper. Refrigerate overnight so that the moisture of the cheeseball will soften the dried peppers. Arrange on a plate garnished with fresh cilantro and clusters of small, dried red peppers (chiles japónes). Serve with crusty, garlicky croutons.

NOTE: This cheeseball gets better with age and keeps well in the refrigerator for several weeks.

MENU SUGGESTIONS

Festive Hors d'Oeuvres or Garden Luncheon (*Clockwise*) Basil Torta with Sun-dried Tomatoes; Mardi Gras Montrachet; (*On bamboo tray, right to left*) Salad Burnet Sandwiches, herb butters garnished with flowers, Garden Pesto with roma tomato slices, freshly grated Parmesan and fresh basil sprigs, Mustard and Marigold Mint Chicken, herb butters garnished with flowers.

MENU SUGGESTIONS

A Spicy Southwestern Supper

Queso Fundido with Warm Tortillas
Tomatoes Rellenos
Flank Steak in Cilantro, Citrus, and Gold Tequila Marinade
Velvety Lemon Verbena Flan
Mexican Beer/Fiesta Tequila/Sangría

A Fiesta Happy Hour

Tequila Margarita Cheeseball
Quesitos
Tri-Color Roasted Poblano Peppers
Pollo Picado with Tostada Chips
Mexican Beer/Fiesta Tequila/Sangría

An Elegant Evening

Mardi Gras Montrachet
Sopa de Ajo
Spring Greens Salad
Pork Tenderloin Stuffed with Roasted Red Peppers
Pommes Peabody
Sangría Sorbet

A Special Celebration

Lovely Lemon Verbena Poundcake
Ripe Strawberries and Valentino Cream
Champagne/White Wine/Mexican May Wine

A Festive Spring Dinner

Basil Cheese Torta
Greek Salad
Butterflied Leg of Lamb Laced with Garden Herbs
Lemony Rice with Toasted Almonds

A Savory Summer Picnic

Chicken Breasts Stuffed with Chives and Fresh Herbs
Sliced Baguette with Herb Butter
Dilly Potato Salad
Savory Green Bean Salad
Fresh Lemonade with Rosemary Sprigs

A Festive Fall Luncheon

Golden Corn Soup with Roasted Peppers and Epazote or
Tortilla Soup from Pátzcuaro
Crisp Greens with Sun-Dried Tomatoes, Pine Nuts, Marigold
Mint Vinaigrette
Sangría

▼▼▼▼▼▼▼▼▼▼▼▼▼▼▼▼▼▼▼▼▼▼▼▼▼▼▼▼

SOURCES

BOTANICAL CENTERS WITH HERB GARDENS: A wonderful place to see herbs growing in a natural environment. Highlights of these regional garden centers of special interest to this book are listed.

Denver Botanic Gardens
1005 York Street
Denver, Colorado 80206
(303) 575-2547

Culinary gardens feature many herbs (some Mexican herbs); book-store; annual plant sale/bazaar in May.

Desert Botanical Garden
1201 North Galvin Parkway
Phoenix, Arizona 85008
(602) 941-1225

Chiles, Mexican oreganos and other plants of the Southwest and Mexico; books and gifts.

Huntington Library, Art Collections and Botanical Gardens
1151 Oxford Road
San Marino, California 91108
(818) 405-2100

A variety of herbs (Mexican herbs included); herb plants for sale; books.

The J. Paul Getty Museum
17985 Pacific Coast Highway
Malibu, California 90265
(213) 458-2003

Features a Mediterranean culinary garden; bookstore; call for parking reservations.

Los Angeles State and County Arboretum
301 North Baldwin Avenue
Arcadia, California 91006
(818) 446-8251

A variety of herbs (Mexican herbs included); books and gifts.

▼▼▼▼▼▼▼▼▼▼▼▼▼▼▼▼▼▼▼▼▼▼▼▼▼▼▼▼▼▼▼

Mercer Arboretum
22306 Aldine Westfield
Humble, Texas 77338
(713) 443-8731

Warm weather herbs featured in lovely surroundings.

National Arboretum
The National Herb Garden
3501 New York Avenue N.E.
Washington, D.C. 20002
(202) 475-4865

Holly Shimizu curates two acres of herb gardens featuring over 1,000 culinary, medicinal, utilitarian, and ornamental herbs from around the world; joint project of The Herb Society of America and the Arboretum.

Quail Botanical Gardens
230 Quail Gardens Drive
Encinitas, California 92024
(619) 436-3036

Latin American and Southeast Asian herb gardens—some herbs for sale; formal herb gardens; books, gifts.

San Antonio Botanical Center
555 Funston Place
San Antonio, TX 78209
(512) 821-5115

Hoja santa and many Mexican herbs; garden for the blind; books, gifts.

Tucson Botanical Garden
2150 North Alvernon Way
Tucson, Arizona 85712
(602) 327-9123

Herbs and native crops from the Southwest and Mexico; books, gifts.

University of California at Santa Cruz Gardens
Santa Cruz, California

Intensive raised bed gardens including herbs, flowers, and vegetables pioneered by the late Alan Chadwick can be viewed here; classes.

▼▼▼▼▼▼▼▼▼▼▼▼▼▼▼▼▼▼▼▼▼▼▼▼▼▼▼▼▼▼▼

SEED MAIL ORDER COMPANIES: This is a list of some of the most reputable seed sources. Cost of catalog is noted, as well as hard-to-find seeds pertinent to this book. Common names are used. Consult index for botanical names listed in some catalogs.

Heirloom Garden Seeds
P.O. Box 138
Guerneville, California 95446

$2.00; a unique collection of over 200 non-hybrid culinary, historical, ornamental and rare seeds.

J. L. Hudson Seedsman
P.O. Box 1058, Dept HH
Redwood City, California 94064

$1.00; a complete catalog of rare and unusual seeds (many Mexican herbs such as epazote, Mexican marigold, and chile peppers); books.

Le Marché Seeds International
P.O. Box 190
Dixon, California 95620
(916) 678-9244

$2.00; nicely illustrated catalog featuring gourmet vegetable, herb, and chile pepper seeds; authors of The New American Vegetable Cookbook *($12.95).*

Native Seeds/SEARCH
3950 West New York Drive
Tucson, Arizona 85745
(602) 327-9123

$1.00; herb, vegetable, and native plant seeds for arid regions (Mount Pima oregano, Mexican marigold, Mount Pima anise, Mrs. Burns' lemon basil); books, baskets.

Otto Richter & Sons
Goodwood, Ontario, Canada LOC 1 AO
(416) 640-6677

2.50; many common and unusual herb plants and seeds including Vietnamese coriander (Rau-ram), sweet marigold (Tagetes Lucida), Mexican oregano; gardening supplies; books.

Plants of the Southwest
1812 2nd Street
Santa Fe, New Mexico 87501
(505) 983-1548

$1.00; chiles, epazote and many New World vegetables and plants used by native peoples of the Southwest for thousands of years; books.

▼▼▼▼▼▼▼▼▼▼▼▼▼▼▼▼▼▼▼▼▼▼▼▼▼▼

Redwood City Seed Company
P.O. Box 361
Redwood City, California 94064
(415) 325-7333

$1.00; assortment of Mexican herb, vegetable, and chile pepper seeds;
booklet Peppers: Pickled, Sauces and Salsas *($4.75).*

Shepherd's Garden Seeds
7389 West Zayante Road, Dept. HH
Felton, California 95018
(408) 335-5400

$1.00; a beautifully illustrated catalog with tasty recipes
and hints; ethnic culinary seed collections and chile pepper
collection; many varieties of basil, edible flowers and
vegetables; gifts; author of Recipes from a Kitchen Garden *($6.95);*
tour of demonstration garden in summer by appointment.

MAIL-ORDER SOURCES FOR HERB PLANTS: Price of catalog (often refunded with purchase) indicated and hard-to-find herbs noted of particular interest to this book.

Companion Plants
7247 North Coolville
Ridge Road
Athens, Ohio 45701
(614) 592-4643

$2.00; Vast assortment of plants and seeds; companion
planting chart; source for Mexican oregano (Monarda punctada) and
Vietnamese mint (Rau-ram).

Fox Hill Farm
444 West Michigan Avenue
P.O. Box 9
Parma, Michigan 49269-0009
(517) 531-3179

$1.00; informative brochure and catalog with over 300 varieties of
herbs and growing tips; fresh cut herbs and plants shipped; booklets
including What You Need to Know to Preserve Herbs *($4.00) and*
The Basil Book *($8.25); annual Basil Festival at farm.*

Golden Meadows Herb Farm and Emporium
431 South St. Augustine
Dallas, Texas 75217
(214) 398-3479

$2.00; herb plants; dried herbs; herbal gifts and products; booklet on
growing herbs in North Texas available; herb tours.

▼▼▼▼▼▼▼▼▼▼▼▼▼▼▼▼▼▼▼▼▼▼▼▼▼▼▼▼▼▼▼▼

It's About Thyme
P.O. Box 878 - HH
Manchacha, Texas 78652
(512) 280-1192

Greenhouse address: 729 FM 1626, Manchacha, Texas $1.00; excellent source for Mexican herbs such as Mexican oreganos (Monarda punctada, Poliomintha longiflora, and Lippia graveolens), hoja santa, Mexican marigold, epazote; oriental herbs; native Texas perennials; tour of greenhouses; classes; wholesale-retail.

Nichols Herb & Rare Seeds
1190 North Pacific Highway
Albany, Oregon 97321
(503) 928-9280

No charge for this information-packed catalog; plants; seeds; books; organic pesticides; gifts; source for oriental herbs, non-bolting cilantro, Thai basil and purple ruffles basil.

Rio Grande Herb Farm, Inc.
Joan Loitz
Route 4, Box 157 N
Belen, New Mexico 87002
(505) 864-3122

Over 90 varieties of herbs available to wholesale trade; shipped in New Mexico and nearby states. Send S.A.S.E. for list.

The Sandy Mush Herb Nursery
Route 2 Surrett Cove Road
Leicester, North Carolina 28748

$3.95; a beautifully calligraphed and illustrated catalog with over 600 unusual and common herbs, seeds, books, gifts, hints, and recipes.

Sunnybrook Farms
9448 Mayfield Road
P.O. Box 6
Chesterland, Ohio 44026
(216) 729-7232

$1.00; good assortment of herb plants, seeds, gifts, books, and dried herbs.

Taylor's Herb Gardens Inc.
1535 Lone Oak Road
Vista, California 92084
(619) 727-3485

$1.00; catalog includes recipes, color photographs and growing tips; largest shipper of herbs with many varieties of herbs (organically grown); seeds; tour farm first Saturday each month.

▼▼▼▼▼▼▼▼▼▼▼▼▼▼▼▼▼▼▼▼▼▼▼

Well Sweep Herb Farm
317 Mount Bethel Road
Port Murray, New Jersey 07865

$1.00; Herb plants (many Mexican herbs), seeds, gifts, lectures, tours.

FOR YOUR INTEREST

HERB CONSULTANTS

Culinary and Herb Garden Design
Carole Saville & Melinda Taylor
2936 Briar Knoll Drive, Dept. HH
Los Angeles, California 90046
(213) 656-0515

Design and installation of kitchen herb gardens (view their culinary herb and edible flower garden at Spago restaurant in Los Angeles); call or write for further information.

Herbscapes by Lane Furneaux
6474 Norway Road
Dallas, Texas 75230
(214) 368-4235

Herb garden consultant, lecturer, and herbal symbolism specialist; tour of her garden by appointment.

SPECIALTY FOOD PRODUCTS OF INTEREST TO THIS BOOK

Balducci's
424 Avenue of the Americas
New York, New York 10011
1-(800) 822-1444

Visit this family style European market brimming with gourmet items including fresh herbs, edible flowers, vinegars, spices, cheeses, pastas, etc.; or send for catalog (personalized shopping and gift baskets available); mail order address—334 East 11th Street, New York, N.Y. 10003

Campion Greenhouses
Southwest 42nd, Academy
Loveland, CO 80537
(303) 667-5362

Wholesale herbs and flowers to restaurants (especially Aspen, Vale, Denver area); retail herb plants in Spring; greenhouse located on ground of private academy.

▼▼▼▼▼▼▼▼ ▼▼▼▼▼▼▼▼▼▼▼▼▼▼▼▼▼▼▼▼▼▼▼ ▼

Dean & Deluca
121 Prince St.
New York, New York 10012
1 (800) 221-7714

$2.00; Browse through this shop filled with gourmet products; hard-to-find cookware and implements; excellent custom blends of herbs and spices and many international ingredients; mail order address—110 Green St., Suite 304, New York, N.Y. 10012.

G.B. Ratto International Grocers
821 Washington St.
Oakland, California 94607

Don't miss this catalog packed with gourmet items: olive oils, vinegars, spices, garlic strands, seasonings, ethnic products and much more. Send for catalog.

Han-D-Pac Products
2700 North Piedras
El Paso, Texas 79930
(915) 562-4093

Dried herbs and chile peppers; Mexican products. Send S.A.S.E. for product list.

Mozzarella Co.
2944 Elm Street, Dept HH
Dallas, Texas 75226
(214) 741-4072

Paula Lambert's wonderful cheeses laced with ancho chiles, Mexican marigold, epazote, basil and other exciting herbs may be purchased at factory or shipped (gift baskets also available). Send S.A.S.E. for product list.

Paradise Farms
P.O. Box 436
Summerland, California 93067

Pam and Jay North pioneered the edible flower craze and wholesale their top-quality organically grown herbs and flowers to restaurants and produce companies (also available at some California markets); write for beautifully illustrated recipe booklet ($7.00)

Pepper Tree Shop
912 W. Commerce
El Mercado (Produce Mart)
San Antonio, Texas
(512) 222-9187

Good quality and variety of dried Mexican chiles; dried Mexican oregano, and other Mexican products and cooking utensils. Send S.A.S.E. for product list.

▼▼▼▼▼▼▼▼▼▼▼▼▼▼▼▼▼▼▼▼▼▼▼▼▼▼▼

Select Origins Inc.
Box N
Southampton, N.Y. 11968
1 (800) 822-2092

Fine selection of herb and spice blends (I adore their whole pepper melange), vinegars and oils, and other delectable gourmet items.

Simon David
7117 Inwood Road
Dallas, Texas 75209
(214) 352-1781

$1.00 for mail-order catalog; a gourmet's delight; fresh herbs, edible flower and minature vegetables; exotic condiments and wide selection of ethnic foods; excellent meat market; gift baskets; new store to open in Austin, Texas.

Timber Crest Farms
4791 Dry Creek Road
Healdsburg, California 95448
(707) 433-8251

Fabulous dried tomatoes and recipe booklet; unsulfured dried fruits (organically grown); gourmet products; nuts; send for product list.

FARMS, NURSERIES, GARDENS AND SHOPS: This list is by no means comprehensive, but includes places that relate to the topics in this book.

Blue Moon Gardens
Route 2 Box 2190
Chandler, Texas 75758
(214) 849-6554 or 849-2252

Wholesale to East Texas and Dallas area only.

Caprilands
Silver Street
Coventry, Connecticut 06238

Don't miss this charming farm when in the area. Herb plants, seeds, gifts, programs; founder, Adelma Simmons, author of many wonderful herb books available by mail order.

Gardenville of Austin
6266 Hwy 290 West, Dept. HH
Austin, Texas 78735
(512) 288-5971

▼▼▼▼▼▼▼▼▼▼▼▼▼▼▼▼▼▼▼▼▼▼▼▼▼▼▼▼▼▼▼

Organic gardening headquarters featuring compost, soils, natural pesticides, books, herbs, tools, and plants suited for the area. S.A.S.E. for further information and product list.

The Herb Bar
200 West Mary
Austin, Texas 78704
(512) 444-6251

Quaint store with herb plants, dried herbs, books, baskets, gifts, classes.

Herb Valley
204 John McCain Road, Dept. HH
Colleyville, Texas 76034
(817) 498-6362

Fresh cut wholesale (including Southwestern varieties) herbs delivered in Dallas-Fort Worth metroplex; garden design and installation; presentations to groups; call or send S.A.S.E. for further information.

Hilltop Country Inn
P.O. Box 1734
Cleveland, Texas 77327
(713) 592-5859

Country inn restaurant run by Madalene Hill and Gwenn Barclay (formerly of Hilltop Herb Farm). Call for directions and reservations.

The Hunt Herbary
Route 1 Box 156 B
Hunt, Texas 78024
(512) 238-4944

Wholesale only to Central Texas area specializing in herbs grown in large containers.

Lucia's Garden
2213 Portsmouth, Dept. HH
Houston, Texas 77098
(713) 523-6494

An enchanting herb cottage in the middle of the city—plants, dried herbs, wreaths, gifts, books, and more. Send S.A.S.E. for list of products.

Natures Herbs
2415 Glen Ivy
San Antonio, Texas 78213
(512) 341-1118

Herb plants and fresh cut herbs—many Mexican (oreganos, Mexican marigold, epazote) and Oriental herbs (rau ram).

▼▼▼▼▼▼▼▼▼▼▼▼▼▼▼▼▼▼▼▼▼▼▼▼▼▼▼▼▼

9T Farms
Route 5 Box 72
Ennis, Texas 75119
(214) 875-8369

Large selection of herbs at this nursery; retail and wholesale.

Patty's Herbs, Inc.
Route 1 Box 31 J
Pearsall, Texas 78061
(512) 334-3944

Fresh cut culinary herbs (available at many Central Texas supermar-
kets); flowers and baby vegetables; spring and fall garden tours and
luncheon (reservations); plants; booklet on herbs available.

The Peaceable Kingdom School
P.O. Box 313
Washington-on-the-Brazos, Texas 77880
(409) 878-2353

Non-profit organization teaching classes on all aspects of herbs at
their 152 acre farm; fresh cut herbs sold to restaurants; gifts. Send for
catalog for schedule of classes.

Roger's Gardens
2301 San Joaquin Hills Road
Corona del Mar, California 92625
(714) 640-5800

Fantastic 8 acre nursery with extensive collection of herbs including
many Mexican and Oriental herbs.

Saso Herb Gardens
14625 Fruitvale Avenue
Saratoga, California 95070
(408) 867-0307

Beautiful gardens featuring a wide assortment of herbs; organically
grown herbs for sale; lectures, workshops. Send S.A.S.E. for further
information.

Varneys-Chemist-Laden
242 West Main Street
Fredericksburg, Texas 78624
(512) 997-8615

No charge for catalog featuring quality herbal cosmetics, books and
gifts. Quaint shop in historic town with herb plants, gardens, and
classes.

▼▼▼▼▼▼▼▼▼▼▼▼▼▼▼▼▼▼▼▼▼▼▼▼▼▼▼▼▼▼▼▼▼▼

Windstar
2317 Snowmass Road
P.O. Box 503
Snowmass, Colorado 81654
(303) 923-2145

Founded by John Denver and Thomas Crum. 1,000 acre educational and research ranch with on-site demonstrations and classes uniting man and the environment; herb gardens and solar-geodesic greenhouses. Write for further information about classes, workshops, etc.

ETC

Clayworks Studio
1209 E. 6th Street, Dept. HH
Austin, Texas 78702
(512) 474-9551

Stoneware herb markers (Southwestern herbs included); garden signs, and wall lamps; send S.A.S.E. for list (special requests as well).

Root and Vine
P.O. Box C-51
Westport, Massachusetts 02790
1 (800) 334-8033 (orders only!) or (617) 636-5155

Vinegar making supplies, labels, caps and bottling equipment; booklets.

CONTRIBUTING RESTAURANTS: Make sure to visit these fine restaurants which feature fresh herbs in their cuisine.

Baby Routh
Amy Ferguson, executive chef;
Carla Wood, sous chef/butcher
2708 Routh Street
Dallas, Texas 75201
(214) 871-2345

Cafe Annie
Robert del Grande, chef/owner
5860 Westheimer
Houston, Texas 77057
(713) 780-1522

▼▼▼▼▼▼▼▼▼▼▼▼▼▼▼▼▼▼▼▼▼▼▼▼▼▼▼▼▼▼▼

City Grill
401 Sabine
Austin, Texas 78701
(512) 479-0817

Clarksville Cafe & Jeffreys
Mick Vann, Chris Shirley & Raymond Tatum, chefs
1202 West Lynn
Austin, Texas 78703
(512) 474-7279

Coyote Cafe
Mark Miller, chef
132 W. Water Street
Santa Fe, New Mexico 87501
(505) 983-1615

The Mansion at Turtle Creek
Dean Fearing, executive chef
2821 Turtle Creek Boulevard
Dallas, Texas 75219
(214) 526-2121

Routh Street Cafe
Stephan Pyles, chef/owner
3005 Routh Street
Dallas, Texas 75201
(214) 871-7161

Sea Dragon (Chinese/Vietnamese Cuisine)
8756 Research Boulevard
Austin, Texas 78758
(512) 451-5051

PUBLICATIONS: Sources for valuable herbal information.

The Business of Herbs
Portia Meares, editor
P.O. Box 559
Madison, Virginia 22727

Bi-monthly newsletter full of information for the herb trade as well as the herb gardener/cook, $18.00 yearly.

▼▼▼▼▼▼▼▼▼▼▼▼▼▼▼▼▼▼▼▼▼▼▼▼▼▼▼▼▼▼▼▼▼▼▼▼

Foster's Herb Business Bulletin
P.O. Box 454
Mount View, Arkansas 72560
(501) 368-7439

Published four times a year with information on herb sources and products; book reviews; of particular interest for herb trade. ($8.00)

The Herb Basket
P.O. Box 1773
Brattleboro, Vermont 05301

A series of four small informative books available each season (some out-of-print herbals, some new); $20.00 yearly.

Herban Greenhouse News
Chris Utterback, editor
Route 1 Box 130
Carpenter Road
New Hartford, Connecticut 06057
(203) 489-0567

A bi-monthly herb newsletter for cooks, gardeners, crafters and hobbyists. $18.00 yearly.

The Herb Quarterly
Sallie Ballantine, editor
Box 275
New Fane, Vermont 05345

Quarterly magazine with informative articles, sources, recipes, etc.; $24.00

HerbalGram
Mark Blumenthal and Rob McCaleb, editors
P.O. Box 12006-HH
Austin, Texas 78711

Quarterly comprehensive review of research, legal, media and networking in herb movement; $15.00 yearly.

Potpourri from Herbal Acres
Phyllis Shaudys, editor
Pine Row Publications
Box 428
Washington Crossing, Pennsylvania 18977

Networking quarterly newsletter of interest to herb hobbyists and businesses; packed with valuable information; $15.00 yearly (includes all issues of current series).

BIBLIOGRAPHY

Andrews, Jean. *Peppers, the Domesticated Capsicums.* Austin: University of Texas Press, 1984.

Bailey, Liberty Hyde and Ethel Zoe Bailey. *Hortus Third.* New York: Macmillan, 1976.

Batcheller, Barbara. *Lilies of the Kitchen.* New York: St. Martin's Press, 1986.

Bentley, Virginia Williams. *Let Herbs Do It.* Boston: Houghton Mifflin, 1973.

Brennan, Jennifer. *The Original Thai Cookbook.* New York: GD/ Perigee, 1981.

Bye, Robert A. "Medicinal Plants of the Sierra Madre: Comparative Study of Tarahumara and Mexican Market Plants." *Economic Botany.* 40 (1986):103-124.

Curtin, LSM. *Healing Herbs of the Upper Rio Grande.* Los Angeles: Southwest Museum, 1974.

Daisley, Gilda. *The Illustrated Book of Herbs.* New York: American Nature Society Press, 1982.

de Baggio, Thomas. "1987 Spring Plant Catalog." *Earthworks.* Spring 1987.

Foster, Gertrude B. and Rosemary F. Louden. *Park's Success with Herbs.* Greenwood, South Carolina: Geo. W. Park Seed Co., 1980.

Foster, Steven. *Herbal Bounty!: The Gentle Art of Herb Culture.* Salt Lake City: Peregrine Smith Books, 1984.

Grieve, Mrs. M. *A Modern Herbal.* 2 vols. New York: Dover, 1971.

Hall, Dorothy. *The Book of Herbs.* New York: Charles Scribner's Sons, 1972.

Hampstead, Marilyn. *The Basil Book.* New York: Long Shadow Books, 1984.

Hemphill, John and Rosemary Hemphill. *Herbs: Their Cultivation and Usage.* Poole, England: Blandford Press, 1983.

Joly, Luz Graciela. "Feeding and Trapping Fish with Piper Auritum." *Economic Botany.*

Kennedy, Diana. *The Cuisines of Mexico.* New York: Harper & Row, 1972.

Kennedy, Diana. *Recipes from the Regional Cooks of Mexico.* New York: Harper & Row, 1978.

Lathrop, Norma Jean. *Herbs: How to Select, Grow and Enjoy.* Tucson: HP Books, 1981.

Latorre, Dolores. *Cooking and Curing with Mexican Herbs.* Austin: Encino Press, 1977.

Linares, Ma. Edelmira and Robert A. Bye, Jr. "A Study of Four Medicinal Plant Complexes of Mexico and Adjacent United States." *Journal of Ethnopharmacology.* 19 (1987).

Linares, Ma. Edelmira, Robert Bye and Beatriz Flores Penafiel. *Tés Curativos de Mexico.* Mexico, D.F.: Fonart, 1984.

Martinez, Maximino. *Catalogo de Nombres Vulgaros y Científicos de Plantas Mexicanas.* Mexico, D.F.: Fondo de Culturo Económica, 1979.

Meltzer, Sol. *Herb Gardening in Texas.* Houston: Gulf Publishing, 1983.

Mendizabal, Guillermo, Antonio Basurto and Ariel Rosales. *El Yerberito Ilustrado.* Mexico City: Editorial Posada, 1976.

Michael, Pamela. *All Good Things Around Us.* New York, Holt, Rinehart and Winston, N.Y.

"Oriental Herbs and Vegetables." *Plants & Gardens: Brooklyn Botanic Garden Record* Summer 1983:1-76.

Owen, Millie. *A Cook's Guide to Growing Herbs, Greens, and Aromatics.* New York: Alfred A. Knopf, 1978.

Root, Waverley. *Food: An Authoritative and Visual History and Dictionary of the Foods of the World.* New York: Simon and Schuster, 1980.

Simmons, Adelma Grenier. *The Little Book of Thyme.* Coventry, Connecticut: Caprilands Herb Farm, n.d.

Simmons, Adelma Grenier. *The World of Rosemary.* Coventry, Connecticut: Caprilands Herb Farm, n.d.

Stanley, Paul C. and Julian A. Steyermark. "Flora of Guatemala." *Fieldiana: Botany* vol 24, part III. Chicago: Natural History Museum Press, 1952.

Stobart, Tom. *Herbs Spices and Flavorings.* New York: Overlook Press, 1970.

Yepsen, Roger B. ed. *The Encyclopedia of Natural Insect & Disease Control.* Emmaus, Pennsylvania: Rodale Press, 1984.

INDEX

▼▼▼▼▼▼▼▼▼▼▼▼▼▼▼▼▼▼▼▼▼▼▼▼▼▼▼

▼▼▼▼▼▼▼▼▼▼▼▼▼▼▼▼▼▼▼▼▼▼▼▼▼